UPROOTED

UPROOTED

STORIES FROM THE SRI LANKAN TAMIL DIASPORA

Ana Pararajasingham

Monitor Publications

Copyright © Ana Pararajasingham 2025

All rights reserved

ISBN: 978-0-6486722-6-5

Published by Monitor Publications,

September 2025, Sydney, Australia

To all those who remained—
who, having endured a brutal war that claimed their kith and kin, continue to rebuild their lives with courage, dignity, and hope.

CONTENTS

Acknowledgements 1

Foreword 3

Introduction 5

ARTISTS 9

Mathangi Maya Arulpragasam: M.I.A. – The Sound of Rebellion 11

Anton Ponrajah: Bridging Cultures Through Theatre 21

Shakthi Shakthidharan: Weaving Stories, Bridging Worlds 31

Mira and Dipha Thiruchelvam: Singing the Story of Exile 40

WRITERS AND JOURNALISTS 47

George Alagiah: Reporting from the Margins 49

Shankari Chandran: Redefining the Australian Story 57

HUMANITARIANS AND HUMAN RIGHTS DEFENDERS ... 67

Ahilan Arulanantham: Defending the Displaced 69

Arunn Jegan: On the Front Lines of Humanity 79

Luxshi Vimalarajah: Mediating Paths to Peace 89

SURVIVORS AND STORYTELLERS 97

Umes Arunagirinathan: A Mango Tree with Roots in Two Worlds 99

Raj Rajaratnam: In the Face of Uneven Justice 109

Roy Ratnavel: A Tale of Resilience and Triumph 119

SOCIAL ACTIVISTS 131

Shaun Christie-David: The Privilege of Escape, the Responsibility to Act 133

Max Jeganathan: The Politics of Grace 141

Ambalavaner 'Siva' Sivanandan: Fighting Race and Class 147

Danny Sriskandarajah: Power to the People 157

EDUCATORS AND SCIENTISTS 167

C J Eliezer: Scholar, Advocate, and Global Educator 169

Suresh Canagarajah: Reimagining the English Language 181

Elagu Elaguppillai: Science, Service, and Entrepreneurship 191

Brindha Shivalingam: Leading the Way in Brain Surgery 199

Nadarajah Sreeharan: A Life in Service and Science 207

Nadarajah Sri Sriskandarajah: A Quest for Justice and Sustainability 215

POLITICIANS 225

Gary Anandasangaree: From Refugee to Canadian Cabinet Minister 226

Uma Kumaran: Redefining Representation and Resilience 237

Samantha Ratnam: Championing Justice and Inclusion 245

CULINARY CHAMPIONS 253

Brin Prathapan: MasterChef 257

Tharshan Selverajah: Winner of the Best Baguette in Paris Award 261

Tanesh Thanaratnam: *Coupe de France du Burger* Regional Winner 265

Tharsiny 'Thas' Thanendran: Finalist *Den Store Bagedyst* 266

SPORTING HEROES 269

Rigivan Ganeshamoorthy: Strength in Stillness 273

Amuruthaa 'Amu' Surenkumar: Batting for the Future 275

Kenirujan 'Kenu' Suthakaran – The Tamil Tiger of the Cage 277

Vimal Yoganathan: Footballer, Trailblazer 279

A Story of a Returnee 281

About the Author 283

"Resilience is the ability to attack while running away."
— **Wes Fessler**

"A good half of the art of living is resilience."
— **Alain de Botton**

Acknowledgements

I am deeply grateful to everyone whose support and contributions made this book possible.

My sincere thanks to **Karunyan Arulanantham** for his encouragement and for generously sharing his network of contacts. I am also thankful to **Kulasegaram Sanchayan** for discussing the concept, connecting me with several subjects, and offering support in many other ways.

I thank **Anton Ponrajah**, a subject in this book, for kindly introducing me to another subject, Umes Arunagirinathan.

A special thanks to my daughter-in-law, **Davina Dressler**, for her meticulous editing and insightful feedback, which helped ensure the narrative remained clear, engaging, and well-structured. Equally, I am grateful to my son-in-law, **Prasanna Chandrakumar**, for his creativity and care in designing a cover that beautifully captures the essence of the book. Their thoughtful contributions enriched the work in ways that went far beyond expectation.

My heartfelt gratitude to **Professor Bruce Kapferer** for his generous foreword. His lifelong commitment to anthropological inquiry has been, and continues to be, a source of inspiration.

Each of these contributions, in their own way, has helped shape this work into what it is today.

Foreword

Western Colonial and Imperial expansion, their retreat and collapse, the nationalisms and wars emergent in their wake, have played a huge role in the formation of contemporary global realities giving vent to extraordinary population movements born of displacement, dispossession and dire existential suffering. While a process of cultural and social destruction it is also a history of recreation and regeneration. This is what this remarkable book is about. It tells how children of families fleeing the violence of oppression and displacement have found new lives, and are active in the rebuilding of their communities in new lands, communicating understanding of the history of their plight and, most of all, contributing to the formation of a better more tolerant world.

The stories told in *Uprooted* are ones of achievement and success, often against what might seem to be insurmountable odds. They confound common criticisms often rife with dehumanizing prejudices that paradoxically repeat sentiments integral to the forces which impelled the suffering and migration. This is a book about the overcoming of the forces of destruction that is not self-seeking but whose projects aim to help others in the communities concerned and many others including those of the societies they join and whose cultural and social realities they enrich. The individuals that come to life in these pages commemorate those whose struggle gave them motivation, the courage and opportunity to work towards the generation of new transcendent realities that refuse the horrors of the past and open to new awarenesses, hopefully creating a heterogeneous more hybrid open world without exclusion.

More concretely, the chapters here are about young vital members of the Sri Lankan Tamil diaspora created in years of ethnic civil war in the post-colonial context of nationalist oppression and dispossession. What happened is being repeated in many other parts of the world, the situation of Palestinians and Ukrainians are outstanding examples among numerous others. The situation is being exacerbated by major geo-political transitions and political-economic crises that are driving inflation and growing inequalities in the global north and the south bringing with them further wars and in some instances the revival of old prejudices.

This is a book very much of the current historical moment and acutely relevant to it. We are in a radically changing world situation when the shadows of the past are appearing in new form. This is starkly apparent with current developments in the US and also in Europe (e.g. in Brexit UK). Populisms rising in the countries of refuge are starting to threaten, re-inventing misunderstandings and prejudices that are at the root of the difficulties overcome in the lives presented here.

The reader could have no better guide than Ana Pararajasingham, a voice of the Tamil diaspora and a highly regarded scholar of the Tamil crisis in Sri Lanka.

Bruce Kapferer
Professor Emeritus, University of Bergen
Professorial Fellow, University College London
Director, European Research Council Advanced Grant on Egalitarianism

Introduction

Throughout history, those forced to flee their homelands have shown remarkable resilience, making the painful choice to leave everything familiar to escape danger. The trauma of this uprooting often echoes across generations. *Uprooted* explores these experiences. It captures stories of individuals who, despite displacement, found ways to adapt, thrive, redefine success in new lands.

This book focuses on the displacement of Sri Lanka's Tamil people, whose original presence on the island stretches back several millennia. In recent decades, a significant proportion of this community has fled the country. The extent of this exodus is starkly illustrated by a personal memory: of the thirty-odd Tamil children who started kindergarten with me, only three remain in Sri Lanka, the rest scattered across the globe—part of the million-strong Tamil diaspora.

This book presents the stories of thirty-four Tamils of Sri Lankan origin—some who were displaced themselves and others born to those who were uprooted. They identify in various ways, including as Sri Lankan Tamils, Eelam Tamils, and, depending on where they now live, as British, American, Australian, Canadian, or European Tamils. Within Europe, many identify by their specific country of residence, such as French, German, or Swiss Tamils, reflecting the unique cultures of their adopted homelands.

These stories are not just accounts of individuals who left and later rebuilt their lives elsewhere. They are deeply intertwined with the political upheavals, state policies, and global events that compelled them or their families to leave.

Since the 1950s, Tamils have fled Sri Lanka in successive waves, creating a diaspora with parallels to Jewish, Armenian, and Palestinian communities. Initially labelled economic migrants, Tamils were in fact forced out by systemic policies and violence. In the 1950s and 1960s, policies such as the Sinhala Only Act made Sinhala the sole language for government work, marginalized Tamil speakers from public service. State-condoned violence directed against Tamils who protested against these measures caused further alienation. During this time, many professionals and academics left Sri Lanka, facing both systemic discrimination and intimidation from state-condoned anti-Tamil violence.

In the 1970s, the exodus extended to include young Tamil students subjected to the "Standardization" policy, which forced them to achieve higher entrance scores than their Sinhala peers. Although relatively few were directly barred from university by this rule, its very existence—and the sense of injustice it fostered—prompted many more to leave in search of fairer opportunities abroad.

Following the 1977 election, which saw widespread support for Tamil independence, violence against Tamils intensified, prompting another wave of migration among young professionals.

The late 1970s saw a turning point as frustrated Tamil youth took up armed resistance. In response, the Sri Lankan government intensified its repression, leading to the anti-Tamil violence of July 1983, now known as Black July. During this period, targeted attacks resulted in the deaths of over 3,000 Tamils. Fleeing the violence, thousands sought refuge in `Canada, Australia, and Europe.

Black July was not an isolated incident but the seventh[1] in a series of violent attacks against Tamils dating back several decades. These coordinated assaults—carried out with the complicity or inaction of the state—are collectively referred to as pogroms, a term used to describe organised massacres of a targeted ethnic or religious group.

In the aftermath of Black July, some Tamils stayed to fight for independence, finding support in Tamil Nadu, India. Regional dynamics led India to initially support the Tamil fighters but later to a failed attempt to disarm them through a 1987 accord with Sri Lanka, which resulted in further conflict and migration. In the early 2000s, a Ceasefire Agreement offered brief hope, but renewed conflict forced even more Tamils to leave. The war culminated in 2009, ending with a government victory. At the end of the war, many young Tamils, suspected of being former fighters, faced detention and torture, prompting yet another wave of departure as they sought safety around the world.

Across continents, these uprooted Tamils have overcome the many challenges of adapting to new societies. Their achievements reflect the endurance, strength, and determination of the Tamil community. *Uprooted* tells their stories, celebrating their resilience and the contributions they have made globally despite a legacy of hardship. The individuals featured in these pages represent but a fraction of the uprooted Tamils whose journeys and triumphs deserve to be told. Countless others—across every continent and in every walk of life—have similarly navigated exile, rebuilt

---

[1] S J Tambiah, *Sri Lanka Ethnic Fratricide and the Dismantling of Democracy*, Chicago, University of Chicago Press, 1986, p13

communities, and forged new identities without ever relinquishing the ties that bind them to their heritage. While these stories span diverse backgrounds—gender, profession, generation, and geography—an effort has been made to maintain a balanced representation across these varied categories. As migration continues and new generations come of age, the number of stories grows ever larger, each echoing the same themes of perseverance and hope. *Uprooted* is merely the opening chorus in a much larger chorus of voices, affirming that these narratives are far from finished—and that, in sharing them, we bear witness to a community that not only survives but flourishes.

The biographies are grouped alphabetically into the following categories.

Artists
Writers and Journalists
Humanitarians and Human Rights Activists
Survivors and Storytellers
Social Activists
Educators and Scientists
Politicians
Culinary Experts
Sportspeople

The only exception is Professor C. J. Eliezer, whose particularly notable impact places him first in the "Educators & Scientists" category.

Together, these categories reflect the diverse ways in which Sri Lanka's Tamil diaspora has enriched societies around the world. By showcasing voices from the arts, sciences, humanitarian efforts, journalism, activism, politics, sports, culinary arts, and more, this collection honours not only individual achievement but also the collective spirit of resilience and creativity. Each biography is designed to stand alone. As a result, events affecting multiple individuals may be mentioned more than once. This repetition is intentional, ensuring each voice is complete and self-contained.

As you explore these stories, you will discover how each person—whether a trailblazing educator, a boundary-pushing artist, or a compassionate advocate has carried forward a legacy of hope. May their journeys inspire you to recognize the many paths through which one can transform adversity into opportunity, root identity in action, and truly thrive despite being uprooted.

As this book also delves into the circumstances that compelled individuals to flee Sri Lanka—the war, political repression, targeted violence, and systemic discrimination—it is my hope that readers in Sri Lanka, particularly those who lived through these times or witnessed this exodus firsthand, will gain a deeper understanding of the human cost behind those departures. These are not abstract tales of migration, but lived experiences of trauma, loss, and survival. By illuminating the personal and often painful decisions that led so many to leave, these stories also speak to a broader, global audience—inviting empathy, connection, and reflection from anyone who has experienced or grappled with displacement, forced migration, or the search for safety and dignity. In this way, the Tamil experience becomes part of a shared human story, resonating far beyond national or ethnic boundaries.

My own journey in researching and curating this collection—through online sources, in-depth interviews, and personal conversations—has been a deeply humbling experience. Wherever possible, I spoke directly with the individuals featured, listening to their stories in their own words. In some cases, however, this was not possible: a few subjects are no longer among the living, and others could not be contacted despite considerable efforts. In such instances, I relied on a wide range of offline and online sources, including published interviews, archival material, public records, and media coverage. This research was exhaustive, and every effort was made to ensure that the information presented is accurate, reliable, and verifiable. As I delved into the lives of these thirty-four men and women, I was struck by the extraordinary resilience, commitment, and passion that define their stories. Each of them has faced challenges—whether in adapting to the dominant culture or navigating the tension between their parents' heritage and the society they now inhabit. Many have experienced a profound sense of 'otherness', yet they have found ways not only to cope, but to thrive and contribute meaningfully to the communities in which they now live.

The final chapter is a brief account of someone who has walked the reverse path—returning to the homeland after years abroad. Here the bittersweet weight of nostalgia and the tension of living between two worlds offer a poignant reminder that home can be both a place we carry within us and a landscape we revisit in memory.

ARTISTS

Mathangi Maya Arulpragasam: M.I.A. – The Sound of Rebellion

From Council Estate to Global Stage

Growing up in a council flat in South London, Maya Arulpragasam could hardly have imagined that she would address the Oxford Union one day. Yet, on a bright spring day in May 2017, there she stood—a refugee raised by a single mother—making her voice heard at the heart of the British establishment. With her long, dark brown hair cascading over her shoulders, expressive eyes and wide, genuine smile, Maya exuded confidence. She showed no signs of being intimidated by the surroundings. The legendary Oxford Union was the most prestigious society at the University of Oxford. Since 1823, it has been a platform for world figures from every field—politics, business, sports, and the arts—to share their thoughts. The roster of past speakers reads like a who's who of history: U.S. Presidents Reagan, Carter, and Clinton, Henry Kissinger, Mother Teresa, Desmond Tutu, Albert Einstein, Malcolm X, Dame Judi Dench, and Michael Jackson, to name just a few. Maya had earned her place in this illustrious group through her revolutionary music—a bold fusion of hip-hop, electronic beats, and global rhythms, interwoven with hard-hitting political messages that challenged the status quo.

Maya's first two albums, *Arular* (2005) and *Kala* (2007), were smash hits. Her single, *Paper Planes*, soared to number four on the US Billboard Hot 100 and scored a nomination at the 51st Annual Grammy Awards for Record of the Year.

Defying all odds—growing up with a single mother in a low-income neighbourhood—Maya's sharp mind and fearless confidence helped her rise above every challenge thrown her way.

This is Maya's story:

A Childhood in the Shadow of War

Maya was originally named Mathangi, a name her fellow Brits struggled to pronounce, so she adopted "Maya," a simpler alternative. Maya was born in Hounslow, London in 1975, but when she was just six months old, her parents decided to return to Sri Lanka.

It was in war-torn Sri Lanka that she spent the first decade of her life. Her father's political involvement took the family to Northern Sri Lanka, the heartland of the Tamil homeland. Maya's first album *Arular* was named after her father, Arulpragasam. He was a founding member of the Eelam Revolutionary Organisation of Students (EROS), a Tamil political group that began as a think tank of young Tamil students in London but soon evolved into a militant group fighting for the independence of Tamil Eelam in Sri Lanka through armed resistance. EROS, though not as active on the front lines as other militant groups, focused on spreading the ideology of armed resistance among the Tamil people.

At the beginning. Maya lived with her family on her grandparents' remote farm, a collection of huts without electricity or running water. After a year, as her father's involvement in militant activities increased, Maya, her older sister Kali, and their mother moved to Jaffna in the far north of the country, where Maya's younger brother Sugu was born.

Within a year of Maya's return to Sri Lanka, in August 1977. yet another bout of anti-Tamil violence was unleashed, forcing hundreds of Tamils to flee the Sinhala-dominated South and seek refuge in their Northern homeland. Just after her sixth birthday, in 1981, Maya heard of the Jaffna Public Library being burned down—a shocking act of cultural genocide, later revealed to have been overseen by four of Sri Lanka's cabinet ministers. By the time Maya was eight, the infamous Black July of 1983 had erupted, claiming thousands of Tamil lives and displacing hundreds of thousands more. This marked the transformation of a low-key militancy into a full-scale civil war—the armed struggle for Tamil independence had begun.

Maya's father left the family to join the armed rebellion making contact with him strictly limited. His occasional sporadic visits were in secret, slipping through the window at night and being introduced to the children as "an uncle" so that his identity and whereabouts would not be given away to the army which dropped in frequently to question the family.

As the war escalated, the family was forced to endure the oppressive presence of the Sri Lankan military in the Tamil homeland. They experienced the terror of being caught in the aftermath of ambushes by the Tamil fighters, as civilians were rounded up by the Sri Lankan army in retaliation. The blockade of food and medicine imposed by the government left Maya and many other children malnourished, while the relentless raids by the Sri Lankan army forced her family to move from place to place. The army, breaking out of its barracks to punish the people who had given birth to the Tamil guerrillas and often sheltered them, created an atmosphere of constant fear and instability.

Recognizing the mounting danger, Maya's father decided to send the family back to England while he stayed behind to continue his fight. This time, they returned to England as refugees. Maya's return to London was just a week shy of her eleventh birthday.

The return to London was far from straightforward. The family first relocated to Madras (now Chennai), India, where they moved into a derelict house miles away from the nearest road or neighbour. They managed to survive there for a while, with occasional visits from Maya's father. The girls excelled at the local school. However, as money grew tight, the children fell ill—Kala contracted typhoid—and the family struggled to get by with limited food and water. Concerned for their well-being, a visiting uncle moved them back to Jaffna. But with the violence escalating once again, they tried to flee to India. After several failed attempts, Maya, her siblings, and their mother finally made it to India before eventually returning to London in 1986.

Returning as a Refugee

In London, Maya's mother worked hard to provide for her children. The rest of Maya's childhood and teenage years unfolded on the Phipps Bridge Estate in South London, where she learned to speak English and adapted to her new surroundings. She lost all contacts with her father. Here, she was exposed to Western radio for the first time, hearing broadcasts emanating from her neighbours' flats. Her affinity for hip-hop and rap began there. The uncompromising attitudes of *Public Enemy, Big Daddy Kane, Roxanne Shante* and *N.W.A.* clicked with a frustrated, energetic war child trying to relate to grey and foreign surroundings. Those records were rhythmic, so whether you understood the language or not, you could understand the music.[2]

A talented and creative student, Maya earned a spot at London's prestigious Central Saint Martin's College of Art and Design, where she studied fine art, film, and video. It was here that she began to weave together the various strands of her life experiences. In an early version of what would later become her unique style, she juxtaposed her multiple cultural identities—blending rap iconography with the imagery of warfare

---

[2] https://tamilnation.org/diaspora/unitedkingdom/mia

from her youth, mixing Asian British culture with American new-wave filmmaking, and fusing St. Martin's fashion-forward style with the perspective of a refugee. Maya was soon on the cusp of a successful career; this seemed to be her destiny for a while.

In 2001, she held her first-ever public exhibition at the Euphoria Shop in Portobello, London. It featured candy-coloured, spray-painted stencil pictures of the Tamil rebellion, with gratified tigers among palm trees mixed with green and pink camouflage, bombs, guns and freedom fighters on chipboards and canvases. However, it was not art but in music that she would excel.

The Turning Point: Searching for the Missing

Later that year, Maya received a small grant from a TV company to make a documentary about her cousin, who had gone missing- one of the many Tamils abducted by the Sri Lankan state and never to be heard of again. Two years earlier, in 1999, a study by the United Nations found that Sri Lanka had the second-highest number of disappearances in the world and that 12,000 Sri Lankans had disappeared after being detained by the Sri Lankan security forces. Upon arriving in Sri Lanka, she quickly realized that filming and conducting interviews could lead to her arrest. Shifting her focus, she delved into learning more about her family—a personal journey of self-discovery. This experience not only deepened her understanding of the conflict that permeated every aspect of Tamil life but also profoundly shaped the trajectory of her own life from that moment on.

Birth of M.I.A.: Music Without Borders

Maya's path to music began while designing artwork for *Elastica's* second album. On tour with the band, electro-clash artist Peaches introduced her to the Roland MC-505,[3] sparking her confidence in making music. Back in London, Maya used a basic setup to create a demo tape, marking her entry into the music world.

Maya's music and career soared at a pivotal time when the internet was just beginning to flourish. She harnessed the power of platforms like

---

[3] The Roland MC-505 is a self-contained electronic music production instrument known as a "groove box." Released in 1998, it combines a synthesizer, drum machine, sequencer, and MIDI controller into one unit, designed primarily for creating dance, techno, and electronic music

Myspace and file sharing to swap ideas, defy cultural and geographical boundaries, and connect with a global audience. Young people everywhere were sharing and celebrating their creativity outside the control of major corporations, and Maya's music struck a powerful chord with this generation.

She called herself M.I.A., a play on her name and "M.I.A." for "Missing in Acton," reflecting her time living in Acton. Later, she revealed that M.I.A. also referenced her missing cousin, one of the many who disappeared during the war in Sri Lanka—a country notorious for leading the world in enforced disappearances at the time.

Provocative, Political, Unapologetic

In 2004, Maya drew attention to the ongoing struggle in Sri Lanka through her powerful track *Sunshowers,* drawing from the unwavering resolve of the Tamil Tigers, who had pledged never to surrender. The music video featured young women clad in the style of Tamil Tiger soldiers, interspersed with symbolic images of a tiger and a lion. The song's bold, defiant verse paid tribute to the Palestine Liberation Organization (PLO), who had provided military training to her father's group, EROS, with lyrics that rang loud and clear:

"You wanna go?
You wanna win a war?
Like P.L.O I don't surrender."

MTV demanded she clarify the song's message before airing the video, but Maya didn't back down. She responded boldly, "When you watch the news, that's what's shown, and they don't have to censor that. I wrote this song as a chicken-and-egg story: who's attacking who, who is good, who is evil? You can't grab someone by the neck and choke them and then complain they're kicking you. If you're going around oppressing people, they will fight back."[4]

Her response—sharp, unapologetic, and fearless—was a testament to her quick wit and refusal to be silenced. MTV refused to play the video until the reference to the PLO was removed, Maya did not relent. She expanded on her early experiences now informed by her life-altering recent visit, "I'd seen people die by the time I left. That's as bad as it could get when you see people from your village disappearing and not coming back.

---

[4] https://www.infolanka.com/ubb/Forum2/HTML/000370.html

One minute they're doctors and respected and the next they're in wheelchairs because they've been 'accidentally' shot. My school was burned down. My family's house was burned down. When we tried to leave Sri Lanka with my mom, the buses we were on would get stopped in the middle of nowhere and people would be taken off and killed."[5]

It was a powerful indictment of the Sri Lankan government, and for this, along with her other outspoken comments, Maya would later face death threats against both her personally and her son.[6]

From *Arular* to Activist

Her first album, *Arular* was released in December 2005, propelling her into the limelight. Maya used her newfound fame to shine a spotlight on the plight of her people—Sri Lanka's Tamils, locked in conflict with the Sri Lankan state. As the war escalated and atrocities against the Tamil people went largely unnoticed by Western media, Maya took it upon herself to expose the truth. For her efforts, she became a target of the Sri Lankan regime, while the Western media framed the conflict in terms of terrorism, casting Maya as a terrorist sympathizer. She found a reaction by Oprah Winfrey emblematic of the Western establishment's attitude, even among those who were otherwise progressive. Winfrey was happy to pose for a photograph with Maya but refused to engage with her message, dismissing her concerns and implying that she was just another "crazy terrorist".[7]

Unfazed, Maya doubled down, openly declaring her stance.

She used her voice—both lyrically and symbolically—to advocate for the voiceless. In a September 2005 interview with *The Guardian* after the release of *Arular*, she articulated her mission: "I was a refugee because of war, and now I have a voice in a time when war is the most invested thing on the planet. What I wanted to do with this record was to give every refugee kid who came after me something good to feel about."[8]

Maya vs. the Mainstream

Despite being vilified for her political views, Maya's bold creativity kept

---

[5] https://www.infolanka.com/ubb/Forum2/HTML/000370.html
[6] https://www.greenleft.org.au/content/mia-modern-media-assassin
[7] https://www.usmagazine.com/celebrity-news/news/mia-slams-oprah-winfrey-ex-boyfriend-diplo-in-rolling-stone-chat-2015203/
[8] MIA, Myself and I, *The Guardian*, 5 September 2005

her in the global spotlight. In 2009, *Time Magazine* named her one of the 100 most influential people in the world. *Esquire* ranked M.I.A. among the 75 most influential people of the 21st century, and *Billboard* recognized her as one of the "Top 50 Dance/Electronic Artists of the 2010s."

In April 2010, Maya once again used her platform to highlight the plight of the Tamil people, who were identifying the atrocities in the final stages of the war in Sri Lanka as genocide. She released the song and video *Born Free*, a provocative piece depicting red-haired adolescents being forced to run across a minefield, symbolizing the brutal realities of oppression. The video sparked controversy due to its violent imagery, but it was quintessential Maya—fearlessly drawing attention to uncomfortable truths and using art to confront the world's indifference.

The New York Times' response was typical of how the establishment handles revolutionaries—through dismissal and ridicule. On 25 May 2010, writer Lynn Hirschberg penned a hit piece that downplayed Maya's understanding of Sri Lanka's political landscape and labelled the powerful imagery in *Born Free*, as "exploitative" and "hollow." Hirschberg also aimed at Maya's personal life, criticizing her for moving to an upscale Los Angeles neighbourhood and marrying Benjamin Bronfman, the son of a wealthy mogul, accusing her of wanting to balance bold political statements with a luxurious lifestyle. The critique was as predictable as it was narrow, missing the deeper revolutionary message Maya was championing. Ever quick-witted, Maya humorously responded on Twitter, encouraging people to call for her side of the story—and cheekily posted Hirschberg's phone number, jamming her line with calls.

Maya's anti-establishment stance came through boldly and unexpectedly during her performance at the American Super Bowl in 2012. When performing alongside Madonna, she flashed her middle finger to the camera. True to her unapologetic and irreverent style, Maya humorously explained it as a 'Hindu' spiritual gesture, turning the moment into a playful jab at the National Football League. It was classic Maya—fearlessly challenging conventions and ridiculing the establishment, all while maintaining her trademark wit.[9]

---

[9] The legal dispute with the NFL lasted several years and, according to some observers, pushed Maya to lean further into her bold, politically charged artistry, strengthening her voice as a cultural provocateur.

A Rebel with a Cause

In 2015, Maya's track *Borders* and its accompanying video sparked controversy and conversation. For Maya, though, this was familiar territory—it was about refugees, a theme deeply personal to her. The video depicted Syrians, Iraqis, Libyans, Afghans, and Eritreans fleeing war and conflict, as part of Europe's growing Migrant Crisis. With over a million people arriving in Europe that year, a sharp increase from the 153,000 in 2008, Maya's self-directed video brought to life the struggle of refugees—young, brown men packed onto fishing boats, scaling razor-wire fences—humanizing their experience in a way few others could.

In 2020, Maya was awarded the Member of the Order of the British Empire (MBE) for her contributions to music—a recognition from the very establishment she had long challenged. Some saw it as an attempt to pacify her outspoken activism, perhaps hoping she would step back. But Maya's resolve remained unshaken, and she continued to elevate the voices of the marginalized.

In 2023, Maya became Christian, having previously identified as Hindu. While this was a personal decision, it wasn't entirely unexpected, as her mother had become a Christian, and her father, Arulappu Richard Arulpragasam,[10] as his name suggests, was at least nominally Christian. Maya quickly reassured her fans that this change hadn't altered her Tamil identity, saying, "I kind of couldn't let go of the Tamil side. That's why 50% of the record is still like that. Because I'm still me. That's still my language."[11] Her new faith is unlikely to diminish her support among the predominantly Hindu Tamils, as Tamil nationalism is rooted in language and culture, not religion.

Maya, an artist of immense talent, is keenly aware of the challenges she faces as a woman of colour in the West, particularly when delivering a political message that calls out those in power. Her boldness makes her controversial, but she knows controversy is a powerful tool to ensure her message is heard. By actively courting it, she stays relevant, and makes the world aware of the plight of her people. Deliberately showcasing the tiger, a symbol of Tamil nationalism, she countered the way both Western and Eastern establishments used the same symbol to demonize the Tamils and

---

[10] https://www.wikiwand.com/en/articles/Arul_Pragasam
[11] https://www.movieguide.org/news-articles/m-i-a-defends-her-conversion-to-christianity-amid-biggest-backlash-in-her-career.html#:~:text=%E2%80%9CI%20kind%20of%20couldn't,That's%20still%20my%20language.

undermine their quest for independence.

Yet Maya also understands that her people's struggle is part of a much larger global picture—one of power imbalance. This drives her to align herself with figures like Julian Assange and to speak out on issues such as poverty, revolution, gender and sexual stereotypes, war, and the conditions of the working class in London. Her presence on the US Homeland Security Risk List in 2006, US government visits to her website, and visa denials by the US are proof that her message is taken seriously.

Reflections

In many ways, Maya's artistic activism parallels the intellectual rigour of Noam Chomsky, the investigative journalism of John Pilger, and the unapologetically progressive politics of Jeremy Corbyn. While Chomsky dissects power structures through academia, Pilger exposes injustice through the lens of journalism, and Corbyn fights inequality in the political arena. Maya took to the global stage using her art as a vehicle of resistance. Through her music, performances, and public statements, she continuously challenged the status quo, fearlessly calling out systems of oppression, inequality, and hypocrisy. Her fusion of music with powerful political messaging allowed her to reach audiences far beyond academic and political circles, turning her songs into anthems for the marginalized and the voiceless. Whether addressing issues of war, displacement, or class, Maya's activism, much like these figures, sought to disrupt the establishment's complacency, making her not just an artist, but a revolutionary voice for justice in her own right.

Anton Ponrajah: Bridging Cultures Through Theatre

Honouring a Trailblazer

On a crisp spring evening in 2005, the City of Lucerne honoured one of its own, Anton Ponrajah, for his contribution to Swiss theatre—a remarkable recognition in view of his extraordinary journey. More than a celebration of artistic achievement, the honour acknowledged Anton's unique role in using theatre as a bridge between cultures. Through his productions, workshops, and community engagement, he brought together people from diverse backgrounds—immigrants and locals, young and old—fostering dialogue, understanding, and a shared sense of belonging. At a time when questions of identity and integration were becoming increasingly pressing in Switzerland and across Europe, Anton's work stood as a powerful example of how the arts could transcend barriers and nurture cohesive, inclusive communities.

Acting Across Cultures

When Anton arrived in Switzerland as a refugee in 1985, he spoke no German. Over the years, Anton overcame significant challenges to become an accomplished actor in Swiss-German films and television. More importantly, he used theatre as a powerful medium to bridge two seemingly disparate communities: the German-speaking Swiss and the asylum-seeking Tamil diaspora.

In 1985, Tamil asylum seekers arriving in Switzerland faced significant challenges: cultural differences, an unfamiliar language, food, and climate, all in addition to the trauma of fleeing their land of birth. These hardships were compounded by the Swiss public's lack of understanding of the reasons behind the sudden presence among them an alien people. Adding to their plight was the Swiss government's controversial policy of deporting asylum seekers back to Sri Lanka—a practice that had tragically resulted in at least one returnee being tortured upon arrival.

Amid these challenges, Tamil asylum seekers found invaluable support from Caritas, a Swiss organization dedicated to supporting vulnerable groups that included the poor, single parents, the unemployed, and asylum seekers.

Facing Ignorance and Prejudice

Within a short time of his arrival, Anton had become a prominent spokesperson for Tamil asylum seekers due to his ability to communicate in English. Assisted by Caritas, Anton began visiting schools, aiming to explain the reasons behind the Tamil presence in Switzerland. During these visits, he was struck by the widespread ignorance about Sri Lanka among Swiss students. Many did not know about the political turmoil that had forced Tamils to flee their homeland, while others only knew of the narrative presented by local media, which often reflected the Sri Lankan state's perspective.

Anton was astonished that some students were unaware that a country called Sri Lanka even existed. As a child in Sri Lanka, he and his peers had learned much about Switzerland, and the stark contrast between the awareness levels of the "first world" about the "third world" and vice versa was both perplexing and thought-provoking.

Although Anton knew he was making progress in clarifying the circumstances that had led thousands of young Tamils to seek asylum in Switzerland and other countries, significant prejudice persisted. *Blick*, a widely circulated Swiss newspaper, played a particularly damaging role in shaping negative perceptions of Tamil asylum seekers. The publication frequently exaggerated crimes committed by individual Tamils, portraying the entire community as criminals. It accused Tamil asylum seekers—who were legally prohibited from working during the initial period of their registration—of living off Swiss taxpayers. Furthermore, the paper sensationalized images of Tamil people gathering in railway stations during winter, framing these scenes as intimidating.

Blick also gave undue prominence to right-wing politicians opposed to asylum seekers, reinforcing public hostility. One of the most damaging narratives perpetuated by the newspaper was the association of Tamil asylum seekers with drug trafficking, often relying on tenuous evidence. This relentless negative publicity had tangible consequences: Swiss authorities began isolating detention centres for Tamil asylum seekers, locating them far from populated areas, which made finding employment nearly impossible. Even those who managed to secure jobs struggled to find accommodation, as landlords were reluctant to rent to individuals from a community tarnished by such widespread stereotyping.

Meanwhile, the Tamil community, feeling culturally alienated and demonized, began to turn inward, becoming more insular. Anton recognized that his efforts—visiting schools and other venues to provide explanations—were not enough. Something more impactful was needed.

A New Stage: Theatrical Beginnings with Caritas

It was at this pivotal moment that Anton had a fortuitous encounter with Peter Braschler, a Swiss representative from Caritas. Peter approached Anton with an idea Caritas had devised: to use theatre to tell asylum seekers' stories. The plan involved producing plays that brought together Swiss actors and members of the refugee communities to share their narratives on stage.

For Anton, the proposal resonated deeply. He had acted in school plays, participated in inter-school drama competitions, and performed in local dramas in his village. His passion for theatre had further led him to attend drama school in Jaffna, where he was trained by the renowned A.C. Tarcisius. Tarcisius, a disciple of the Stanislavski Technique, imparted its principles to Anton. Developed by Konstantin Stanislavski, this technique emphasized creating authentic, believable characters by enabling actors to fully immerse themselves in their roles. Stanislavski viewed theatre as a powerful art form with the potential to educate and transform society. Anton's guru, Tarcisius, was not only an exponent of the Stanislavski method, but one who had integrated the ancient Tamil art of *koothu*, a powerful medium for transmitting cultural narratives to produce a distinctive style of theatre.

Anton quickly realized that his theatrical training and experience perfectly aligned with Peter's vision. With his unique skills and understanding of storytelling, he saw the opportunity to bridge the divide between the Swiss and Tamil communities while shedding light on the struggles of asylum seekers.

From the outset, Anton and Peter connected deeply, united by a shared vision of using theatre as a bridge and this bond quickly extended to the Swiss actors involved in the project. Despite some initial reservations, they gradually found common ground with Anton and the Tamil troupe. As their collaboration grew, Anton became affectionately known as "Tony," following the Swiss custom of shortening the name Anton as a variation of Antony.

Swiss director Arlette Zurbuchen admitted feeling somewhat

apprehensive at first, particularly due to the language barrier and the predominantly male presence within the Tamil asylum-seeking community at the time. However, these initial hesitations began to fade as collaboration unfolded.

What stood out to observers was the Tamil troupe's eagerness to engage with Swiss culture and foster genuine intercultural dialogue. Albin Bieri, a social anthropologist involved in the project, admired this openness: "You know, as a social anthropologist, I was very impressed by how open the Tamils were to Swiss society in doing the theatre work. They were genuinely looking for intercultural dialogue. That was, for me, something astonishing. Normally, many refugee groups go somewhere and hide themselves out of sight. But the Tamils were open; they were actively seeking this dialogue. That was, for me, very impressive."[12]

In one such attempt to begin a dialogue, Anton conducted a workshop for the Swiss Police force on the topic of "Communicating and Comprehending Aliens." At the end of three sessions, Anton realised that the workshop had served not only to bring about some understanding of the plight of the 'aliens' amongst the policemen but also helped Anton understand the situation from the point of view of the police.

This openness and willingness to collaborate helped break down cultural barriers, forging connections that went beyond the stage and laid the foundation for mutual understanding between the two communities.

Maralam: Theatre as a Cultural Bridge

Peter entrusted Anton with the task of writing the plays for their project. Anton decided to create six short plays, each running 15 to 20 minutes. Five of these plays highlighted the plight of Tamils both in their homeland and as asylum seekers in Switzerland, while the sixth focused on the experiences of African refugees, who were also part of the Caritas initiative. When it came to naming the series, the Swiss actors made a suggestion that intrigued Anton—they proposed calling it "Marala Marala" because, to their ears, Tamil sounded like that. Amused by the suggestion, Anton and his compatriots embraced it, adapting the name to *"Maralam"* to give it a distinctly Tamil touch.

Maralam premiered at the Luzerne Spielleute Pavillon on May 2, 1986.

---

[12] Anton Ponrajah, Swiss Made (private video recording), 8 November 2024, shared privately in an mp4 format.

The response to the first performance far exceeded Anton's expectations. The audience's applause was so sustained that it continued even after the actors made five curtain calls and only subsided when Peter intervened to thank them. Among the six one-act plays, the standout piece depicted a fictional scenario in which Swiss people sought refuge in the Tamil homeland. It humorously portrayed their struggles with unfamiliar food, culture, language, and climate, with Swiss actors playing the role of refugees and Tamil actors as the confused hosts. This play resonated deeply, engaging the audience with its wit and role reversal.

Maralam ran for three days at the Luzerne Spielleute Pavillon and later toured other parts of the Canton of Lucerne as well as neighbouring Cantons, including Berne, Basel, Zurich, and St. Gallen. Each performance was followed by discussions that encouraged dialogue and understanding. The production garnered positive media coverage, countering the negative publicity that had tarnished the Tamil community's image. It became a resounding success, fostering greater acceptance of Tamils within Swiss society and creating pathways for integration.

For Anton, *Maralam* marked the beginning of a transformative journey. It not only bolstered the Tamil community's standing in Switzerland but also opened doors for him personally, leading to prominent roles in Swiss TV, radio, and stage productions.

Expanding the Stage: Anton's Growth as an Actor and Playwright

Anton's first performance as a professional actor in Switzerland was in *Aijoh*, directed by Otto Huber in 1988. This multilingual play was staged in Zurich—the Swiss capital—and at the Kulturepanorama in Lucerne.

The success of *Aijoh* was a deeply humbling experience. For Anton—who had arrived in Switzerland as a refugee with no knowledge of German—taking centre stage in a Swiss production marked a profound personal milestone. The enthusiastic reception confirmed that he was no longer seen as just an outsider or asylum seeker. He had crossed a threshold: he was now part of the cultural fabric, recognised and respected as an actor in the Swiss mainstream. It was a moment of quiet affirmation—an arrival that didn't inflate his ego, but instead deepened his gratitude for the journey that had brought him there.

In 1989, Anton, with the help of his reconnected mentor Tarcisius, translated a Tamil play, *Ēn Odukirai* (Why Are You Running?) into

German and English. With Peter Braschler's assistance, the play was transformed into *Sri Salami*, a multilingual German-Tamil production that intriguingly incorporated the ancient Tamil art form of *Koothu*. That same year, Sri Salami won the prestigious Vestag-Preis awarded by the Canton of Lucerne.

Encouraged by Peter Braschler, *Malaram* embraced the Forum Theatre format—a style developed by Brazilian theatre practitioner Augusto Boal in the 1970s. This form invited audience members to intervene and explore the issues presented on stage, creating dynamic discussions.

One such production, Brune Sack, tackled workplace discrimination in a Forum Theatre setting. In this play, Anton portrayed an apprentice under Peter Braschler's direction. The play was staged in fifteen of the German-speaking Cantons in Switzerland. In 1991, an invitation was extended for Brune Sack to be performed in Sibiu in Romania which had a strong German connection and where German is spoken.

Anton soon realized that Forum Theatre shared many qualities with the traditional Tamil art form of *Therukoothu* (street theatre), which is performed in outdoor spaces, further extending *Maralam's* reach.

Anton considers his participation in Invisible Theatre—a form of street theatre—to be one of his most memorable experiences. In this art form, performances take place in public spaces, with the unsuspecting audience believing that the events unfolding before them are real. In one such performance designed to highlight the challenges faced by asylum seekers, Anton portrayed a young refugee denied permission to marry his Swiss fiancée because he was on the verge of deportation. The act sparked debates about the plight of refugees. The performance was so convincing that real police intervened, stopping the couple; Anton was even taken to the police station and ordered to vacate the area.

This early engagement with politically charged performance deepened Anton's commitment to socially conscious theatre. It also broadened his range as an actor, enabling him to take on more complex and nuanced roles in formal stage productions. In 1994, he performed in *Moskau-Petuschki*, a bilingual play in Russian and German, staged in Switzerland and later in Saint Petersburg. Tackling themes of dislocation and existential longing, the play further expanded his linguistic and cultural repertoire.

As his career evolved, Anton continued to explore themes of identity and belonging through character-driven narratives. The theme of interracial love was central to *Grenzliebe* (Border Love), a play directed by Peter Braschler in which Anton portrayed Shiva, a young Tamil man. The production offered a thoughtful yet humorous exploration of love and marriage from both Swiss and Tamil cultural perspectives.

He also took on the role of narrator in *Bruder Klaus und die Pandava Prinzen*, a unique production that wove together Tamil theatrical forms such as *Therukooth*u with Swiss storytelling traditions. The play was a cultural fusion, bringing together the tale of Bruder Klaus—the mythical Swiss hero and patron saint of Switzerland—with that of the Pandavas, the legendary heroes of the ancient Indian epic, the *Mahabharata*. For Anton, it was another opportunity to experiment with form and content, and to blend his Tamil heritage with his adopted Swiss identity on stage.

Redefining Swiss Icons: Happy Birthday TELL

In 2005, Anton co-directed and acted in *Happy Birthday TELL*, a bold reinterpretation of Switzerland's national hero, co-created with Urs Graf.

The original William Tell (German: Wilhelm Tell), written by Friedrich Schiller in 1804, dramatizes the legendary Swiss marksman's role in the 14th-century struggle for independence from the Habsburg Empire. During the play's bicentennial in 2004, Anton was struck by the range of modern takes on the Tell legend presented across Swiss media. One particular debate— "William Tell: Freedom Fighter or Terrorist?"— resonated with him deeply.

Happy Birthday TELL reimagined Tell as an elderly man navigating contemporary Switzerland. His son Walter is cast as a hardline right-wing politician, while his other son, also named William, is a liberal Catholic priest. The play offered a sharp commentary on current political tensions, with Walter voicing anti-refugee views and William providing a humanist counterbalance. Infused with elements of *koothu*, the production brought a rich intercultural dimension to a Swiss icon.

In the lead-up to the premiere, Anton received threats from right-wing extremists angered by what they saw as a foreigner's encroachment on national tradition. Undeterred, he pressed on—and the play was ultimately met with enthusiastic praise from the mainstream media.

On Stage and Screen

As mentioned, Anton's debut as a professional actor in Switzerland was in *Aijoh* in 1988. He continued his career in theatre. In 2010, Anton acted in the film *Madly in Love*, directed by Swiss director Anna Luif. This romantic comedy portrayed love as a force stronger than cultural differences and traditions.

Anton's last play was *Ein Mann und Eine Frau* (One Man, One Woman) in 2015, directed by Otto Huber—the same director who had given Anton his first professional role in *Aijoh*. The production was memorable for more than one reason. On the day of the performance, Anton had been diagnosed with a damaged intestine, received medication, and was ordered to rest. Determined not to disappoint his fellow artists, he showed up for the performance despite his condition, only to find that his mouth was so dry he could hardly speak. With a valiant effort, he overcame this setback and began to perform. Although he remembers very little of that day, he recalls the deafening applause that followed. Remarkably, he managed to perform in several shows over the next few days, with the play being staged 20 times.

To-date Anton's acting career span over thirty-years included numerous other performances in theatre, film, and radio.

Networking and Advocacy

Anton's public life, however, was not confined to acting. His concerns extended beyond the challenges faced by Tamil asylum seekers in Switzerland to the unfolding events in his homeland. While his work in theatre significantly improved relations between the Tamil and Swiss communities, Sri Lankan propaganda continued to shape the narrative in Swiss media. Recognizing the need for a platform to share the Tamil community's perspective, Anton, with the support of his Swiss theatre colleagues, launched a German-language newsletter titled *Stimme der Menschenrechte: Informationsbulletin (Voice of Human Rights: Information Bulletin)* First published in November 1987 with a circulation of 300 copies, the newsletter quickly grew to over 3,000 and eventually evolved into a journal called *Vannakam*, which expanded its reach beyond Switzerland to Germany. The publication ceased in 2000 as online platforms emerged and the Sri Lankan conflict became better understood globally, reducing the need for the journal.

Anton also engaged with international advocacy, becoming involved in periodic UNHCR sessions. In 1995, he was appointed the permanent delegate of International Education Development, an NGO dedicated to human rights advocacy, which enabled him to participate in sessions focused on Sri Lanka's human rights issues. In 2004, Anton played a pivotal role in forming the Centre of Just Peace and Democracy (CJPD), an initiative that began by formalizing existing networks within the Tamil diaspora and beyond. These groups had long worked to achieve a just peace in Sri Lanka. With the support of the Berghof Foundation and the Norwegian Government, the network was institutionalized in 2007 with a hub in Switzerland, becoming actively involved in track 2 diplomacy aimed at ending the conflict in Sri Lanka.

Reflections

Anton Ponrajah's remarkable journey—from a refugee with no knowledge of German to a celebrated actor and cultural ambassador—stands as a testament to his resilience and vision. Through his groundbreaking work in theatre, film, and advocacy, he bridged divides between Swiss and Tamil communities, inspiring dialogue and mutual understanding. His enduring legacy continues to remind us that art and compassion can transform lives and bring about meaningful change.

Shakthi Shakthidharan: Weaving Stories, Bridging Worlds

Redefining Australian Theatre

A bare stage, a few simple props, and a cast that shifts roles and languages with ease. The play, *Counting and Cracking* unfolds like a theatrical miracle. What begins as an empty square becomes, in moments, a Sydney apartment, a Colombo courtyard, a beach, a train station—traversing continents and generations with elegant simplicity. At the heart of this ambitious, genre-defying work is S. Shakthidharan, the playwright and co-director of *Counting and Cracking*. Eamon Flack was the director and associate writer.

When *Counting and Cracking* played for the first time at the Sydney Town Hall in 2019, critics described it as "warm and witty." It soon proved to be much more than that winning numerous awards, including the NSW Premier's Literary Award, the Victorian Premier's Literary Award; and the 2019 Helpmann Awards for Best Play, Best New Australian Work; Best Sound Design, and Best Scenic Design, among many others. Five years later, when the play was performed again at Carriageworks, it was declared by *ArtsHub*, an independent online forum, to be the best Australian play of the 21st century.

Roots in Jaffna: A Personal and Political Legacy

The play drew inspiration from the family history of Shakthidharan, also known as Shakthi, whose ancestral roots trace back to Jaffna, in the northern part of Sri Lanka. The central character, Manickavasagar, is loosely based on Shakthi's great-grandfather, C. Suntharalingam, a prominent Tamil politician.

Shakthi left Sri Lanka as a toddler in the aftermath of Black July, a state-sponsored wave of violence that targeted Tamil homes, businesses, and live during July 1983. His mother, Anandavalli, was a renowned Bharatanatyam dancer and his father, Jayantha Sivanathan, was an electrical engineer. Both hailed from Colombo's well-established Tamil community, known for its strong ties and enduring relationships with their

Sinhala counterparts. Yet, even they were forced to flee, underscoring the devastating significance of Black July as a turning point in Sri Lanka's history.

Growing Up in Western Sydney

Shakthi grew up in the Western suburbs of Sydney not knowing much about the reasons for fleeing Sri Lanka. His mother, never spoke of it, because leaving the country had been so painful.

It was his grandmother who gave him his name, Shakthidharan. In Hindu theology, Shakthi is feminine power. Naming him thus was a way of including the feminine power of Shakthi within a male name. For Shakthi, his name carries the weight of this legacy. It is a daily reminder of his grandmother's wish to instil that same indomitable spirit within him. He is the only child of a single mother after his parents divorced

Shakthi's mother, Anandavalli, established a dance school in 1985 after settling in Australia. Growing up amid his mother's Bharatanatyam dance company, Shakthi was surrounded by strong, resilient women. These women, hailing from conservative communities in Colombo and Jaffna, were navigating the challenges of starting anew in Australia while battling systems that often sought to render them invisible. Shakthi recalls his mother as a formidable presence—intimidating at times and quick to raise her voice, undeniably strong and a survivor in every sense of the word. To Shakthi, she is a testament to the strength required for these women to make their voices heard in a world that often tried to silence them.

Surrounded by the vibrant energy of his mother's dance school, Shakthi witnessed firsthand the transformative power of the stage and its ability to enchant audiences. Drawn to storytelling and its potential to influence society, he was captivated by the stage's magic.

Sacred and Radical

As Shakthi recalls, observing the backstage workings, he realized it was a place where "anything can happen." He saw it as both a "sacred space" and a "radical space," acknowledging its potential for transformation and innovation.

Shakthi's solitary childhood fostered a deep connection to art. He spent countless hours immersed in books and music, finding solace and inspiration in these creative outlets. Art became a powerful tool for him to make sense of the world and express himself.

Despite her artistic background, Anandavalli was hesitant to let her son pursue a career in the arts. Guided by traditional Tamil values and acutely aware of the challenges faced by artists, she encouraged Shakthi to choose a stable and respectable profession, such as a doctor, engineer, or accountant. Seeking a compromise, Shakthi opted for journalism—a profession he hoped would satisfy his mother and extended family while staying true to his creative aspirations.

Community Artist

In 2003, while at university, 21-year-old Shakthi channelled his passion into founding an arts company called *CuriousWorks*, dedicated to amplifying diverse community voices. Through this initiative, he embraced the role of a community artist, helping others share their stories with the world. Later, he left *CuriousWorks* to start a new venture called *Kurinji*—named after a South Indian flower that blooms once every twelve years—alongside his long-time collaborator, composer, actor, and wife, Aimée Falzon.

Like many children of diasporas, Shakthi eventually came to realize how little he knew about his own story and the journey of displacement that brought his family to Australia. Questions about his roots began to stir within him: how had his family ended up in Australia? What had truly happened in Sri Lanka? These questions sparked a deep need to understand his past.

Reclaiming the Past

Driven by this quest, Shakthi began speaking to members of the Tamil diaspora, both in Australia and across the world, connecting with people from all walks of life. His growing curiosity and research soon made it clear that a visit to Sri Lanka was essential.

However, his mother was strongly opposed to the idea. Defying her wishes, Shakthi travelled to Sri Lanka to visit his uncle and uncover his family's history. There, his uncle handed him a shoebox of letters written by his great-grandfather, revealing hidden chapters of his family's legacy. This discovery ignited an even deeper dive into Sri Lanka's turbulent history and Shakthi's own identity. Further conversations with members of the Tamil diaspora—from politicians to asylum seekers—fuelled a narrative that would ultimately blossom into his groundbreaking three-hour theatrical production, *Counting and Cracking*.

What Shakthi uncovered about his family history revealed an intimate connection to the events that led to his parents' uprooting from their homeland. At the centre of this story was his great-grandfather, C. Suntharalingam, a figure deeply intertwined with Sri Lanka's political and social evolution.

Suntharalingam, an Oxford-educated mathematician from the village of Urumpirai in northern Sri Lanka, entered politics in the 1940s. In 1947, he won a seat in parliament and became a minister in the newly independent government as a member of the United National Party. However, his political journey was marked by principled defiance. Though he initially supported the controversial Ceylon Citizenship Act, which stripped citizenship from 11% of the population—primarily Indian Tamils—he resigned from his ministerial position during the act's second reading, unable to reconcile his conscience with its implications. From that point on, he became a staunch advocate for the rights of the disenfranchised Indian Tamils.

Re-elected to parliament in 1952, Suntharalingam's focus shifted to resisting the imposition of Sinhala as the sole official language of the country. In 1955, he famously warned that if Sinhala were enshrined as the only state language, Tamils would demand an autonomous state of "*Thamil Ilankai*" for Tamil-speaking peoples. By 1963, Suntharalingam became the first Sri Lankan politician to call for an independent Tamil state, which he termed "*Eylom*." Despite his political convictions, he maintained enduring personal relationships with the Sinhala political elite.

In a letter to Sri Lanka's Deputy Prime Minister in 1961, Suntharalingam sharply critiqued the misuse of democracy to justify oppression. He asserted that "democracy means the counting of heads within certain bounds and cracking of heads beyond those bounds," foreshadowing the intensifying struggle of the Tamil people. By the late 1970s, under Sri Lanka's unitary constitution, Tamils faced systemic discrimination through constitutional amendments that exacerbated their marginalization. These injustices propelled a younger generation of Tamils to embrace Suntharalingam's defiant philosophy.

How Art Helped Healing

Shakthi, deeply cognizant of his family's history and his great-grandfather's legacy, drew inspiration for *Counting and Cracking* from this lineage. The central character of the play was a tribute to Suntharalingam, and its title echoed his great-grandfather's pointed metaphor about democracy—a testament to the enduring relevance of his ideas.

The staging of *Counting and Cracking* proved to be a deeply cathartic experience for Anandavalli. Shakthi observed how it allowed her to reconnect with positive memories of her homeland, enabling her to reclaim a more nuanced identity. Reflecting on her journey, she expressed, "My Sri Lankan identity is more than just that week in 1983. It's all of these moments, like a river of time, that have shaped who I am." Like his mother, Shakthi's Tamil identity exists within the broader framework of a Sri Lankan identity, a perspective shared by many Tamils whose families have lived for generations in the southern parts of the island.

The extent of Anandvalli's liberation from her fears became evident when she took on the central role in Shakthi's next play, *The Jungle and the Sea*, which delved into the Sri Lankan conflict and the harrowing end of the civil war.

The Jungle and the Sea: War, Loss, and Belonging

The Jungle and the Sea, staged in late 2022 at Sydney's Belvoir Theatre, was a resounding success, playing to packed audiences. It was co-produced with Eamon Flack, who was also the Director and associate writer on *Counting and Cracking*. While the first spanned several decades, capturing the sweeping historical arc of the second half of the 20th century and the early 21st century, The *Jungle and the Sea* focused more narrowly on the final decade of the 20th century and the first decade of the 21st. Like its predecessor, this play also revolved around a Tamil family torn apart by war and forced to live in two countries: war-torn Sri Lanka and Australia. It powerfully depicted the struggles of a family displaced, dispossessed, and forced into exile.

The family in *The Jungle and the Sea* is portrayed as upper-middle-class, westernised, and anglicised—conscious of their Tamil heritage but detached from the nationalist narrative of Sri Lanka's Tamil masses. The play's climax unfolds during the final, brutal phase of the Sri Lankan civil war and its immediate aftermath. At the same time, the Tamil diaspora in Sydney takes to the streets to protest the massacres occurring in Sri Lanka. In a striking moment, one character refers to these protests as being led by "Sri Lankans," a label that feels incongruous given the context. Later, she admits to having secretly contributed money to the Tamil Tigers, highlighting the inner conflict of the Sri Lankan Tamil upper-middle-class—torn between their Tamil identity and their broader Sri Lankan affiliation.

This nuanced depiction resonates with the work of Professor Karthigesu Sivathamby, whose collection of articles on Tamil identity was aptly titled *Being a Tamil and Sri Lankan*. Shakthi, aware of and perhaps grappling with this same duality, appears to have woven this tension into *The Jungle and the Sea*, offering a poignant exploration of identity, belonging, and the complexities of diaspora life.

The Craft of Storytelling

Shakthi's success as a storyteller stems from his thoughtful approach and philosophy. He deeply understands the power of storytelling to shape perceptions and impact lives. He believes that every story carries the potential to leave a mark, and that it's crucial to approach storytelling with intention. For him, storytelling isn't merely about recounting events; it's about conveying truth in all its complexity. He strives to tell stories that foster understanding, offering audiences a clearer and more compassionate perspective on the intricate layers of reality.

Central to Shakthi's philosophy is the interconnectedness of humanity. He believes that despite our differences, we share a fundamental commonality. This belief enables him to connect with audiences on a profound level.

Through his work, Shakthi seeks to create spaces where healing can occur—not just for individuals but for communities. His stories are crafted to resonate with those who carry wounds, providing a shared experience that encourages both reflection and renewal. In wielding the power of storytelling with care and intention, Shakthi aims to inspire transformation and connection, bridging divides and helping audiences move closer to a shared sense of humanity.

Shakti's Model of Creation

At the same time Shakthi understands that stories like these don't emerge in isolation; they require a radically different approach to storytelling. In an interview with *The Saturday Paper*'s Celina Ribeiro, he dismissed the romanticized notion of the lone creative genius scribbling away in solitude, calling it "bullshit." For Shakthi, telling these stories demands a new way of writing—one rooted in collaboration and inclusivity. It requires rethinking every aspect of the process, from production to casting, from marketing to staging.

This approach brings new voices to the forefront, voices often overlooked by the mainstream. It means audiences from diverse backgrounds—those with surnames the establishment struggles to pronounce and from suburbs it rarely acknowledges—finally seeing themselves reflected on stage. Shakthi's storytelling is as much about reimagining the system as it is about the stories themselves, creating spaces where everyone belongs and every voice is heard.

When advising Chenturan Aran, an Australian-born Tamil playwright whose work delves into themes of memory, migrant families, and technology, Shakthi shared a key insight into his creative philosophy. He emphasized the importance of authenticity, saying, "The image you put out to the world is what people think you're offering. If you pitch something that, isn't you and it goes well, you are kind of screwing yourself because they're going to want more of that. It's incumbent upon us to work from our instincts, because that's the version of us we want the world to want more off." [13]

Shakthi recognises the complexity of the Tamil people who are central to his plays *Counting and Cracking* and *The Jungle and the Sea*. He understands their passion and strong opinions and acknowledges that responses to grief can vary greatly.

Shakthi approaches success with a unique perspective. He distances himself from traditional definitions, focusing instead on the intrinsic value and impact of his work. He is grateful for the recognition his play Counting and Cracking has received, particularly its celebration as a significant migrant and Sri Lankan story within Australia. This success has allowed him to move beyond the need for self-validation. While he acknowledges the industry and societal success of his plays, his ultimate satisfaction lies in the healing and connection they have fostered among audiences.

Reflections

Shakthi's journey, rooted in his personal history and Sri Lankan Tamil heritage, reflects a profound commitment to storytelling as a tool for connection, healing, and understanding. Through his groundbreaking works, he has illuminated the complex narratives of displacement, identity,

---

[13]https://saaricollective.com.au/culture/blog/we-dont-want-to-be-divided-in-conversation-with-playwright-s-shakthidharan/

and resilience, offering audiences a chance to grapple with uncomfortable truths while finding shared humanity. By creating spaces for underrepresented voices and challenging conventional paradigms of storytelling, Shakthi continues to redefine the cultural landscape, leaving an indelible mark on Australian theatre and beyond.

Mira and Dipha Thiruchelvam: Singing the Story of Exile

A Moment of Affirmation

It was a surreal moment on 24 April 2024, as Norwegian-Tamil sisters Mira and Dipa Thiruchelvam stepped onto the stage to accept the Spellemannprisen—Norway's equivalent of the Grammy Awards. Their band, *9 Grader Nord*, had just won in the open category for *Yalpanam*, a bold 2023 album that fuses ancestral Tamil rhythms with Western folk-rock, pulsing with cultural pride and sonic defiance.

This wasn't their first brush with acclaim. Their 2019 debut album *Jaffna* had already made waves in Norway's music scene, earning Mira the prestigious Edvard Prize in the 'Challenger' category—one of the country's highest honours for composition.

Echoes of Jaffna on a Norwegian Stage

The name of the band and the titles of their award-winning albums are deeply rooted in Jaffna, located in the north of Sri Lanka and the spiritual heartland of the island's Tamil population. For many in the global Tamil diaspora, Jaffna is more than just a place—it is a symbol of origin and memory.

9 Grader Nord—meaning "9 degrees north"—points directly to the geographic latitude of Jaffna, anchoring the band's music in the homeland of their ancestors. The song *Yalpanam* revives the city's original Tamil name, restoring what was altered through centuries of colonial rule. Jaffna fell under Portuguese control in 1619, followed by Dutch rule from 1685 to 1796, and then British rule until Sri Lanka's independence in 1948. For over three centuries, the region was governed by Western powers. The shift from "Ya" to "Ja" in names like *Yalpanam* to Jaffna reflects the linguistic displacements common under colonisation—subtle but powerful changes that distort, erase, or overwrite local identities and histories.

By reclaiming these names and infusing them into their music, Mira and Dipha are not just making art—they are telling a story of roots, resistance, and reconnection. Their sound is a celebration of both heritage and hybridity, weaving together rock and pop with South Asian rhythms, and giving voice to a generation of young Tamils forging identity in exile.

Formation of the Band

In 2017, sisters Mira and Dipha —both accomplished flautists— founded *9 Grader Nord*, a band born out of a desire to honour and reimagine their cultural roots. Daughters of Tamil refugees who fled Sri Lanka's brutal civil war in the 1980s, the sisters were raised on stories of loss, resilience, and survival. Music became their way of making sense of this inheritance—a language of remembrance, resistance, and revival.

Mira, who also serves as the band's composer and producer, began writing music while still in high school. Guided by their father—himself a flautist and their first teacher—and influenced by a wide range of global sounds, she started shaping a musical identity that was both diasporic and deeply personal. As her passion for composing and producing grew, so did her vision: she wanted to form a band. She reached out to percussionist Jakob Sisselson Hamre, a kindred spirit who shared her interest in rhythmic innovation. He readily joined—and brought along his friend, bassist Jakob Sønnesyn. With Hamre and Sønnesyn on board, the ensemble was complete.

9 Grader Nord officially came into being—a bold fusion of ancestral memory and contemporary sound, anchored by the creative force of Mira and Dipha.

9 Grader Nord's music stands out not only for its distinctive sound but also for its lyrical choice—in Tamil. Despite the potential language barrier, their performances have resonated widely with Norwegian audiences, a testament to the band's ability to communicate emotion and meaning beyond words. Their sound transcends borders, inviting listeners into a richly textured world of cultural memory and lived experience.

Blending tradition with modernity, the band skillfully weaves together instruments like the bamboo flute and cajón with electric bass and synthesizers, crafting a soundscape that is at once grounded in heritage and daringly contemporary.

Claiming Identity Through Sound

9 Grader Nord's music explores themes of cultural identity, migration, and the preservation of roots in unfamiliar soil. Their work captures the complexities of diasporic life—the tensions between belonging and assimilation, the weight of inherited sacrifice, and the evolving relationship between first- and second-generation Tamils in Norway. Through sound and storytelling, the band offers a powerful celebration of Tamil heritage and its dynamic intersections with Norwegian society.

Jaffna, their debut album, is a vivid exploration of cultural identity—a journey that was far from straightforward. Like many children of the diaspora, Mira and Dipha initially felt a quiet pressure to blend in and prove their belonging within Norwegian society. Mira recalled in an interview with *Tamil Guardian*[14] how, at school, they became skilled at hiding their true selves, often feeling self-conscious about their parents accented Norwegian and different background. But around the age of eighteen or nineteen, Mira experienced a profound shift—a sudden, fearless urge to fully embrace her identity. This awakening became the catalyst for *Jaffna*. More than just a collection of songs, the album is a bold and unapologetic celebration of Tamil culture in its raw and authentic form. This pride is expressed not only through the music but also through their choice to wear traditional saris and sing in Tamil. With *Jaffna*, Mira and Dipha claimed their heritage loudly and proudly, positioning themselves as the voice of their community's stories, resilience, and spirit.

Looking back, Mira reflects that their earlier need to hide wasn't just personal—it was shaped by the Norway they grew up in. "At the time, there wasn't much room for difference," she recalled. "Multiculturalism wasn't really part of the national conversation. The expectation was clear: adapt, fit in, don't stand out." That quiet pressure seeped into everything. But things have changed. "Now, there's more space to be who we are—to show up fully as Tamil and Norwegian," she says. For Mira, embracing her identity wasn't just an act of personal liberation; it was a response to a society slowly opening its eyes to the richness of difference. And this shift works both ways. As Norway becomes more multicultural, mainstream Norwegians are also growing more curious, more open, and more enthusiastic about other cultures—including Tamil music. "We sing in Tamil, and they don't just listen—they celebrate it," Mira says. "That's something I never imagined as a child. It's like we're finally being heard in our own language."

---

[14] *Tamil Guardian* 8 April 2024

Voices of Resistance and Recognition

The award-winning album *Yalpanam* features several powerful tracks that delve into pressing contemporary issues. As their second album, it marked a clear evolution in the band's artistic direction. Reflecting on this shift, Mira explained that *Yalpanam* was "totally different from our first in that it digs deeper into our roots. It's not about convincing the Norwegians—it's about finding ourselves and exploring the more vulnerable spaces between the two cultures."[15]

One song in particular, *Vayppu*, gives voice to the generational tensions within the Tamil diaspora in Norway. It pays tribute to the first wave of Tamil refugees who arrived in the 1980s, many of whom found work in the fishing industry. While the song honours their hard work, loyalty, and sacrifice, it also questions the silence surrounding the injustices they endured. Many in that first generation, having fled war and persecution, were understandably reluctant to question the system that gave them refuge—even when it was unequal or exploitative. For Mira and Dipha, this unquestioning gratitude is something the younger generation must reckon with. While they deeply respect their parents' sacrifices, they believe that those born and raised in Norway have the freedom—and responsibility—to reflect more critically on the structures they've inherited. *Vayppu* encourages listeners to move beyond passive thankfulness and confront the ways inequality can persist when left unchallenged.

The song sparked difficult conversations at home for the sisters. Their parents, still feeling a deep sense of indebtedness to Norway, were uneasy about its more critical message. But for Mira and Dipha, expressing these tensions is essential. *Vayppu* reminds us that gratitude and critique are not opposites—that to truly honour the present, we must have the courage to question the past.

Perhaps it is not only gratitude that shapes their parents' response. Having fled a state that not only discriminated but actively persecuted them, they are acutely aware that, as minorities in Norway, they have been treated with far more fairness and dignity than they ever experienced in their homeland.

---

[15] *Tamil Guardian* 8 April 204

A Unique Voice Within a Shared Culture

Another standout track, Victoria, is a powerful anthem celebrating women's independence, resilience, and triumph over adversity. Drawing inspiration from the legendary Tamil poet C. Subramania Bharati, the song centers around his iconic phrase *"Atcham illai"*—meaning "I have no fear." This phrase captures the spirit of courage and fearlessness that *9 Grader Nord* seeks to embody. Victoria honours the woman as the architect of her own success, emphasizing that her achievements arise not from external forces, but from her own determination and strength.

Mira highlights *Adayalam* as one of the most significant tracks on their second album—a song rooted in questions of identity. It's an unapologetic assertion of Eelam Tamil distinctiveness. While many in the diaspora gravitate toward the more dominant Tamil pop culture of Tamil Nadu, *Adayalam* pushes back, asking: do you want me to write like Vairamuthu or sing like Janaki and to tell her story? As Mira expanded on this when she told the Tamil Guardian, "We support Indian Tamil artists, but we don't support our own [...] Yes, we are Tamil, but we are Eelam Tamils. We have a unique history. We've been through genocide. Our story is different." *Adayalam* isn't just a song—it's a demand for recognition, a call to own and honour the narrative of a people shaped by loss, resilience, and resistance."

Reflections

Through *9 Grader Nord*, Mira and Dipha have created more than just a band—they've built a living archive of cultural memory, identity, and resistance. Their music gives voice to a generation caught between worlds: shaped by the pain of exile, the pull of ancestry, and the pressures of assimilation. Albums like *Jaffna* and *Yalpanam* are not simply musical triumphs—they are declarations of identity, woven from the dual threads of belonging and defiance.

With tracks like *Vayppu,* they honour the resilience of the first generation while refusing to let gratitude silence necessary critique. With Victoria, they uplift women's strength and self-determination, rewriting narratives long ignored. And with *Adayalam,* they make their most personal statement yet—staking claim to the distinct identity of Eelam Tamils. It is a call to the diaspora to stop erasing their own uniqueness in favour of the more dominant Tamil Nadu mainstream. It asks difficult, necessary questions: Who are we telling stories for? And whose stories are we choosing to tell?

By singing in Tamil, performing in saris, and fusing ancestral instruments with electric sounds, Mira and Dipha don't cater to the mainstream—they challenge it. They invite Tamil and non-Tamil listeners alike into a sonic space that is at once intimate and defiant, where language, memory, and music converge.

In doing so, *9 Grader Nord* has carved out more than a place in Norway's music scene—they've claimed space for a diasporic identity that is often misunderstood or overlooked. Their work reminds us that music can be a home—a place to remember, to resist, and ultimately, to belong.

WRITERS AND JOURNALISTS

George Alagiah: Reporting from the Margins

Bearing Witness with Compassion

One day in December 1992, George Alagiah stepped carefully through the dust and despair of a Somali refugee camp. Around him, chaos swirled—emaciated children cried for food, aid workers barked instructions, and camera crews jostled for the most harrowing shots. But George wasn't there for spectacle. Amid the noise, he spotted Amina, a mother who had trekked for days with her children clinging to life. He put down his notebook, sat beside her, and listened—not for soundbites, but for truth. Long before he became a trusted face in British living rooms, George was already doing what he did best. Bearing witness not to headlines, but to humanity.

In his subsequent report, George told Amina's story in detail, giving viewers a window into her daily struggles and resilience. His coverage helped humanize the crisis, reminding audiences that behind every headline were individuals with names, dreams, and dignity. It was this approach-putting ordinary people at the centre of extraordinary events-that became a hallmark of his journalism and set him apart as a storyteller who truly listened.

George became one of the BBC's most respected and recognisable journalists, serving as a leading foreign correspondent covering major global conflicts before becoming the main presenter of the BBC News at Six for two decades. His calm authority, empathy, and integrity made him a fixture of British television news and a trusted voice for millions of viewers

As he recounted in his memoir *A Passage to Africa*, while others chased breaking news, he sought out the quiet voices—refugees, survivors, and ordinary people—whose lives were shaped by conflict and injustice. It was in these moments, far from the studio lights, that he forged his reputation as a journalist who believed the world was best understood through the eyes of those most often overlooked.

Early Life and Displacement from Sri Lanka

George was born on 22 November 1955 in Colombo, the capital of Sri Lanka (then Ceylon), to Tamil parents, Donald and Therese Alagiah. His father was a civil engineer, and the family belonged to the Tamil community, which faced increasing ethnic tensions and discrimination on the island.

In May 1958, when George was just three years old, Sri Lanka was rocked by a violent anti-Tamil pogrom. Mobs from the largest ethnic group, the Sinhalese, targeted Tamil homes and businesses, resulting in widespread arson, looting, and killings. Hundreds of Tamils were murdered, with many more injured or displaced. The violence was so severe that the Sri Lankan state declared a state of emergency.

George later recalled in *A Passage to Africa* the fear that gripped his family during these events. He described how his family members were separated and terrified, each caught in the web of hatred that enveloped the city. He wrote:

"Anyone who sounded or looked like a Tamil was being singled out for a thorough beating... I was three at the time, oblivious of the politics of hatred, but, no doubt, conscious of the fear that was creeping around our home. My elder sisters knew something sinister was happening. They could hear the shouts of a crowd on the main road and knew the voices were raised in anger... All we could do was wait: for the noise to die down, for my father to return, for the rage to ebb away."

Recognizing the growing danger, George's father decided to leave Sri Lanka. As George explained in a 2019 interview, "Tamils very quickly found that they were on the wrong side of history... In 1958 there were some pretty bad riots, so my father was one of the first people who said: 'It's time to get out.'"

In December 1961, the Alagiah family moved to Ghana, West Africa, joining other Tamil families who fled Sri Lanka during this period. George began his primary education at Christ the King International School in Accra, Ghana. As George told *The Guardian*,[16] "

After moving to Ghana for safety and opportunity, the family's togetherness was further fractured when George and his sisters were sent to different boarding schools in England. From then on, they rarely lived as a family, reuniting only during brief school holidays. The sacrifices made by his parents, driven by the need to escape ethnic persecution, meant that

---

[16] *The Guardian* of 17 July 2010

the simple comfort of everyday family life was lost to them" It was a poignant portrayal of uprooting experienced by people forced to flee.

Education and Move to the UK

After several years in Ghana, George continued his education in England, attending St John's College, an independent Roman Catholic school in Portsmouth. He later studied politics at Van Mildert College, Durham University, where he became editor of the student newspaper Palatinate and served as a sabbatical officer of the Durham Students' Union.

Broadcasting Career

George began his journalism career in print, working for South Magazine and eventually becoming its Africa Editor. In 1989, he joined the BBC, initially as a Developing World correspondent based in London, and later as Southern Africa correspondent in Johannesburg.

He became one of the BBC's leading foreign correspondents, reporting on major international events such as the Rwandan genocide, the civil wars in Afghanistan, Liberia, Sierra Leone, Kosovo, and Somalia, and the plight of the Marsh Arabs in Iraq. He interviewed prominent figures including Nelson Mandela, Archbishop Desmond Tutu, Kofi Annan, and Robert Mugabe.

The major milestones of his career reflect both journalistic excellence and an unwavering commitment to human rights. In the early 1990s, his award-winning coverage of the famine and war in Somalia brought global attention to a devastating humanitarian crisis, distinguished by his empathetic and unflinching storytelling.

In 1994, he was nominated for a BAFTA for his courageous reporting on Saddam Hussein's genocidal campaign against the Kurds of northern Iraq, a testament to his ability to navigate complex and perilous environments with clarity and depth. That same year, Amnesty International named him Journalist of the Year for his work on the civil war in Burundi, recognising his dedication to ethical journalism and the defence of human dignity. His contributions were formally honoured in 2008, when he was appointed an Officer of the Order of the British Empire (OBE) for services to journalism—solidifying his place as one of the UK's most respected and trusted voices in the field.

Migration and Multiculturalism

Throughout his life, George reflected on the impact of displacement and the opportunities he found in the UK. He acknowledged the challenges faced by Tamils in Sri Lanka and the gratitude he felt for the life his family was able to build after fleeing violence. In 2021, In an article that he wrote for the *Financial Times, Migration, Memory and Me*, George noted "As the years unfolded, we understood that this country had given us opportunities that we would never have had in a Sri Lanka, where Tamils like us were systematically disadvantaged."

George was a patron of the Migration Museum in London. The Migration Museum explores how the movement of people to and from the UK across the ages has shaped who the British are – as individuals, as communities, and as nations. Indeed, George was instrumental in the formation of the Migration Museum.

As Sophie Henderson reflected, after reading George's warm and witty memoir *A Home from Home: From Immigrant Boy to English Man*, it was clear he supported the idea of a permanent Migration Museum in Britain.

In fact, he openly questioned in his book why such an institution didn't already exist—one that would place stories like his at the forefront and celebrate the vital role migrants have played in shaping Britain's culture, institutions, and everyday life. What she hadn't anticipated, however, was just how devoted an advocate George would become. later, as a trustee, George brought not only his public presence but also a rare blend of passion, positivity, attention to detail, and thoughtful critique that elevated the work of the entire Board. "[17]

George often reflected on his multicultural upbringing and the impact of displacement on family life. He spoke about the challenges of explaining his heritage to his British-born sons and the importance of connecting them to their Sri Lankan Tamil roots. His personal journey informed his empathy and ability to connect with audiences on issues of migration, identity, and belonging.

Other Interests

Beyond journalism, George Alagiah had a wide range of interests that

---

[17] In Memory of George Alagiah, https://www.migrationmuseum.org/in-memory-of-george-alagiah-obe/

reflected his deep social and cultural engagement. He was a regular presence at major literary festivals and spoke at prestigious institutions such as the Royal Geographical Society and the Royal Society of Arts. A keen supporter of the arts, he served on the board of the Royal Shakespeare Company. His commitment to global justice was evident in his role as a patron of the Fairtrade Foundation and his support for microfinance initiatives. He also championed family welfare as a patron of Parenting UK. In addition, Alagiah was a published novelist—his debut, *The Burning Land*, was shortlisted for a Society of Authors award in 2020. Through these pursuits, he extended his impact far beyond the newsroom, using every platform available to promote fairness, creativity, and understanding.

Personal Life and Legacy

George married Frances Robathan, whom he met at Durham University, in 1984. They had two children and lived in North London.

He was diagnosed with stage four bowel cancer in 2014 but continued to work and advocate for cancer awareness until his death on 24 July 2023, at the age of 67. He was much loved and admired.

Statements by colleagues and public figures demonstrated this as tributes poured in. *Question Time* presenter, Fiona Bruce called him "that rare thing – a first-rate journalist and an all-round lovely human being," noting that "integrity and decency shone through him." Veteran BBC broadcaster John Simpson said, "A gentler, kinder, more insightful and braver friend and colleague it would be hard to find." BBC Presenter Clive Myrie described him as "a mentor, colleague and friend," while Allan Little praised his "empathy" and ability to "win [people's] trust" from all walks of life. Former BBC correspondent Jon Sopel added: "Tributes will rightly be paid to a fantastic journalist and brilliant broadcaster – but George was the most decent, principled, kindest, most honourable man I have ever worked with. What a loss."

George is remembered as one of Britain's most respected journalists and broadcasters, as well as one of the early members of the Tamil diaspora. What shines through his life story is how deeply it reflects the shared experiences of countless uprooted Tamils—of loss, resilience, and the search for belonging.

Reflections

George's life and career stand as a testament to resilience, empathy, and the enduring power of storytelling. Forced to leave Sri Lanka as a child due to ethnic violence, he transformed the challenges of displacement into a deep understanding of the world's complexities, bringing rare compassion and insight to his reporting. From covering some of the most harrowing conflicts as a foreign correspondent to becoming a trusted presence in millions of homes as the face of *BBC News at Six*, George combined journalistic excellence with warmth and integrity.

Even in the face of personal adversity, he saw life as a gift and remained grateful for the opportunities and connections he found along the way. Remembered for his kindness, courage, and unwavering commitment to truth, George leaves behind a legacy that continues to inspire colleagues, viewers, and all who value the role of journalism in bridging divides and giving voice to the unheard.

Shankari Chandran: Redefining the Australian Story

Breaking Through the Literary Wall

When Shankari Chandran learned she had won the *Miles Franklin Literary* Award 2023—Australia's most prestigious literary honour—she was in disbelief. This recognition, awarded annually to a novel that best represents Australian life, felt unreal, especially given the challenges she had faced as a writer. She was told that her debut novel, *Song of the Sun God*, was "not Australian enough" for local publishers, forcing her to seek publication in Sri Lanka. Her second novel, *The Barrier*, was only published in Australia after she altered the protagonist's ethnicity from South Asian to white American to satisfy what she by then perceived to be the Australian publishing industry's demands.

Convinced that her books would no longer find a home in Australia's publishing world, Shankari decided to write a novel that explored her understanding of racism in the country. Liberated from the pressure to conform to industry expectations, and free from the fear of rejection, she poured her heart into this new project. The result was *Chai Time at Cinnamon Gardens,* a work of stunning authenticity and insight, which resonated so deeply that it earned her the highest Australian literary accolade—a testament to both her writing talent and the power of the story she chose to tell.

While the publishing industry was reluctant to engage with her, others offered invaluable support. Without the New South Wales government's Writers Fellowship and the Beckett Trust Scholarship, *Chai Time at Cinnamon Gardens* might never have been written. This support allowed Shankari the freedom to fully explore the themes she was passionate about, providing the space and encouragement she needed to bring the novel to life.

Rooted in Displacement: A Diasporic Childhood

Shankari was born in London in 1974, where her parents, both doctors, had relocated in the early 1970s to pursue further studies.

Any plans to return to Sri Lanka were soon abandoned as the persecution of Tamils in Sri Lanka intensified. Staying in London was not an easy option as migration laws did not allow those on student visas to change their status.[18] Seeking a safe environment to raise their family, they migrated to Australia in 1977. From there, they watched the anti-Tamil pogrom of 1977 unfold on television—a stark confirmation that Sri Lanka was no longer their "home." Then, in July 1983, Sri Lanka witnessed its most brutal anti-Tamil pogrom, a state-orchestrated atrocity marked by gross human rights violations. The severity of the violence led Australia to open its doors to Tamil refugees under a Special Humanitarian Program (SHP), and many of the Chandran family's friends and relatives managed to find refuge in Australia.

By the mid-1980s, Shankari's extended family—grandparents, uncles, aunts, and cousins—had all fled Sri Lanka. Some found refuge in Australia, while others settled in Europe, Canada, and the US. Like many in her generation, Shankari grew up within a global diaspora which included: Australian Tamils, British Tamils, American Tamils European Tamils, and Canadian Tamils. English became the dominant language for those in English-speaking countries, while others adopted European languages. Although Tamil was still spoken, it was no longer the first language for many. Their connection to Sri Lanka was now rooted more in a shared history of displacement than in the land itself. Yet, their ancestral homeland in Sri Lanka, Tamil Eelam, remained important, as a vital link to their past.

From a young age, Shankari was drawn to becoming a writer, using storytelling to explore her inner questions and make sense of the world around her.

Her Grade 5 teacher, Josephine Vandermark, played a pivotal role in nurturing this passion. Shankari fondly recalls how, just before the school holidays, her teacher would hand her rolls of computer paper, encouraging her to keep a journal and document her thoughts and experiences during the break. This simple yet thoughtful gesture helped instil in Shankari the discipline of writing regularly and the belief that her voice and stories mattered.

---

[18] Although qualified doctors pursuing higher studies could apply for exemptions, the process was mired in cumbersome bureaucracy. Countries like Australia appeared more promising for raising families

A Political Legacy and the Long Reach of War

Shankari's family was deeply politically engaged with the happenings in their homeland. Her uncle, Ravi, held a key position in the Australasian Federation of Tamil Associations (AFTA), an umbrella organization representing Tamil communities across Australia and New Zealand. AFTA was at the forefront of advocating for the Tamil cause, raising awareness within the wider Australian public. Similarly, her uncle Rajan, a U.S. citizen, was active in Tamil advocacy in America, while her youngest uncle, Kughan, played a similar role in the UK. Growing up, Shankari was acutely aware of the ongoing atrocities in Sri Lanka and the gross violations of human rights inflicted on the Tamil people. She understood that she had escaped this fate only because her parents had left Sri Lanka before the civil war erupted.

The war, a brutal twenty-six-year conflict, had a profound impact on Shankari's life, even from a distance—she was nine years old when it began and thirty-five when it ended. Speaking at the Sydney Writers' Festival in May 2024, fifteen years after the war's violent conclusion, Shankari explained how it impacted the likes of her because "War is dispossession on many levels. It's not just those directly affected who are dispossessed, but also future generations. We have watched it, and we have felt the grief and rage of having survived it. "[19] Aware that the Tamil experience reflected the broader, universal issue of displacement and loss, Shankari explored different facets of this dispossession in each of her five books. Her insights shed light on how intergenerational trauma has taken root among younger generations of Tamils, even for those like her who grew up far from the physical battlegrounds of the war.

Between Two Worlds: Growing Up in Canberra

Shankari's life in Canberra—a city characterized by its whiteness, monoculturalism, and orderliness—was far removed from the war-torn, tropical Tamil homeland of northern Sri Lanka.

While Canberra shaped her everyday experiences as she navigated school, homework, shops, and the library, her homeland remained an ever-

---

[19]https://www.arc.unsw.edu.au/blitz/interviews/sydney-writers-festival-2024/shankari-chandran

present factor in her life's trajectory. News from the war front, the ongoing suffering of her people, and frequent atrocities perpetrated by Sri Lanka's armed forces were accessible through a phone line offering pre-recorded updates from the battleground. To bypass the censorship imposed by the Sri Lankan state and counter its propaganda, the Tamil resistance established direct radio communications with the diaspora. This information was transcribed and faxed worldwide, ensuring that Tamils in the diaspora, including Shankari's family, remained informed. However, this also led to frustration when Australian media echoed Sri Lanka's biased narratives. Shankari learned early on that unchecked power could lead to injustice—a realization that would shape her views and future work.

While Shankari's weekdays were similar to those of other residents in Australia's capital city, her weekends were deeply immersed in Tamil culture. Along with many Tamil families who had migrated to Canberra, her parents spent their weekends socializing within the Tamil community. Many of the children worshipped at Tamil temples and churches and later, as the community grew, they also attended Tamil school, learning to read and write a language that shaped their identity, while others practiced Bharatanatyam. These gatherings provided a strong cultural and spiritual connection for a people uprooted from their homeland.

Growing up in this way, Shankari straddled two worlds. During the weekdays, she navigated the predominantly monocultural environment, trying to live a life similar to her Western peers. On weekends, however, she was immersed in Tamil culture, and expected to adhere to its values and traditions. This dual existence inevitably led to conflicts. Like many children of immigrants, Shankari did not participate in much of the social life of her Anglo-Australian friends., as her parents found it overly liberal. At the same time, she resisted some of the cultural norms of her Tamil heritage, realizing that it was shaped by her parents' generation. She came to understand that she was neither "white enough" to fully embrace (or be embraced by) Western culture nor "brown enough" to meet (or be completely bound by) the expectations of her Tamil upbringing.

Faith, Racism, and Resistance

One area where Shankari did not expect to encounter barriers was religion. The predominantly Hindu Tamil community practiced a form of Hinduism known as *Saivam*, which embraced a universal and inclusive approach not bound by holy books. It allowed for the coexistence of different beliefs—monotheism, polytheism, reincarnation, or even none at all—while still identifying as Hindu. This flexibility was captured in the Tamil saying "*onre kulam, oruvene thevan*" ("All mankind is one, God is one"), a sentiment popularized by the Tamil Saivite mystic Tirumular. Shankari and other Tamils expected similar religious tolerance in Australia but instead encountered subtle, yet pervasive, religious intolerance from some sections of the wider community. This form of racism—questioning whether one's culture or religion made them "less Australian"—became a troubling undercurrent in Shankari's experience growing up in Australia.

It wasn't just religious intolerance; the prejudice was much broader than that. Shankari recalls a few instances where people hurled racial slurs at her in school—nothing particularly inventive, things like "Blackie" or "Abo." But on a subtler level, there were more insidious forms of racism, harder to pinpoint yet ever-present. It required non-white individuals to fit in without drawing attention to the underlying inequalities. If someone dared to raise issues about racism, society, or cultural politics, the conversation was often shut down. Shankari understood that if she persisted, she risked being labelled an "angry brown woman," which would hinder her ability to move forward. As a result, the system pressured her to self-censor, suppressing her thoughts and preventing her from questioning the status quo.

Shankari was deeply angered by all forms of injustice, and reading To Kill a Mockingbird, inspired her childhood belief in the importance of defending fairness. Her decision to study law stemmed from a belief that the legal system held the potential to address such wrongs. She enrolled at the University of New South Wales and, through an exchange program, completed her final semester at McGill University in Canada. While there, she made a pivotal choice—enrolling in a Political Science course, "South Asian Post-Colonial Politics," which was outside her law curriculum. She needed to get special permission from the Dean of the Law faculty to pursue the course and write her thesis on —this topic. This decision had a profound impact on her life.

The course helped her understand how colonialism and the manipulation of history and religion had shaped post-colonial South Asia. It helped her realise how Sri Lanka's political elite had invented 'Political Buddhism' to gain power. She was particularly drawn to the works of scholars like Professor Stanley Tambiah, whose insights helped her understand the conflict in Sri Lanka in ways that she could later communicate to a Western audience.

Shankari came to understand that confronting the deep-rooted injustices faced by the Tamil people meant engaging with those who held power—and that power lay in the West. She believed that further training in law had equipped her to navigate and challenge that power effectively.

Law, Justice, and Global Advocacy

A British citizen by birth, Shankari arrived in the UK in 1999 and quickly found employment—not in the field of Human Rights, which was her passion, but at the prestigious law firm Allen & Overy, where she aimed to sharpen her legal skills. Within a year Shankari was appointed to the firm's pro-bono program —a role that marked the end of her corporate legal career and the start of her journey into social justice. She would come to love this position and hold for a decade.

At the time, in 2000, it was one of the first dedicated pro bono roles in the legal sector, and Shankari's task was to convince the firm—particularly its partners—that pro bono work was not only the right thing to do but also beneficial to the firm in the long run. Her job for the next ten years was to develop pro bono initiatives that aligned with the firm's values and interests, helping them recognize that success and profit could take non-financial forms. With the firm's growing support, Shankari worked to assist vulnerable communities and the organizations that served them, solidifying her role in advancing social justice.

In 2002, the Pro Bono Division of Allen & Overy was approached by the Human Rights Institute of the International Bar Association to assist in filing amicus briefs in the US courts, regarding the legal rights of Guantanamo Bay detainees to challenge their detention. Shankari's task was to convince the firm to accept the brief. The Guantanamo Bay case helped Shankari redefine what success in pro bono work truly meant. Following the 9/11 attacks, the US began detaining individuals, often with tenuous connections to the attacks, and transporting them to Guantanamo Bay, where they were subjected to torture or, as it was disingenuously called, "enhanced interrogation."

These detainees had no access to legal representation, no trial, and were held indefinitely in inhumane conditions. Shankari believed the US was violating the fundamental right of habeas corpus. She successfully argued to the partners that the resulting publicity would benefit the firm, while also presenting a compelling moral argument to the public: if we fail to defend people's rights to legal representation, a fair trial, and freedom from torture, we lose the moral authority to demand those same rights for ourselves.

Shankari continued to lead Allen & Overy's Pro Bono activities, overseeing work across 31 offices worldwide for the next seven years, until her return to Australia in 2009. These years were both challenging and fascinating for her. The Britain Shankari experienced during this time was vastly different from the Britain of the 1970s and 1980s—Asians were now an integral part of British society. As a British Asian, Shankari felt valued and appreciated, finding her place in a more inclusive, multicultural Britain.

Coming Home to a Changed Nation

Returning to Australia, however, came as a shock. The country she had grown up in seemed unfamiliar. She was disturbed by the widespread hostility towards asylum seekers, the public fear mongering about "boat people," and the tendency to blame migrants for societal issues. Beneath the rhetoric of border security, Shankari sensed a deep xenophobic undercurrent. Australia, under successive conservative governments, appeared to have regressed from the progressive policies of the Hawke-Keating era, fostering an environment of fear and division. The shift left her grappling with the reality of how much her country had changed while she was away.

Shankari was deeply concerned that Australia was in denial about its multicultural reality, clinging to an outdated identity. This denial, she believed, jeopardized her children's right to be seen and accepted as Australians. She wanted Australia to embrace its multiculturalism and face its issues with asylum seekers. Rather than simply complaining, she sought to contribute to the conversation through her writing.

In her debut novel, *Songs of the Sun God*, Shankari explored the lives of a Tamil family who migrated from Sri Lanka to Australia, tracing the experiences of subsequent generations. The novel is semi-autobiographical, with the lead character inspired by her grandmother, *Ammama*.

It also seeks to shed light on the atrocities committed in Mullivaikkal during the final stages of Sri Lanka's civil war—and on how such events were allowed to unfold.

In May 2009, as the war drew to a close, government forces advanced into a narrow strip of land in Mullivaikkal that had been designated a no-fire zone. Despite this designation, relentless shelling and attacks led to catastrophic civilian casualties. United Nations estimates suggest that between 40,000 and 70,000 Tamil civilians may have been killed, though some sources cite even higher figures. Most tellingly, these massacres have been compared to the later atrocities in Gaza—with one critical difference: the Mullivaikkal massacre took place without witnesses.

In her second novel, *The Barrier*, Shankari confronted the monocultural nature of Australia's publishing industry, reluctantly changing the ethnicity of her protagonist—originally a South Asian character—to a white man to make the book more marketable. This need to "whitewash" her book to have it published left Shankari devastated and confused. *Chai Time at Cinnamon Gardens* addressed the complexities of racism, while her fourth book, Safe Haven, examined Australia's harsh detention policies and the plight of asylum seekers. This last book was inspired by the real-life story of the Murugappan family, widely known across Australia as the "Bilola Family", a Tamil asylum seeker family whose struggle garnered widespread public sympathy in Australia.

Shankari's legal training not only shapes her writing but also guides the in-depth research she conducts for her books. More importantly, it influences the stories she chooses to tell, as her work is often driven by a desire to address issues of justice and inequality.

Reflections

Shankari Chandran believes in the law as a powerful means to combat injustice, a conviction that guided her advocacy for fair trials for Guantanamo Bay inmates. Yet her faith in legal systems has been shaken by governments that violate human rights with impunity, undermining the law's credibility as a tool for justice.

Reflecting on her own experiences in Australia, Shankari acknowledges the country's progress despite enduring issues such as refugee policies, subtle racism, and an unwillingness to fully address its colonial legacy.

Her parents faced pressure to assimilate and preserve their culture amidst racism, while she herself struggled with not fitting neatly into either the Tamil or white Australian communities. In contrast, her children now grow up in an environment that encourages pride in cultural identity and grants them the freedom to define what that identity means. For Shankari, this marks meaningful progress.

Now a mother of four, Shankari balances part-time legal work with writing—driven by the anger she feels at persistent injustice and the burden of having to constantly prove herself as a person of colour. She transforms this rage into stories rooted in empathy and understanding, finding in writing both a refuge and a means of resistance.

A self-described modern feminist, Shankari also finds empowerment through Thai boxing, a physical practice that reflects her deeper belief in confronting challenges directly. Both in her activism and her creative life, Shankari embodies resilience, strength, and a commitment to redefining identity and justice in contemporary Australia.

HUMANITARIANS AND HUMAN RIGHTS DEFENDERS

Ahilan Arulanantham: Defending the Displaced

A Genius for Justice

In 2016, Ahilan Arulanantham, then 43, received one of the most prestigious accolades in the United States: the MacArthur Fellowship, often called the "Genius Grant." This prestigious award, recognizes those Americans whose extraordinary originality, dedication, and self-direction, have led to remarkable accomplishments in their field. With its no-strings-attached grant of $625,000, the fellowship affirmed that Ahilan's tireless commitment to justice and human rights was nothing short of genius.

As an American human rights lawyer who specializes in immigrants' rights, particularly the rights of people facing deportation from the United States, Ahilan's work stands at the intersection of justice and humanity giving voice to the voiceless and hope to the hopeless. Ahilan is a professor from practice & Faculty co-director of the Center for Immigration Law and Policy (CILP) at the UCLA School of Law. and has been a lecturer at the University of Chicago and University of California, Irvine law schools.

Roots of Compassion

Ahilan was born in the United States to Sri Lankan Tamil parents who had migrated to escape sporadic violence and widespread discrimination against Tamils in their homeland. By the time Ahilan was ten years old, Sri Lanka had descended into civil war, forcing most of his extended family to flee. Many of them found refuge in the US with some of them living with his family for several years.

As a child, Ahilan witnessed firsthand the profound pain and challenges caused by displacement. He watched the war upend three generations of families were uprooted en masse in the face of brutal violence. Some of his cousins arrived without their parents, leaving a deep impression on him. In later years, these experiences resonated with the plight of Central American children separated from their families, making the issue profoundly personal and immediate for him.

A Calling Forged by Crisis

Ahilan's journey into human rights law began when he worked as an Equal Justice Works Fellow for the American Civil Liberties Union (ACLU) Immigrants' Rights Project in New York. After the 9/11 terrorist attacks, he witnessed firsthand how the ACLU responded to the wave of anti-immigrant backlash that followed. It was during this period that he learned from human rights advocates "that leadership in times of crisis requires a combination of moral clarity, rigorous analysis, and courage."[20]

Ahilan provided legal assistance to immigrants arrested on immigration charges and wrongfully detained in connection with the 9/11 attacks, and also supported the ACLU's advocacy against The Patriot Act, which was passed in the wake of 9/11. These individuals came from diverse regions of the world—South Asia, North Africa, Indonesia, and the Caribbean, among others. Some were undocumented, while others had lawful immigration status. Despite their ethnic and legal differences, they shared one undeniable truth: *Not a single one of them had anything to do with the 9/11 attacks.*[21] They were also all people of colour.

Racial Bias at the Border

Ahilan had a personal story to share on this topic.

Shortly after the Patriot Act's passage, he attended a legal conference in Tucson focused on immigration issues like detention and expedited removal. Following the first day, he joined younger attorneys in a border protest highlighting migrant deaths in the desert. Later, they crossed into Nogales, Mexico, for dinner.

At the time, crossing the border required only a driver's license. Over dinner, someone proposed an experiment: they would re-enter the U.S. one by one to see if Ahilan, the only non-white member, would be stopped. Ahilan agreed, and bets were placed. The question was settled when Ahilan was sent to secondary inspection and Matt Adams, a colleague, had to intervene, vouching for him, in order for Ahilan to be released. The experience illustrated a systemic bias: a white witness's word was required to secure his re-entry into his own country.

Ahilan points out that the need for a white person to validate one's

---

[20] https://law.yale.edu/studying-law-yale/alumni-student-profiles/ahilan-t-arulanantham-99
[21] https://prime.dailybruin.com/arulanantham

legitimacy is rooted in a troubling historical precedent. During the Chinese Exclusion Era, characterised by discriminatory laws and policies, the 1893 Supreme Court case *Fong Yue Ting* upheld the "one white witness" rule, Chinese immigrants had to provide testimony from a white person affirming their prior residency to prove their entitlement to live in the US. Although that law is no longer in effect, the case has never been overruled, and the doctrine it established continues to influence modern immigration law.

The Case of Ahilan Nadarajah

In 2006, in a landmark early victory, Ahilan secured the release of a Tamil asylum seeker who shares his first name. Ahilan Nadarajah, who had been detained in the U.S. since 2001 on unfounded suspicions of ties to the Liberation Tigers of Tamil Eelam (LTTE), a group designated as a terrorist organisation by the United States. Nadarajah had fled Sri Lanka after enduring brutal torture by the Sri Lankan Army, including beatings, cigarette burns, and suffocation. Despite an immigration court granting him asylum in 2003, the U.S. government continued to detain him, claiming the authority to hold suspects indefinitely under post-9/11 anti-terrorism policies.

In 2006, the U.S. Court of Appeals for the 9th Circuit ruled his detention "unreasonable, unjustified, and in violation of federal law." The court firmly rejected the government's argument, with Judge Sidney R. Thomas declaring that no alien could be held indefinitely without legal basis. Ahilan, then a staff attorney with the ACLU of Southern California, emphasized the broader implications of the case: "The government got it completely wrong. My client is a torture victim, not a threat to our country".[22] This decision not only secured Nadarajah's freedom but also challenged the government's overreach, setting a precedent for other asylum seekers unjustly detained. Although Ahilan Nadarajah was released, he had spent the four and a half years incarcerated without justification.

Other Successes and Challenges

Ahilan's other early successes include securing the release of a client by

---

[22] US Court Frees Tamil Detainee, *Tamil Guardian*, 21 March 2006 https://www.tamilguardian.com/content/us-court-frees-tamil-detainee

challenging the U.S. military's detention, in Iraq, of a U.S. citizen accused of being an enemy agent (*Kar v. Bush*, et al.); opposing the government's policy of forcibly drugging noncitizens prior to removal *(Diouf v. Chertoff)*; and contesting the policy that denied workers arrested in immigration raids the right to consult with counsel (*NLG v. Chertoff*).

In 2009, Ahilan co-litigated a landmark case against Immigration and Customs Enforcement (ICE) over the inhumane conditions at its "B-18" detention facility in Los Angeles. The facility, notorious for overcrowding, lacked basic necessities like soap and drinking water. Through his efforts, the lawsuit resulted in a comprehensive settlement that not only addressed these appalling conditions but also ended ICE's practice of shuttling detainees between local jails to circumvent rules against long-term detention at B-18. This victory was another step in Ahilan's relentless fight to uphold the dignity and rights of those caught in the immigration system.

One of Ahilan's devastating losses came in 2016 with the case *J.E.F.M. v. Lynch*, a class action lawsuit seeking to establish the right to appointed counsel for children facing deportation. For Ahilan, the case was deeply personal and urgent, as thousands of children fleeing violence in El Salvador, Guatemala, and Honduras faced life-threatening danger if deported. Despite the moral and legal clarity of the case, the court ruled against the class action, stating that children seeking counsel must appeal individually within their own immigration proceedings. The decision struck at the heart of Ahilan's mission, leaving thousands of vulnerable children to navigate a complex and adversarial system on their own. The case remains a poignant reminder of the systemic barriers in the fight for justice and the high stakes involved when human lives hang in the balance.

Such losses were not uncommon for Ahilan, who has throughout his career, confronted formidable obstacles that were often beyond his control.

"The rightward shift of the federal judiciary, the rising tide of anti-immigrant sentiment, and the intensifying partisan divide have all posed significant challenges to his mission of creating a more humane and just immigration system. Over time, these forces have shrunk the space available to create incremental progressive change toward a more humane and fair immigration system",[23] he reflects. "I don't know that I have overcome these obstacles, but the successes I have had, have come through constantly reassessing tactics in response to changing

---

[23] *A Fighter for Justice*, https://law.yale.edu/studying-law-yale/alumni-student-profiles/ahilan-t-arulanantham-99

conditions."²⁴

Ahilan's ability to adapt, recalibrate, and persevere in the face of such challenges underscores his dedication to advancing justice, even when the path forward seems uncertain.

Inspired by Gandhi

In October 2024, while accepting Equal Justice Works' Distinguished Alumni Award, Ahilan reflected on how Mahatma Gandhi's philosophy had guided him through the inevitable setbacks of his career. He shared his admiration for Gandhi's decades-long, peaceful struggle for the decolonization of South Asia—one of history's greatest triumphs for freedom. Quoting Gandhi, Ahilan said, *"It's the action, not the fruit of the action, that's important. You have to do the right thing. It may not be in your power, may not be in your time, that there will be any fruit, but that does not mean you stop doing what is right. You may never know what results come from your action, but you know if you do nothing, there will be no result."*²⁵ For Ahilan, this perspective offered clarity and resilience. Even when outcomes seemed uncertain or victories elusive, Gandhi's words reminded him that persistence in pursuing justice was itself a meaningful and necessary act.

Personal Heros

Among the figures who inspired Ahilan's journey in human rights is the late Dharmaratnam Sivaram, whose life and work are chronicled in *Learning Politics from Sivaram* by Mark Whitaker. This book heads Ahilan's list of essential reads, reflecting Sivaram's profound influence on him. Ahilan had the opportunity to meet Sivaram and speak with him in person for several hours not long before he was assassinated. Sivaram was more than a journalist; he was a thinker, activist, and advocate for Tamil justice in Sri Lanka, blending intellectual rigor with fearless commitment to truth. His life exemplified the courage needed to challenge oppression and the power of individuals to shape history. Little wonder that for Ahilan, Sivaram's legacy serves as both an inspiration and a reminder that intellectual clarity and advocacy can amplify marginalized voices and drive

---

²⁴ *A Fighter for Justice*, https://law.yale.edu/studying-law-yale/alumni-student-profiles/ahilan-t-arulanantham-99
²⁵ Ahilan T Arulanantham Accepts 2024 Distinguished Alumni Award https://www.youtube.com/watch?v=2xS7Ocl5cbg

meaningful change.

Another figure Ahilan admires is Mark Dow, author of *American Gulag: Inside U.S. Immigration Prisons* (2004). Aimed primarily at a legal audience, the book exposes the appalling conditions endured by immigration detainees in detention centres scattered across the United States—an "archipelago" of suffering hidden in plain sight. Dow's mission, as he puts it, is to "leave a record ... of something the U.S. government has long preferred to keep far from view." He challenges the misconception that the mistreatment of immigration detainees began after September 11, 2001, arguing instead that abuse and the systemic denial of civil and human rights have been persistent issues in the immigration detention system. According to Dow, the post-9/11 era didn't create this mistreatment; it merely provided cultural justification for practices long entrenched in the system.

Recognition

In 2010, the American Immigration Lawyers Association (AILA) honoured Ahilan with the prestigious Arthur C. Helton Human Rights Award. As then-Director of Immigrants' Rights and National Security advocacy at the ACLU of Southern California, Ahilan was recognized for his groundbreaking litigation that profoundly benefited countless vulnerable non-citizens, safeguarding their rights and dignity.

The award commemorates Arthur Helton, a distinguished advocate for refugees and asylum seekers. Ahilan embodies Helton's legacy, demonstrating the compassion, intellect, tenacity, and strategic thinking that define excellence in the fight for human rights.

Ahilan's exceptional contributions to immigrants' rights have earned him widespread recognition. He was named one of California Lawyer magazine's Lawyers of the Year in both 2007 and 2013—once for his work protecting the due process rights of thousands of detained immigrants to obtain hearings where they could seek release on bond, and six years later for his work to establish a right to appointed counsel for immigrants with serious mental disorders facing deportation. Ahilan has also consistently appeared on the Daily Journal's list of Top 100 Lawyers in California over the past decade. In 2014, he received the Jack Wasserman Memorial, honouring his impactful litigation to protect the rights of vulnerable immigrants.

Fighting Racism in Immigration Law

Ahilan, recognising the deep-seated racism embedded in the application of immigration law, understood the urgent need to confront it. Among the significant actions he pursued were:
- **Ramos v. Nielsen, (October 2018)** First as the Legal Director of the ACLU of Southern California and then as Co-Director of the Center for Immigration Policy, Ahilan led a group of attorneys who sought to stop the first Trump Administration from ending the Temporary Protected Status program for approximately 400,000 long-time residents from six countries. Ahilan argued that the Trump Administration's actions were motivated by racism, in part because Trump labelled the TPS holders "people from shithole countries" in a meeting where he rejected a bipartisan proposal to grant them lawful permanent residence. A court ruled in the TPS holders' favour, and the ruling was ultimately upheld on appeal. That decision remained the only nationwide injunction against a Trump administration policy on anti-discrimination grounds that survived all four years of the Administration. As of this writing, every person who held Temporary Protected Status in 2016 remains eligible for it today.
- **United States v. Rodrigues-Barios (March 2022):** As Co-Director of the Center for Immigration Policy, Ahilan collaborated with the Aoki Center for Critical Race and Nation Studies and the Southern Poverty Law Center to file an amicus brief in the Ninth Circuit Court of Appeals. The case addressed a pivotal racial justice issue. The defendant, Mr. Rodrigues-Barios, argued that the criminal illegal re-entry statute—a primary driver of mass incarceration for Mexicans—was unconstitutional because it was originally enacted to discriminate against Mexicans based on their race.
- **Reversing Racist Precedent (August 2023):** Ahilan authored a groundbreaking paper titled Reversing Racist Precedent advocating that courts should overturn prior decisions rooted in racial animus, as such precedents violate the Constitution's anti-discrimination principles. This insight emerged from his experiences litigating immigration cases against the federal government, where he repeatedly encountered government attorneys citing cases from the Chinese Exclusion Era. These

cases, laden with overtly racist reasoning, were still being used to justify legal positions, highlighting the urgent need for their repudiation.
- **Protections for Venezuelans Pending a Final Decision (March 2025)**: Ahilan played a key role in securing protections for Venezuelans facing uncertainty in the United States. As counsel for the plaintiffs, he successfully challenged the federal government's attempt to strip Temporary Protected Status (TPS) from Venezuelan nationals. Had the government's actions prevailed, approximately 350,000 Venezuelans could have lost their work authorization and faced the risk of deportation. The case preserved critical protections while a final decision remains pending.

Through these efforts, Ahilan has sought to expose and dismantle the structural racism perpetuated through immigration laws and their enforcement.

Reflections

Ahilan's unwavering commitment to justice has defined his career, as he challenges systemic biases and racial discrimination embedded in immigration law. From securing landmark victories for asylum seekers and detained immigrants to confronting the racist legacies of historical legal precedents, he combines legal acumen with a deep sense of humanity. His work not only seeks to rectify past injustices but also to inspire a more equitable future, where the rule of law protects rather than oppresses.

The values that guide Ahilan's legal advocacy are rooted in a broader intellectual tradition shaped by figures who modelled fearless engagement with power and injustice. The writings and legacy of Dharmaratnam Sivaram offered Ahilan a profound example of how rigorous thought and moral clarity can serve as tools of resistance. Sivaram's life and work impressed upon Ahilan the importance of coupling critical analysis with the courage to speak uncomfortable truths.

Similarly, Mark Dow's *American Gulag* sharpened Ahilan's understanding of how state systems conceal cruelty behind bureaucratic walls. Dow's insistence on bearing witness to hidden abuses in immigration detention resonates deeply with Ahilan's own mission: to bring visibility to injustice, uphold the humanity of the marginalized, and hold the state accountable to its own ideals.

Together, these influences have helped shape a vision of justice that is unflinching in its critique and grounded in compassion. In the courtroom, the classroom, and the public arena, Ahilan continues to advocate for a legal system that defends dignity and restores faith in the promise of equal justice.

Arunn Jegan: On the Front Lines of Humanity

On the Ground in Palestine: A Human Perspective

In 2024, Arunn Jegan, led Médecins Sans Frontières's (MSF) projects in one of the world's most volatile regions—Palestine. His journey to date, shaped by years with MSF and other humanitarian organisations, has taken him to some of the world's harshest crisis zones: Yemen, Afghanistan, Syria, Iraq, and beyond. Each assignment has deepened his understanding of the stakes, as he witnessed firsthand the devastating toll of violence and deprivation on ordinary lives. For Arunn, being an aid worker transcends the task of delivering resources; it is about ensuring solidarity to people in their darkest times. To those he works with, his presence is a powerful reminder that the world has not turned its back on them, that their suffering is seen, and that, against all odds, they are not forgotten.

In November 2023, Arun, then in Sydney spoke to Australia's *Channel Seven* about the grim reality at Al-Shifa Hospital in Gaza. He recounted how the hospital, already crippled by severe shortages of medical supplies, faced unimaginable challenges. Doctors were forced to perform amputations and surgeries without anaesthesia. But the crisis extended beyond resource scarcity; the hospital itself was under relentless attack. Even ambulances carrying injured children to Al-Shifa were bombed, killing both patients and the driver. Arunn shared the growing dangers faced by MSF staff, whose work was becoming nearly impossible under these conditions. As he described it, it was a deeply personal and urgent appeal— "one of my worst days as a humanitarian." His account was a powerful reminder of the dire realities civilians and aid workers face.

With independent news coverage severely limited, and Palestinian voices being unfairly screened and silenced, voices like Arunn's have become the last line of communication, bearing witness to the devastation and carrying a message to the global community. In these moments, aid workers act not only as humanitarians delivering desperately needed assistance, but as critical witnesses, carrying the stories of Gaza beyond the borders of silence and into the world's conscience.

A Deadly Assignment in Jerusalem

In 2024, Arunn's posting during the Gaza war proved to be one of his most challenging assignments. Aid workers and journalists were facing unprecedented dangers, with record fatalities reported. The United Nations documented the highest death toll for aid workers in a single crisis in Gaza[26], and *Al Jazeera*[27] confirmed this alarming trend, reporting that of the 280 aid workers killed globally in 2023, over half lost their lives in just the first three months of Israel's war on Gaza after Hamas' attacks.

The Legacy of War and Family

In April 2024, Arun told journalist Greg Thom of the Institute of Community Directors Australia, that what drives him to risk his life on the front lines of humanitarian crisis was his, "lived experience as a Tamil during the civil war in Sri Lanka , that was always my motivation."[28] This sentiment resonates deeply with many Tamils who, whether in the battle zone or dispersed through diaspora, bore witness to the painful final days of the conflict. For Arunn, however, the motivation is even more personal. His father was an aid worker in the war zone, often untraceable—known only to be among civilians targeted in attacks widely described as "genocidal." This legacy of resilience and sacrifice became a driving force for Arunn, inspiring him to take up his father's mission and serve in the world's most dangerous places.

The Tamil Experience and the Power of Witnessing

Arunn's dedication is deeply rooted in his awareness of the atrocities committed against the Tamil people during the final phase of the Sri Lankan civil war, when the Sri Lankan state barred international non-government organisations (INGOs) and UN agencies, effectively creating a "war without witnesses." Growing up as a Tamil child in Australia, Arunn was acutely aware of these unreported atrocities, which rarely surfaced in the international media. However, news of the violence occasionally

---

[26] https://www.un.org/unispal/document/statement-by-iasc-23sept24/
[27] https://www.aljazeera.com/news/2024/8/19/un-reports-gaza-war-caused-major-spike-in-aid-worker-deaths-in-2023
[28] https://www.communitydirectors.com.au/articles/running-toward-the-guns-to-help-others

trickled through. His decision to pursue a career in humanitarian work was shaped significantly by his early exposure to the efforts of organizations like MSF and ICRC (International Committee of the Red Cross), whose work in conflict zones left a lasting impression on him.

He understands that today's conflicts often face similar conditions, even with an international presence. The more powerful side can control the narrative, allowing only their version to prevail. For Arunn, INGOs hold a critical responsibility: to bear witness and speak out against atrocities, providing a semblance of solidarity amid the chaos.

First Steps into Humanitarian Work

After the conclusion of the Sri-Lankan civil war, Arunn's career in humanitarian work began not with an aid organization but with the Australian Centre for Independent Journalism, where he researched media coverage of climate change and advocated for increased scrutiny on media monopolisation in Australia.

He later joined the International NGO Safety Organization (INSO), which led to his first deployment in Afghanistan in 2014 and 2015. There, he faced the challenge of negotiating with non-state actors and providing advice to ensure the safety of humanitarian workers. At the time, the US-backed Afghan government was facing intense resistance from the Taliban, and Arunn was stationed in areas contested by the group.

From Afghanistan, Arunn moved to cover Syria, another conflict zone, where he assumed a similar role but with expanded responsibilities as Deputy Director of the NGO. In this position, he was tasked with setting up offices across the region and managing relations with various non-state armed groups, as well as coordinating with US and EU diplomatic missions.

Joining MSF: From Bangladesh to Emergency Response

While working with INSO, Arunn collaborated with several NGOs including MSF, whose work left a strong impression on him. In 2016, he joined MSF, beginning a career that would take him to numerous countries. His first posting was in Bangladesh, where he served as a Project Coordinator, leading initiatives to combat sexual and gender-based violence in the slums of Kamrangir Char. This challenging role involved providing medical and psycho-social support to marginalized groups, including sex workers, trans-women, and women abandoned by their husbands.

Facing Genocide: The Rohingya Crisis Unfolds

While Arunn was working on the MSF project in Bangladesh, the Rohingya in Myanmar faced a brutal attack by the Burmese military. In August 2017, the military launched a genocidal campaign against the Rohingya, marked by mass killings, sexual violence, and the destruction of entire villages. This crisis forced around 800,000 Rohingya to flee Myanmar within six weeks, seeking refuge in Bangladesh. MSF, already on the ground, was one of the first to respond, and Arunn, stationed in Bangladesh, found himself confronting the aftermath of this humanitarian catastrophe.

Arunn and a team of doctors rushed to the border town of Cox's Bazar, where they witnessed one of the gravest human tragedies of modern times—one that received minimal international attention. Over 800,000 Rohingya faced a violent persecution by the Myanmar state, and were all forced to displace into Bangladesh, forming the largest refugee camp in the world. Brutal mass killings, mass-rapes, and scenes of horror were described to all those receiving the refugees in Cox Bazaar. The scale of the crisis was overwhelming; initially deploying a team of 300, MSF found it necessary to expand to over 3,000 staff within three months to address the mounting needs. This was Arunn's first major emergency operation, a rapid and intense response made possible by MSF's independence and self-funding, which allowed the organization to act swiftly without waiting for external approvals. This agility and autonomy were what Arunn found uniquely rewarding about working with MSF, enabling the organization to respond effectively to urgent needs on the ground.

Caught in Conflict: Yemen and a Narrow Escape

In 2018, Arunn was in Yemen in the city of Taiz when he found himself in one of the most dangerous situations while working for MSF. Taiz was highly volatile, with frontlines splitting the city and Islamic State, Al-Qaeda, and other armed groups actively operating there. Due to high abduction risks, only two foreign MSF staff were stationed in the city— Arunn and a surgeon. They stayed at the back of a hospital, maintaining a low profile while still known to the local factions.

During one routine visit by the ICRC, a group blocked the road, ambushed an ICRC vehicle, and killed a Lebanese staff member named Hani. His body was brought to Arunn and his team, who pronounced him dead, shaken by the brutality. Later that night, an explosive device was planted under a car near their hospital, which detonated, causing extensive damage and shrapnel injuries to their building. Fearing they were now targets, Arunn and the team braced for an attack and ultimately evacuated from the hospital at dawn. Though the exact motive for the attacks remains unclear, the experience left a lasting impression on Arunn about the extreme risks aid workers face in war zones. This wasn't the first or the last time, he narrowly escaped danger.

Hands-On Emergency Work in Raqqa

From Yemen, he moved back to Syria where he undertook direct, hands-on emergency work. He was involved in rebuilding the Raqqa National Hospital and managing a trauma project in the city, addressing the critical healthcare needs in the war-torn area.

Blackouts and Breakdown: Crisis in Venezuela

In 2019, Arunn went to Venezuela amid widespread protests and a US-backed attempt to unseat President Nicolás Maduro. The country was already suffering a severe economic crisis, which was exacerbated by massive power blackouts, or *apagones* in Spanish. Arunn witnessed the profound impact of these blackouts: basic functions halted as water pumps, fuel, and electronic transactions became unavailable, leading society to near-collapse despite the availability of food.

Hospitals were in disarray, with medicines expiring on shelves due to systemic corruption and mismanagement. Arunn's work included managing a malaria project in Sucre and operating initially out of Caracas before moving to other locations in the country. This experience highlighted for him that energy crises, not just war, can unravel a society.

Back to Bangladesh: A Senior Leadership Role

After finishing his work in Venezuela, Arunn was asked to return to Bangladesh, this time as the Head of Mission and Emergency Coordinator, marking his first senior management role with MSF. Beginning in late 2019, he oversaw a large-scale operation in Cox's Bazar, which included two hospitals, seven primary health clinics, two large water treatment reservoirs, the construction of one of the largest natural faecal sludge treatment plants in the world, and a substantial €35 million budget. This was one of the largest MSF missions globally, focused on the Rohingya crisis.

Arunn noted that while the camp had evolved, with solar panels and better services, the fundamental issues of suffering and uncertainty remained, as 1.2 million people continued to live in limbo. The Bangladeshi government, initially welcoming but restrictive, denied the Rohingya rights to work, education, or citizenship, expecting them to eventually return to Myanmar. Over time, the Rohingya became politicized, used by opposing political factions as a "political football."

This experience was a turning point for Arunn, who began to see humanitarian organizations as filling governmental gaps they should not have been responsible for, which deepened his understanding of the complexities of humanitarian work and the political manipulation involved.

The Pandemic Pause: A Forced Reset

When Arunn returned to Australia, he was unwell, the intense pressure of his work had taken a toll on him. It took him three months to recover. In early 2020, he decided to rejoin MSF to serve as Head of Mission in South Sudan. However, the COVID-19 pandemic disrupted these plans.

After signing his contract in Amsterdam, where MSF's headquarters are located, global borders closed the following day, leaving him stranded there for three months. During this period, he attempted to secure flights to South Sudan multiple times, facing numerous logistical hurdles with restricted flights and permissions. He even boarded a plane once but was unable to proceed due to transit issues in Ethiopia. Unable to reach his post, he contributed remotely to operations in South Sudan, advising on set-up procedures amid the pandemic. Eventually, with his European visa expiring, he returned to Australia, considering it an opportunity to regroup before determining his next steps.

After returning to Sydney, Arunn had to spend two weeks in hotel quarantine, which he found incredibly challenging despite his prior experiences living alone in remote areas, such as the border-towns of Afghanistan. This isolation triggered a period of reflection about his future, leading him to consider settling in Australia and seeking work locally.

Exploring Art and Identity in Marrickville

Initially, he faced difficulties finding a job due to the pandemic, so he took on as Co-Director role at an art collective called "Join the Dots Workshop" in Marrickville, an inner-city suburb in Sydney, where he became part of the local arts community.

During his time at the gallery, Arunn explored his long-standing passion for the arts, including woodworking and theatre, which he had enjoyed since childhood. He reflected on how art was an integral part of his upbringing, particularly through cultural programs he participated in growing up.

Shifting Focus: Advocacy at MSF Australia

Eventually, after six months, he rejoined MSF in Australia, this time as the Humanitarian Affairs lead. In taking up this role, Arunn took on a position that was a step down from his usual senior roles, but he welcomed the opportunity. He wanted to focus specifically on advocacy, a field in which he had less holistic experience. Previously, he managed entire teams—medical, logistics, HR, administration, finance, and advocacy—but now he aimed to concentrate on one area to understand it better and improve his skills.

At MSF, advocacy involves supporting field projects by addressing issues like insufficient donor budgets for water, hygiene, and sanitation for vulnerable populations, such as the Rohingya, or changing systemic issues, like increased resettlement pathways for refugees stuck in offshore detention on Nauru. Arunn also engaged with the Australian Government, providing independent feedback on how Australian funds were being used in projects, as MSF does not accept Australian Government funding, its reporting was viewed as objective.

The Power of Independence in Humanitarian Action

This independence is fundamental to MSF's mission, and it was a key reason for their separation from the Red Cross in the 1970's—to ensure they could freely speak on issues, such as urging the Australian Government to call for a ceasefire in conflict zones like Gaza. MSF advocacy was also partly responsible for opening up more opportunities for the Rohingya in Australia through the Humanitarian Program.

Returning to the Rohingya: A Lasting Concern

On reflection, Arunn realizes that while all of the assignments he was involved in were important, his work in Bangladesh assisting the Rohingya, was particularly significant. He has been deeply impacted by the Rohingya's suffering, especially because the world largely remains unaware of their plight. The statelessness of the Rohingya is an issue he believes humanity must confront, as the Rohingyas are among the most marginalized people, even within refugee communities. In November 2024, Arunn accompanied Craig Foster, the former Australian soccer player and human rights activist to meet the Australian Minister for Immigration and Foreign Minister in Canberra to allow more Rohingyas to resettle to Australia. For Arun, the Rohingya's silent ethnic cleansing is a powerful reminder of the world's failure to acknowledge their plight.

Challenges

Working with MSF and other organizations in conflict zones has led Arunn to critically assess the humanitarian sector. While these organizations provide essential aid, they are also part of a system that sometimes unintentionally re-enforce cycles of dependency. He observed this dynamic in Palestine, where international organizations are welcomed by Israeli authorities, which, in turn, marginalizes and undermines local Palestinian organizations that embody Palestinian civil society and self-determination.

Before the recent escalation in Gaza, MSF recognized that Palestinian organizations were providing healthcare of such high quality that MSF's presence was not required at scale. This indicated that Palestinians were capable of managing their own healthcare needs. However, MSF is now the primary provider of secondary healthcare—a role that risks supporting a system that, instead of empowering Palestinians, could strip them of political agency. The dilemma is that without these organisations, no one would be providing medical services.

Reflections

Upon reflection, Arunn, whose initial interest in humanitarian work was shaped by the national liberation struggle of the Tamil people, now views conflict not through the lens of nationalism, but as a broader human issue.

Arunn's journey through humanitarian work reflects a profound evolution in his understanding of conflict and its complexities. What began as a deeply personal connection to the Tamil liberation struggle has transformed into a critical engagement with global humanitarian issues. Through his work with MSF and other organizations in conflict zones, he has come to recognize the limitations and unintended consequences of international aid, particularly in situations where it can inadvertently undermine local autonomy and political agency.

Arunn's experiences have led him to reflect on the unique role that humanitarian organizations and workers can play in providing a narrative that often goes unheard in mainstream discourse. He believes that humanitarian organizations, by virtue of their neutrality and independence, are in a position to speak truths that the establishment and mainstream media may overlook or intentionally suppress. In conflict zones like Palestine, where international organizations are often welcomed by state authorities, Arunn sees the potential for these organizations to serve as a voice for the marginalized and to challenge dominant narratives

Ultimately, Arunn's journey is a testament to the importance of questioning the systems we work within and striving for a more just, politically conscious, and truth-driven form of humanitarian action. His belief in the power of humanitarian work to tell stories that the establishment might prefer to ignore is central to his evolving perspective on how the sector can contribute to a more inclusive and honest global dialogue.

Luxshi Vimalarajah: Mediating Paths to Peace

Approach to Peace

"Imagine two children fighting over the last orange," Luxshi Vimalarajah likes to say. "A parent might instinctively cut it in half—fair and equal. But both children end up dissatisfied. Now imagine if the parent asked *why* each child wanted the orange. One might need the juice; the other, the zest for baking. Suddenly, both can have what they truly need. But only if the right question is asked."

This simple story encapsulates Luxshi's approach to conflict resolution. She doesn't advocate for compromise for its own sake—what she calls the lose-lose scenario. Nor does she accept the dominance of one side over another—the win-lose model that often entrenches division. Instead, she believes in probing deeper, uncovering underlying needs, and crafting outcomes where both sides can walk away having gained something meaningful.

Luxshi Vimalarajah is one of the world's most respected peace mediation experts. She is currently the Senior Peace Mediation Advisor at the Berghof Foundation in Berlin, Germany. With extensive experience in high-level negotiation, dialogue facilitation, and mediation support, she works to transform entrenched conflicts by shifting the focus from positional bargaining to mutual understanding. For her, peace is not a halfway measure—it's a creative, context-driven process grounded in listening, trust, and mutual learning.

Fleeing Sri Lanka

Like tens of thousands of other Tamils, Luxshi Vimalarajah and her family were uprooted as Sri Lanka descended into civil war. Their path to safety was neither straightforward nor taken together. Luxshi's father was the first to flee. He fled Sri Lanka in 1984-85. with the hope of eventually bringing the rest of the family over to Germany where he had found sanctuary.

Her two sisters were the next to leave Jaffna, aided by the Red Cross. They made their way to Germany, like many other Tamils did at that time Luxshi and her brother, however, remained with her mother and did not leave until 1986. Luxshi's mother was anxious that the family be re-united. When she finally decided to flee, she told no one—not even close friends or neighbours—fearing that this may jeopardize her plans.

When the moment finally came, it was swift, secretive, and silent. Luxshi was unable to tell anyone—not even her closest friends. She left with just one change of clothes—"a T-shirt or a frock," she recalled—an abrupt and heartbreaking end to her childhood in Sri Lanka.

Because they could not travel directly to Germany, Luxshi, her mother, and her brother first made their way to India, before eventually reaching safety in Germany. Yet the pain of leaving was not only in the journey—it was in the silence that accompanied it. For Luxshi, the most painful part was that she had no chance to say goodbye.

At that time, she was just 13 years old, attending school and living in the quiet village of Uduvil, where her family had recently settled. Their home stood in the middle of a paddy field, a place she cherished deeply. "For me, as a child growing up in that environment," she later said, "surrounded by paddy fields and nature—it was a magical experience." That serenity was suddenly, and violently, taken away—replaced by uncertainty, displacement, and exile.

Growing Up in Berlin

As Luxshi grew up in Berlin, she watched from afar as the war ravaged the land and people she had left behind. Like many who are forcibly uprooted, she carried with her the pain of separation—leaving behind not only her homeland, but also the kith, kin, and memories that had shaped her early life.

In addition to processing this emotional burden, Luxshi had to adjust to an entirely new environment: a different language, unfamiliar customs, and a culture that often felt alien. She credits her early schooling at Uduvil Girls' College in Jaffna for giving her the confidence to face these challenges. As the second-oldest school in Sri Lanka, Uduvil had a long-standing tradition of empowering young women. "It was a progressive place," she reflected, "where girls were encouraged to grow into confident, capable women."

Arriving in Germany, however, she was struck by a stark contrast. "It was a cultural shock," she recalled. "Girls here were not treated equally.

They weren't given the same status or respect as boys." What made this especially frustrating for her was the irony—many Germans seemed to carry the stereotype that women in Asian societies were oppressed, while overlooking gender disparities within their own.

Luxshi also noted that while there was racial prejudice in Germany, it was not always directed at South Asians in the same overt way. Often, people like her were regarded as "exotic," which came with a different set of assumptions. She attributes the relative respect she received to the fact that she spoke fluent English and came from a visibly educated background—both markers that, in her experience, earned her a measure of acceptance.

Luxshi found that her German counterparts knew little about Sri Lanka or the conflict that had forced her to flee. Rather than retreat into silence, she took the time to explain it—planting the seeds of what would become a lifelong commitment to dialogue, understanding, and the pursuit of peace.

The Making of a Mediator

When the war in Sri Lanka appeared to reach a turning point with a ceasefire and the initiation of peace talks, Luxshi allowed herself a measure of hope. Yet, on more than one occasion, that hope was shattered as the two parties—the Sri Lankan state and the Tamil rebels led by the Liberation Tigers of Tamil Eelam (LTTE)—returned to violence, abandoning negotiations.

It soon became clear to her that these talks were marred by deep mistrust, significant power imbalances, and a lack of genuine commitment to negotiate. Both sides clung to maximalist positions, making meaningful progress nearly impossible. Reflecting on these experiences, Luxshi found herself preoccupied with two critical questions: *How are deep-rooted asymmetric conflicts resolved? And how can warring parties be guided toward non-violent political engagement?* These questions shaped her academic and professional path, motivating her to pursue a degree in political science with a specialization in conflict transformation and international relations.

She went on to earn a Master's degree in Political Science from the Free University of Berlin, where she later spent a short time teaching—laying the foundation for a career dedicated to the pursuit of sustainable peace.

A Role in Sri Lanka

In December 2002, the Sri Lankan government and the Liberation Tigers of Tamil Eelam (LTTE) entered into a new ceasefire, this time brokered by Norway. The involvement of international actors gave rise to cautious optimism that the truce might hold. Among those taking an active interest was the Berghof Foundation, a Berlin-based organisation committed to sustainable peace through conflict transformation, peacebuilding, and peace education. Recognising that her background and connections to Sri Lanka could be of value, Luxshi Vimalarajah joined Berghof to support the multistakeholder dialogue process that followed. She relocated to Sri Lanka and soon became involved in what is known in diplomatic circles as Track 1.5 diplomacy.

Track 1.5 diplomacy bridges the gap between official negotiations (Track 1) and informal civil society dialogue (Track 2). It involves facilitating discussions between non-governmental organisations, think tanks, and other non-state actors alongside government representatives. In this capacity, Luxshi worked across a range of stakeholders—a task both complex and demanding, but ultimately deeply rewarding. For a time, the process seemed to hold promise. There was hope that a durable peace might be within reach.

However, the peace process was fragile and deeply entangled in geopolitical considerations. Persistent mistrust between the parties—combined with the reluctance of powerful international actors to engage the LTTE on equal footing with the Sri Lankan state—began to erode confidence. There was growing scepticism, sometimes disingenuously expressed, about the LTTE's intentions. For the LTTE, this reinforced the perception that the ceasefire was being used to entrench an already existing power asymmetry. Statements from hawkish Sri Lankan politicians and editorial commentary in leading newspapers[29] further inflamed tensions.

Ultimately, the ceasefire collapsed, and hostilities resumed. Backed by international powers—including India, China, and key Western governments—the Sri Lankan state decisively defeated the LTTE in a final military offensive. Berghof's hope of transforming the conflict from an armed struggle into a political process was not realised.

---

[29] "The role played by Sri Lanka's leading newspapers cannot be understated—a view supported by Johan Mikaelsson's findings in his study *Building Bridges or Adding Fuel to the Fire? War Reporting in Sri Lanka* (Gothenburg University, Department of Journalism and Mass Communication, December 1999)

For Luxshi, however, it was a baptism of fire. The experience profoundly shaped her understanding of international mediation. While the outcome in Sri Lanka ended in the military defeat of one side, it reinforced her belief in the importance of third-party mediation—not necessarily as a means to immediate resolution, but as a tool to level the playing field and build common ground. Reflecting on this, Luxshi told *Monocle* in November 2024:

"The Sri Lanka conflict helped me to understand the tool of mediation and what assets a third party brings, as a go-between and an honest broker. The third party helps to level the playing field and find common ground." [30]

Departing Sri Lanka

By 2007, while still working in Sri Lanka, Luxshi began to sense a troubling shift. Despite official rhetoric about pursuing peace, it became increasingly clear that the conflict parties were preparing for a final military offensive. She believed it was vital for Berghof to maintain a presence—not only to bear witness to what was unfolding but also to try, however modestly, to mitigate the harm that would inevitably fall on civilians. But that hope was soon dashed.

What followed was what Luxshi later described as a "double trauma." While back in Germany for Christmas, she was summoned by her superior and told that she could not return to Sri Lanka—it was no longer safe. By that time, permits for international peace NGOs and rehabilitation and development organizations had been withdrawn, and visas for foreign nationals were revoked, as had been the case with her boss. The message was unmistakable: return could mean danger.

The news left her devastated. Over the previous five years, she had built friendships, professional networks, and a renewed emotional connection to the country she had once fled. Now, she was forced to leave again—this time without warning, without farewells, and without closure. The pain was compounded by the knowledge that this was not an isolated threat. Since 2005, the government and the LTTE have been widely accused of carrying out extra-judicial killings of dissidents, journalists, and others it viewed as oppositional. The risk was real. And once again, Luxshi had no

---

[30] "Interview: A peace mediation adviser on how to resolve conflict", Monocle, 14 November, 2024
https://monocle.com/affairs/how-to-resolve-conflict/

choice but to leave behind a part of herself—quietly, and without goodbye.

Refining the Craft: Two Decades in Global Conflict Zones

The insight Luxshi gained through her involvement in the Sri Lankan peace process was just the beginning. It served as a foundational experience that deepened her understanding of mediation, power asymmetry, and the role of third-party actors. Over the following two decades, these early lessons were further sharpened and expanded through her engagement in some of the world's most complex conflict zones—including Nepal, Myanmar, the Basque Country, Yemen, North Macedonia, Colombia, Turkey and Catalonia. In each of these contexts, Luxshi provided negotiation support to key conflict parties, facilitated inclusive mediation and dialogue processes, and helped design strategic pathways for sustainable peace. Her work involved not only technical advice but also the delicate task of building trust among actors with long histories of mistrust and violence. These experiences solidified her belief that even in the most protracted conflicts, thoughtful mediation and inclusive engagement can open space for transformation.

When asked recently to recall a particularly memorable moment in the field, Luxshi offered an illuminating example.[31]

"In 2008," she explained, "members of the Basque movement approached the Berghof Foundation to explore whether we could support *Euskadi Ta Askatasuna* (ETA), the armed separatist group and the broader Basque movement in transitioning away from violent politics." At the time, ETA was a proscribed terrorist organisation, but it was willing to consider disarmament—provided it could do so in a dignified manner. The group sought a structured negotiation process and a roadmap for demobilisation. However, the then Spanish administration rejected negotiations. "It was an unusual and complex process," Luxshi reflected. "We had to think not just about the weapons but also about the people—those in exile, in hiding, the active militants, and the wider Basque community. The risk of further radicalisation and polarisation loomed large, especially in the absence of official dialogue." Over two years, Luxshi was deeply engaged in a quiet, behind-the-scenes effort. She facilitated internal strategic discussions among different factions of the Basque movement and brought them into dialogue. She and her colleagues remained involved until ETA's eventual

---
[31] As disclosed to *Monocle* on 14 November 2024

disarmament. It was, as she described, a rare and formative experience, underscoring the delicate balance of trust-building, dignity, and inclusion required to transform a violent movement into a political one.

Luxshi is acutely aware that mediation is a voluntary process—its success depends on both parties being genuinely willing to resolve the conflict. A crucial condition for meaningful engagement is the recognition by both sides that continuing the struggle will inflict greater costs than seeking peace. This is often described in conflict resolution theory as a "mutually hurting stalemate"—a point at which neither side can achieve outright victory. Mediation becomes possible only when both parties reach this impasse and begin to seek a different, more constructive way to engage with one another.

Future Directions

From where Luxshi stands today, the landscape of conflict resolution looks markedly different from when she began her journey. She observes with concern that mediation is increasingly shaped by transnationalism and *realpolitik*—where strategic interests often trump principles of justice, inclusion, and long-term peace.

In the post-Cold War years, she worked within what was known as the "liberal peace paradigm"—an approach grounded in human rights, gender equality, and transitional justice. While it faced significant criticism and had its share of shortcomings, the model aimed, at least in theory, to transform societies by addressing the root causes of conflict. However, this paradigm is now losing its prominence. In its place, a more pragmatic, state-centred approach has emerged, one that prioritizes short-term gains, national interests, and stability, often at the expense of fairness and inclusive dialogue.

For Luxshi, this shift is deeply troubling. She sees how asymmetries are deepening, root causes are being ignored, and peace processes are reduced to temporary fixes—such as ceasefires or humanitarian pauses—rather than meaningful pathways to sustainable resolution. In her view, mediation must remain principled, impartial, and rooted in the lived realities of those most affected by violence.

Yet despite these global setbacks, Luxshi finds powerful sources of hope. Across the world, people continue to take to the streets demanding nonviolent change. Local communities, faith leaders, and civil society actors—often with scarce resources—are leading grassroots peace efforts with courage and creativity. Their resilience, often forged in the face of adversity, affirms her belief that the moral centre of peacebuilding lies not in global boardrooms but in the hands of those closest to the conflict. It is their efforts that renew her conviction that transformative peace is still possible—and still worth striving for.

Reflections

Looking back on a career shaped by some of the world's most intractable conflicts, Luxshi Vimalarajah remains guided by a deep conviction: that even in the most polarised and violent situations, negotiations and dialogue—when pursued with integrity, patience, and cultural sensitivity—can pave the way for transformation. From the bitter lessons of Sri Lanka to the quiet breakthroughs in the Basque Country, and from supporting armed movements in transition, facilitating peace dialogues and negotiations to training negotiators behind the scenes, she has witnessed both the limitations and the quiet power of mediation.

Her experience affirms that peace is never a straight path; it is a layered and often fragile process that demands not only technical skill, but also empathy, trust-building, and a commitment to shared humanity. For Luxshi, the ultimate goal is not merely the cessation of violence, but the reimagining of relationships—so that former adversaries might one day see each other not as enemies, but as partners in building a different, more just future.

SURVIVORS AND STORYTELLERS

Umes Arunagirinathan: A Mango Tree[32] with Roots in Two Worlds

From Terrified Teen to National Voice

In 2018, Umeswaran 'Umes' Arunagirinathan stood on the stage of the German Historical Museum as one of the featured speakers for World Refugee Day and the Day of Remembrance for the Victims of Flight and Expulsion. In the audience sat dignitaries—then Chancellor Angela Merkel and Interior Minister Horst Seehofer. The hall fell into a reflective silence as Umes recounted his harrowing journey from refugee to heart surgeon. After his speech, both Merkel and Seehofer rose to greet him, posed for photographs by his side, and Merkel publicly thanked him, citing his story as a compelling reminder of Germany's moral duty to protect those fleeing war and terror.

Umes was born on 16 March 1978 in Jaffna, northern Sri Lanka, the second of five children in a close-knit household. His early years were marked by the warmth and security of an extended family—parents, siblings, and grandparents all living under one roof. But that sense of safety was shattered when civil war erupted in 1983. At just five years old, Umes's life was upended as his family was repeatedly forced to flee their home, never knowing when or if they could return. Each time they returned, they had to start from scratch, rebuilding their lives in a landscape scarred by fear and uncertainty.

Escape from War

Tragedy struck the family during the height of the war when Umes's

---

[32] In his TEDx talk delivered at TEDx RuhrUniversityBochum, titled "From Needing Help to Helping Others" in May 2018.
(https://www.youtube.com/watch?v=1-6UE2dDBtw), Umes Arunagirinathan likened himself to a mango tree—a ubiquitous presence in the courtyards of homes across the Jaffna Peninsula, but in his case it is a Mango tree with roots in German soil, a powerful metaphor for integration without assimilation. Much of the material for this article was obtained from this TEDx talk.

eldest sister fell gravely ill with kidney failure. With only one functioning hospital in Jaffna and thousands in need, Umes, and his family spent endless hours in overcrowded waiting rooms mostly in vain. By the time his sister turned twelve, she required dialysis, but the necessary medicine and equipment were simply not available. She died shortly after, a devastating loss that left a lasting scar on young Umes—and planted the seed of a dream: to one day become a doctor so others wouldn't have to suffer the same fate. Umes was also aware that his sister's death could have been avoided if not for the horrors of war.

As the conflict escalated, even basic education became a risk. After completing sixth grade, Umes could no longer safely attend school. He joined his father on the streets, selling vegetables, fruit, kerosine, and doing whatever it took to keep the family afloat amid the chaos.

By the time he was twelve, Umes had witnessed boys his age being killed by the military or joining the Tamil resistance to fight government forces. With the war closing in and danger mounting by the day, his mother made a heartbreaking decision: she would send him away, alone, in the hope of saving his life. She sold a piece of family land and borrowed money from an uncle living in Hamburg to pay a smuggler who promised to get Umes to Europe within five days.

On January 6, 1991, Umes said goodbye to his mother. She knelt before him, and he cried, realizing he would be making the journey alone. He promised her three things: he would not drink alcohol, he would not smoke, and he would become a doctor. His journey with two hundred other Tamils also making their escape took him from Colombo to Singapore, then to Dubai, Togo, Ghana, Benin, Nigeria, and finally, after more than eight months, he arrived in Germany via Spain.

A Child Alone in a New Land

At just 13, Umes arrived in Germany alone—stateless, vulnerable, and unable to speak a word of German. He moved in with his uncle in Hamburg and began attending school, where he started learning German from scratch. To his own astonishment, he quickly adapted—eventually becoming class representative and later school speaker, a role that reflected the respect he had earned from his peers. Just as he was beginning to find his footing, his asylum application was rejected. Overwhelmed by fear and despair, he found himself standing on the edge of an 11th-floor building, contemplating the unthinkable. Then, images of his family flooded his mind—his mother's face, the promise he had made to survive. He stepped back.

The next day, he opened up to his classmates and teachers, sharing the full weight of his story. Their response was immediate and heartfelt: they rallied around him, raised money to pay for a lawyer, and gave him the support he needed to stay in school and continue building a future.

Although allowed to stay on in Germany, Umes could not escape the horrors he experienced during his life in Sri Lanka. He would wake up in the middle of the night fearing that the army was about to arrest him; have visions of his sister dying without medicine and fleeing from the army that was about to enter the village. Umes had these recurring nightmares for several years.

A Promise Remembered

Umes went on to fulfil his childhood promise to his mother by studying medicine and qualifying as a doctor in 2008. He often recalled her quiet words, spoken in a hospital waiting room: that one day, someone in their family would become a doctor. Her hope became his purpose, guiding him through the challenges of medical school and giving him the strength to persevere.

In the same year, he became a German citizen, something he could never have imagined at twelve, when he was selling fruit and vegetable on the streets of Jaffna. He celebrated his new citizenship with a joyful gathering, surrounded by friends and mentors who had become like family.

Umes' life in Germany began to flourish.

Reunions and Distance

In 2006, sixteen years after escaping to Germany, Umes travelled to London to see his father, who had come from Sri Lanka to visit his daughter.

It was the first time Umes had seen his father since leaving Sri Lanka. He remembered his father as a jolly, larger-than-life presence from his childhood. Now, standing before him was a frail and ailing old man.

As they greeted each other, his father used the respectful Tamil greeting *"Vaanko"*, a term reserved for elders or strangers—instead of *"Vaa"*, the more intimate and affectionate greeting from a father. There was no embrace. Umes's sister, Nala, gently explained that their father had chosen respect over affection because he admired what Umes had accomplished.

He was no longer addressing a child but a man who had survived, achieved, and surpassed him in many ways.

On the drive home, the air was heavy. Nala tried to fill the silences with light questions, but the mood remained subdued. Umes sensed the discomfort; the dynamic had shifted. The man who had once held authority in the family was now meeting a son who had become more educated, and, in some ways, a stranger. The reversal of roles was painful to witness—for both father and son.

When they arrived at Nala's home, the mood changed. Umes was overjoyed to see his mother again, who he had reunited with only the previous year. By contrast to his meeting with his father, his bond with his mother remained intact, the years apart seemed to vanish in the emotion of their reunion. She had spent the morning cooking his favourite Tamil dishes in the spicy Jaffna style, so hot it burned his tongue. He cooled it down with *payasam*, a sweet dessert, savouring both the food and the comfort of home.

Nala's house was small, and space was limited. Guests were assigned rooms, and Umes shared one with his parents. His father, now physically weak, slept on the floor. Umes shared the bed with his mother, a quiet echo of lost time.

During his stay, Umes made a disturbing discovery: his brother-in-law was physically abusive toward Nala. It was deeply upsetting, but cultural expectations around marriage and family hierarchy restrained his response. In Tamil tradition, a son-in-law is to be treated with deference, making it difficult—if not impossible—for Umes to intervene. The visit was bittersweet: filled with long-awaited reunions, unresolved pain, and a growing awareness of the complicated ties that bind family across distance, time, and silence.

His time with his parents left Umes with a mix of emotions: joy, confusion, and quiet concern. It had brought moments of warmth, but also a profound sense of dislocation. He was no longer the child they had once known, and they were no longer the parents he had remembered. The emotional distance was as real as the physical one that had separated them for years. This dissonance echoed a deeper truth: the lasting pain of uprootal. His parents returned. He did not see them again for many years.

Finding His Place in Medicine

Back in Hamburg, Umes began his specialisation in cardiac surgery. His dedication and leadership soon stood out. He became a spokesperson for the medical staff and was later elected to the doctors' parliament. But after seven years of rigorous training, progress came to an abrupt halt. In 2015, he was told bluntly, *"For you, it's enough."* It was a moment of painful clarity; discrimination had found its way into his professional journey!

Yet Umes refused to be defined by war, racism, or prejudice. Rather than accept limitations imposed on him, he chose to forge a new path. He left Hamburg for Bavaria, where he completed his training and ultimately achieved what he had set out to do: become a cardiac surgeon.

Returning to Say Goodbye

In 2014, his world was shaken by a series of phone call from New York, Toronto, London, Sri Lanka, and Hamburg, all carrying the same devastating news: his father had died. Umes *felt* deep reluctance about returning to Sri Lanka to attend his father's funeral. He openly expressed that he did not want to go back to a country where the military had killed so many Tamil people, and even after the war ended in May 2009, he had never wanted to leave Germany. Despite these strong feelings, he ultimately decided to return—out of respect for his parents' culture and the traditions that demanded he perform the last rites for his father. All siblings now living in different parts of the world also returned.

Uprooted Lives

Umes's family's story is emblematic of many uprooted Tamil families: scattered across the globe. Umes himself is German, his mother remains in Sri Lanka, his brother lives in New York as an American, one sister is Canadian and lives in Toronto, and another sister is British, living in London. Despite their different nationalities and the distances between them, the family came together in Sri Lanka to honour their father, fulfilling the cultural and familial obligations that bind them.

It was during his visit to attend his father's funeral that Umes learned the heartbreaking details of how his grandparents had died. His grandmother, *Ammamah*, had refused to leave the family home. Tired of running, she declared that this was her home and she would never flee again. The house was later bombed, and she perished with it. His grandfather had been taken into custody by the army, tortured, and left to die. All of this had occurred within just a few years of Umes' departure.

Writing His Thoughts

Today, Umes is not only a senior cardiac surgeon at Universitätsmedizin Halle, but also a writer and respected public voice on migration and integration. In 2006, Umesh published his first book, *The Lonely Escape*,[33] giving voice to refugees like himself and helping Germans understand the human stories behind forced migration. Although he wrote the manuscript in 1999, it took seven years to find a publisher. He dedicated the book to his former teacher, Lorenz Köhler—whom he fondly refers to as his "German father in recognition of the unwavering support he received.

His second book, *Der Fremde Deutsche* (The Foreign German), was published in 2017. Written largely in a biographical style, it explores his own experience and that of others like him, who, despite being German citizens or having lived in Germany for many years, continue to be seen as "foreign" because of their appearance, name, or cultural background. The book delves into themes of identity, belonging, and exclusion, and calls for a more inclusive and pluralistic understanding of what it means to be German in a multicultural society.

In his 2018 TEDx talk, *From Needing Help to Helping Others*, Umes likens himself to a mango tree—native to the courtyards of Jaffna but now rooted in German soil. While his appearance may not conform to traditional notions of a "German," he explains, his roots have grown deep through years of study, work, and service in his adopted homeland. The metaphor powerfully conveys the experience of finding resilience in a new land—thriving without losing connection to one's origins.

In 2022, he co-authored *Grundfarbe Deutsch: Warum ich dahin gehe, wo die Rassisten sind (The Primary Colour is German: Why I Go Where the Racists Are)* with journalist Doris Mendlewitsch. In this book, Umes confronts both personal and systemic racism in Germany. His most recent work, *Grenzen akzeptieren wir nicht! (We Do Not Accept Borders!)*, is a dialogue with Holocaust survivor and author Peggy Parnass, who was sent to Sweden as a child to escape Nazi persecution. Umes found parallels between Parnass's story and his own: both were forced to flee their homelands—she from Nazi

---

[33] The direct translation of the German title "*Allein auf der Flucht: Wie ein tamilischer Junge nach Deutschland kam*" is: "Alone on the Run: How a Tamil Boy Came to Germany" ("The Lonely Escape" appears to be an interpretive or alternative English title sometimes used in talks or summaries,)

Germany, he from Jaffna in Sri Lanka then under army occupation. The book offers a layered and moving conversation about migration, displacement, survival, and the enduring human longing for freedom and dignity.

Umes explains that his decision to write about identity, migration, and racism stems from a need to correct the misunderstandings he has frequently encountered. He recalls, for instance, being told at a gym that people like him, "foreigners", should pay in advance. This was despite presenting an identity card confirming his German citizenship. On another occasion, a 17-year-old student laughed derisively during a lecture when Umes referred to himself as German. In both situations, he engaged directly and respectfully, using the moment as an opportunity to challenge assumptions and assert his belonging.

Umes remains deeply grateful to Germany for granting him asylum. He believes that newcomers have a responsibility to communicate not just their presence, but also their commitment to the values of their new homeland.

Writing to Heal and Reform

Umes has also used his voice and experience to engage with some of the most pressing issues facing contemporary German society in respect to healthcare.

In *Der verlorene Patient: Wie uns das Geschäft mit der Gesundheit krank macht* (The Lost Patient) published in 2020, co-authored with Doris Mendlewitsch, Umes offers a pointed critique of the commercialisation of Germany's healthcare system. Drawing on his experiences as a practicing physician, he argues that profit-driven policies undermine patient care and calls for reforms that place human well-being above financial interests. In *Herzensdinge: Die erstaunlichen Leistungen unseres wichtigsten Organs – und wie wir es heilen und schützen können* (Matters of the Heart: How to Heal and Protect Our Most Vital Organ) published in 2024, Umes shifts focus to the human heart, both literally and metaphorically. With clarity and compassion, he explains the heart's incredible functions and offers practical insights into how we can care for it. Combining scientific knowledge with accessible language, he aims to educate readers on the importance of heart health and preventative care.

Reflections

Umes' journey—from a child refugee smuggled out of war-torn Sri Lanka to a respected heart surgeon and public intellectual in Germany is a testament to the resilience of the human spirit and the transformative power of compassion. His life is not only shaped by his own determination, but by the hands that lifted him along the way: teachers, classmates, neighbours, and friends who stood by him when institutions failed. His life stands not only as a testament to personal resilience, but also as a powerful argument for the life-changing potential for humane and inclusive policies.

For Umes, survival was never enough, his passion lies in shaping a better, more humane society. Whether advocating for refugees, critiquing the commercialisation of healthcare, or calling out racism and exclusion, he speaks with the clarity of lived experience and the conviction of someone who believes that systems can change. Through his books, his medical career, and his public engagement, Umes seeks to bridge the divide between newcomers and native citizens, reminding both of their shared humanity.

Raj Rajaratnam: In the Face of Uneven Justice[34]

Return to Homeland

In January 2024, Raj Rajaratnam returned from the United States, where he had lived for the past forty-five years, to Jaffna—the land of his ancestors. His purpose was unmistakable: to help his people rise from the ruins of war and overcome the continued neglect by the Sri Lankan state. Raj was determined to rebuild the Tamil homeland, and with the strength of the local community behind him, he was confident of forging a new path forward.

Tall and broad-shouldered, he stood before a captivated audience in Jaffna, exuding defiance. The crowd—a blend of Tamil businessmen, academics, activists, students, and civic leaders—watched intently as he delivered a powerful message. "Yes, we were defeated by the combined might of India, Pakistan, and Sri Lanka, but we are not out." Even while recalling the civil war that had ended years ago, his words were more than a reflection on the past. They encapsulated his unyielding spirit. For Raj, defeat was only temporary. "Down but not out" was his guiding mantra, a testament to the resilience he had inherited from his roots in Vadamarachchi, the northernmost part of the Jaffna Peninsula. "We from the Vadamarachchi, don't back down; we take it on," he often proclaimed, and it was this indomitable will that had shaped his approach to every challenge in life—facing adversity head-on.

From *Galleon* to Gaol

Raj's journey navigating the American legal system is a testament to his unwavering resilience. As the founder of *Galleon*, one of the most successful hedge funds of its time, Raj's life took a dramatic turn when he was convicted of insider trading in 2011—a charge he vehemently denied.

With a staggering 97% conviction rate for insider trading cases, he faced

---

[34] Much of this chapter draws from Raj Rajaratnam's *Uneven Justice* (Post Hill Press, 2021), as well as interviews with the author and other sources.

a pivotal decision: cooperate with the government, testify against another defendant, and likely walk free, or stand trial and risk losing everything. Raj, true to his nature, chose the latter. His decision followed deep reflection. The charges against him were based on just 0.01% of Galleon's trades—a minuscule fraction of the fund's operations—resulting in a $30 million loss, not a profit. Yet, the looming 97% conviction rate was hard to ignore. Despite the overwhelming odds, Raj stood firm, refusing to compromise his principles. His determination carried him through his ultimate decision and a gruelling seven-and-a-half-year prison sentence, a period that tested but ultimately did not break him.

Writing Behind Bars

In 2021, two years after his release, Raj published *Uneven Justice*, a book that chronicled his experience with the legal system. His goal was to highlight the flaws and imbalances in a system he respected but believed had failed him. Writing the book was no easy feat for a man who had been convicted and incarcerated. Yet, for the son of Vadamarachchi, backing down was never an option. It had to be done, and he did it—head-on, as always. The book was a painstaking effort by Raj who wrote the entire book by hand while in prison.

A Life of Privilege and Purpose

Raj's story stands apart from the typical narratives of fleeing Sri Lanka. Born into privilege, he was the son of a senior executive at a multinational company and enjoyed an elite education that spanned prestigious institutions. From a top preparatory school in Colombo to Dulwich College in London, and later universities in the UK and the United States, Raj's academic journey culminated in his graduation from the renowned Wharton School of the University of Pennsylvania in 1983. He began his career at Chase Manhattan and flourished in the US, rising to become, by 2008, the 262nd richest man in America, according to Forbes.

Raj was undeniably a product of privilege, so why is his story included in this collection? Unlike many others, Raj's journey did not involve the physical displacement or escape from a conflict that so many Tamils endured whereas Raj was overseas and was not exposed to the conflict. Yet, his resilience and his enduring commitment to the Tamil people in the face of adversity makes his story indispensable. What sets him apart is not only his extraordinary success but the unwavering strength he demonstrated when faced with challenges. His battles were often those of an outsider—navigating the complexities of identity, belonging, and survival in a world where acceptance had to be earned.

Moments of Reckoning

During Black July, the brutal pogrom that claimed thousands of Tamil lives, Raj's response was emblematic of his character. While others sought refuge from the marauding mobs, Raj, who was visiting Colombo on holiday, chose to stay with his uncle to defend his home. The house was spared, and Raj returned to the United States, where he later applied for citizenship. However, the experience left him deeply shaken, forcing him to confront the painful reality that he was no longer safe in his own country.

Though Raj's transition to life in the West may have appeared seamless, it was not without its challenges. His uprooting, while different from many others, was no less painful, as he navigated the complexities of identity, belonging, and personal adversity with the same resolve that would define his future battles.

JM Rajaratnam's Defiance

In 1952, Raj's father, Jesuthasan Mylvaganam Rajaratnam (better known as JM Rajaratnam), went to the United Kingdom on a government scholarship to pursue his accountancy studies. At the time, Sri Lanka, then known as Ceylon, had been independent for just four years. In 1956, while he was away, the country passed the Sinhala Only Act, which required all government employees to learn Sinhala. This posed an immediate problem for JM, as a government employee. His scholarship was contingent on his working for the government for a minimum of five years. The Sinhala Only Act meant that he was legally obligated to learn Sinhala.

JM refused to comply. He viewed the law as discriminatory and unfair. He would not be forced to learn Sinhala. But refusing came with consequences. The government demanded that he repay the full cost of his scholarship. This was no small amount, as the scholarship had covered his living expenses for five years in England. To settle the debt, JM borrowed from friends and relatives, sold his meagre assets and used the remainder of his savings.

By doing so, JM freed himself from the obligation to bow to Sri Lanka's odious language policy, standing firm against learning Sinhala by force.

Growing Up Tamil in Colombo

As himself Raj quickly discovered, the culture of a country is often shaped by its leadership, and his school in Colombo. was no exception. Despite its teachings of tolerance, fair play, and equality, some students at St. Thomas harboured chauvinistic and vehemently anti-Tamil sentiments. Raj vividly recalls being taunted by a few Sinhala classmates, who called him a *Kallathoni*, a derogatory term for an illicit arrival by boat. Defiant even in his youth, Raj often found himself in fistfights, enraged by these insults. This hostility wasn't universal. At the time, Colombo's mixed neighbourhoods were still relatively harmonious, with people largely unconcerned about one another's ethnicity. As children, Raj and his friends played together, and even at school, the playground was a melting pot. Yet, there was no denying that the atmosphere was changing.

Raj's childhood was idyllic in many ways. Life moved at a leisurely pace, and he grew up in a large colonial-style home with manicured lawns and a beautiful garden tended by his mother. Sundays were spent at the beach with family and friends, soaking in the simple pleasures of life.

Until the late 1970s, Sri Lanka did not have television broadcasting, and radio was the primary source of entertainment. Like many South Asians, Raj was an avid cricket fan, drawn to the game's nuanced elegance from a young age. Back then, apart from attending local matches in person, the highly anticipated Test matches could only be followed on the radio. For Raj, as for everyone else, it was the radio that allowed him to "see" the match unfold. The slow, deliberate pace of life meant that he, along with countless others, would sit glued to the radio, following the game for five days—the full length of a Test match. In those simpler times, listening to cricket on the radio was a source of great joy.

Connections to Roots

Although Raj was raised in the comfort of Colombo, his parents ensured he remained connected to his roots. Every Christmas holiday, he and his siblings would travel north to Jaffna to visit their maternal and paternal grandparents. There, they joined in daily chores—milking goats, gathering eggs from the coop, and buying fish from the night fishermen returning from the sea. These trips not only kept Raj connected to his heritage but also fostered a deep love for his ancestral land, a spiritual bond that would endure throughout his life.

This attachment to one's roots in the North, despite growing up in the South, fascinated Tarzie Vittachi, the author of *Emergency 58* and one of Sri Lanka's most respected journalists. In his seminal work, Vittachi commented on the English-educated Tamil middle class, to which the Rajaratnams belonged.

"In Colombo or London, they tried to be the model 'Westernized gentleman,' wearing the correct dress with calculated casualness, speaking the correct tongue with cultivated allusiveness, and carefully avoiding the distinctive accents of the denizens of the North. Unlike the English-educated Sinhalese, they preferred to live closer to their traditional soil. They slipped with accomplished grace from their European clothes into their verti and shawl. However deep their roots in Colombo may have run, they found no difficulty being cosmopolitan braves in the city and peninsular Tamils when in Jaffna (which was quite often, since most Tamils maintained their traditional homes in the North and East)"

Vittachi's observation captures the duality of Raj's identity—equally at ease in the Westernized world of Colombo, yet deeply rooted in the traditions of his home in Jaffna.

Studying Abroad

By the time Raj was ready for high school, the country's culture had deteriorated and anti-Tamil sentiments were becoming increasingly widespread. Recognizing the escalating hostility, JM decided to send his son away from the growing unrest. Raj was sent to India to continue his upper school education, far from the turmoil that was beginning to engulf Sri Lanka.

In 1971, the country descended into chaos due to an insurgency led by rural Sinhala youth from the south of the island, endangering lives across the region. In response, JM moved his family abroad with the multinational company he worked for, eventually relocating to the United States.

Raj completed upper school education in India at a boarding school. For eleven-year-old Raj, the transition to this new, austere environment was challenging—a stark contrast to his life in Colombo. Yet, he endured without complaint. He later continued his studies in the UK, completing his General Certificate of Education (GCE) Ordinary and Advanced Levels while at Dulwich College, a prestigious and well-established boarding school, before proceeding with his undergraduate studies at Sussex University.

Confronting Racism

In the UK during the 1970s, racial tensions were high, and it was not uncommon for South Asians to face racial taunts. The entire community, derogatorily referred to as "Pakis," was often targeted. 'Paki-bashing'—violent attacks by British hoodlums, particularly skinheads—was a grim reality, where young Asians were cornered and beaten up simply for their ethnicity.

Young Raj often found himself targeted in these attacks, largely because he refused to run away. Realizing that the assaults usually happened when someone was isolated, Raj, like many other Asians, began moving in groups. Yet, he was always ready to face his attackers alone if needed—armed with something most Asians had easy access to: chilli powder. When ambushed, he was prepared to throw the powder into his attackers' eyes, knowing he wasn't breaking any laws—after all, chilli powder wasn't classified as a weapon like knives or knuckle dusters. Fortunately, he never had to use it.

Raj was acutely aware that the anger fuelling the racism of British hoodlums stemmed from their ignorance of Britain's colonial history. The presence of people from Asia in Britain, he knew, could be explained pithily by the well-known aphorism of Ambalavaner Sivanandan,[35] *"We are here because you were there."*

This clarity about history, power, and injustice didn't just inform Raj's politics—it defined his character. Years later, it was the same defiant sense of principle that led him to reject a plea bargain and face trial, even when conviction seemed certain.

Defiant

His decision to go to trial puzzled many. Why would someone choose an almost guaranteed sentence instead of accepting a plea bargain that might have led to freedom or a significantly reduced sentence?

In Raj's own words, "I went to trial because I was not prepared to plead guilty for something I did not do, no matter what the ultimate cost." [36] This conviction to stand up for himself is rooted in what Raj identified as

---

[35] A fellow Tamil from Sri Lanka and emeritus director of the Institute of Race Relations:

[36] Raj Rajaratnam, Uneven Justice, Post Hill Press, New York 2021, P81

part of his heritage: being a Vadamarachchi man who would never back down. This same unyielding spirit was also displayed by his father, when he refused to comply with the Sinhala-only Act, even at great personal cost. But Raj's strength wasn't inherited from his father alone; his mother had also instilled in him the values of facing adversity head-on, values passed down through stories and lessons from his heritage. As Raj himself put it:[37]

"Night after night, my mother always told us stories; tales and legends that inspired us to find courage, be brave and stand upright. One of my favourites is called "Veerathai" ("Brave Mother") in Tamil. The mother in the story learns that her only son has been killed in battle. Refusing to wait until the body is returned to her, she rushes instead to the battle site to confirm just one thing: whether the arrow has penetrated his chest or his back. Finding that the arrow had pierced his heart, the mother is filled with tremendous pride: her son had not run away from battle.

As a young boy, I thought it odd that a mother could possibly be happy about the death of her only son. My mother would lovingly and patiently explain the moral until I finally understood that courage comes in many forms, including standing up and facing adversity with dignity."

A Seven-year Ordeal

Raj's incarceration, which began on a cold morning in October 2009, culminated in seven and a half years of imprisonment. During this time, Raj learned hard truths. He saw firsthand the glaring inadequacies of the U.S. criminal legal system. He also had to confront his naivety in trusting the wrong people and discovered a reservoir of inner strength he hadn't known he possessed.

Misplaced trusting led to betrayal by his Indian associates, many of whom were former friends. They took plea deals and turned on Raj, a betrayal that stung the most and caused him to deeply regret entering a joint venture with them. In an interview with *Newsweek*, he said: "There are two types of plea bargains. One is, you cooperate with the government. You finger ten other people. The other is a plea bargain without cooperation. The white defendants all pleaded without cooperating; they did not wear a wire. The South Asians all did the plea bargain with fingering. The Americans stood their ground."[38] Although Raj attributed

---

[37] Raj Rajaratnam, Uneven Justice, Post Hill Press, New York 2021, P34
[38] *Newsweek* 23 October 2011, "Excusive: Raj Rajaratnam Reveals Why He Didn't Tak a Plea" https://www.newsweek.com/exclusive-raj-rajaratnam-reveals-why-he-didnt-take-plea-68203

this behaviour of the Indians to the insecurity of being immigrants, and lawyers bullying them into that position, he was unprepared to forgive them.

Early in his ordeal, Raj found a moment of near-vindication when the Securities and Exchange Commission Commissioner Mary Shapiro remarked in May 2011, shortly after his trial, that "the beauty of insider trading laws is the flexibility in interpreting them."[39] This gloating statement underscored the ambiguity and malleability of the very laws under which Raj had been convicted, raising serious questions about the fairness of his prosecution.

Lessons Learnt

Ironically, the ordeal that pushed Raj to the edge of despair ultimately brought him peace and self-awareness. He learned that the human mind is far stronger than most realize, and nothing can break a person who refuses to be broken.

But perhaps the most profound lesson he imparted was teaching his children that standing up for oneself, even when life is unjust, is the only way to truly face adversity. Raj considers his daughters to be his greatest success. His eldest, a lawyer, now works as a civil rights attorney with the Southern Poverty Law Center, a nonprofit organization specializing in civil rights and public interest litigation. His youngest, a healthcare professional, serves in the public sector.

The Final Third: Giving Back to His People and Their Land

Raj's work is far from finished. He has set himself new, critical tasks, with a primary focus on helping rebuild the war-torn Tamil homeland in Sri Lanka. His motivation is rooted in his father's words to him. "In the first third of your life, you learn; in the second third, you earn; and in the final third, you give." Now, as he enters this final chapter, Raj believes there is no worthier recipient of his efforts and resources than the Tamil people of Sri Lanka.

These days, Raj spends at least three months each year in Sri Lanka, typically during the Northern Hemisphere's winter months, investing in businesses and overseeing their operations—a Not for profit, but to ensure

---

[39] *Newsweek*, Oct 23, 2011

that people are employed and the local economy thrives. He has identified several ways to strengthen the economy, focusing on adding value to local products before they leave the Tamil homeland in the North and East. By cutting out the ubiquitous middlemen, Raj aims to ensure that more of the economic benefits flow directly to local communities. Any royalties he earns from his operations in Sri Lanka are donated to charities that work to uplift marginalized and vulnerable populations.

Raj remains confident that, with the resilience of the people, and with the right guidance and resources, they can overcome the devastation and rebuild a sustainable future.

He has resumed working independently, managing his own funds through *Synamon Global* to sustain his activities and generate wealth. True to his father's advice, now that he is in the third stage of life, his intention is to give back.

Reflections

Raj's journey is one of resilience, conviction, and a steadfast commitment to his roots. From navigating the heights of financial success to enduring profound personal trials, his story reflects a spirit unbroken by adversity. His legacy will be defined not by wealth amassed but by the strength he embodied and the impact he leaves behind for future generations.

Roy Ratnavel: A Tale of Resilience and Triumph[40]

Prisoner #1056

Roy Ratnavel never imagined he would be reduced to a mere number, 1056. Yet, for two harrowing months, that's exactly what he became. Roy was imprisoned in one of Sri Lanka's most notorious prisons, Boosa[41], in the Southern Province.

A Childhood Interrupted

Roy was just a teenager when the war in Sri Lanka shattered his world. Born in Colombo, he had returned to Point Pedro in the North, his family's ancestral home. Years before the conflict escalated into a full-blown civil war, Roy's father had moved the family to what he believed would be a safer place.

Point Pedro was a name given to the Tamil town by the Portuguese, who were the first of the colonial powers to conquer the Tamil Kingdom in Sri Lanka—a kingdom that had resisted European domination longer than the Sinhala Kingdoms in the south of the island. The Portuguese called it *Point das Pedras*, meaning the Rocky Cape. The British, the last of the colonial powers, had anglicised it to Point Pedro. However, the Tamils persisted in calling it by its original name, Parithithurai, meaning "Cotton Harbour." Cotton was cultivated in the surrounding areas and exported to India, which had a thriving textile industry for centuries.

Roy enjoyed a fun-filled life during his teenage years in Parithithurai while attending one of Sri Lanka's oldest schools, Hartley College, renowned for its academic excellence. He would cycle along the oceanfront to the school, which was close to his home. During lunch, Roy

---

[40] Much of this chapter draws from Roy Ratnavel's *Prisoner #1056* (Viking, 2023), as well as interviews with the author and other sources

[41] Boosa Camp, officially called the Boosa Detention Centre, is a high-security prison near Galle in southern Sri Lanka. It is notorious for holding people, mostly Tamil accused of links to the LTTE under the harsh Prevention of Terrorism Act (PTA), often without charge or trial.

and his classmates would play cricket, sing boisterous songs from Tamil movies, and indulge in pranks. On some weekends and most vacations, Roy's father would come up from Colombo to spend time with the family. Roy eagerly anticipated these visits, when he and his Appa (dad in Tamil) would cycle together along the byways of Parithithurai, go to the beach to buy fresh fish for the family lunch, and occasionally visit nearby relatives. He cherished these moments, bonding deeply with his father.

Unfortunately, it was too good to last.

The Gathering Storm

The first signs of danger surfaced when rumours began circulating about young Tamil schoolgirls being raped by the Sri Lankan army in July 1983. Soon after, another rumour emerged—this time involving the most prominent of the Tamil militant groups, the Liberation Tigers of Tamil Eelam (LTTE), or Tamil Tigers. It was believed they had avenged the act by killing thirteen Sri Lankan soldiers in a well-planned ambush in Tirunelveli, not far from Parithithurai. This event seemed to set the stage for the bloodletting that followed, as Tamils living in the south among the Sinhalese were subjected to brutal attacks. The anti-Tamil violence continued for two weeks, leaving over three thousand Tamils dead, property worth millions destroyed, and prompting a mass exodus of Tamils from the South to their ancestral villages and towns in the North and East of the island. Many who fled to Parithithurai brought with them horrific tales of the violence they had witnessed. This bout of anti-Tamil violence, now known as Black July, would impact Sri Lanka's history in ways that were impossible to imagine at the time.

Angered by the atrocities perpetrated during Black July, many young Tamils began joining militant groups. While the majority were inclined to join the LTTE, substantial numbers joined another militant group, Tamil Eelam Liberation Organisation (TELO). The anti-Tamil violence had strengthened the belief that Tamils needed to defend themselves. The events of July 1983 transformed a low-intensity militancy into a full-scale war.

Living Under Siege

As the war progressed, Roy's life was turned upside down. There were no more leisurely bike rides to school or cycling adventures with his father.

Instead, Roy found himself hiding under bunkers or lying on the floor at home to avoid being hit by bombs and bullets.

When Roy was only fifteen, he and his brother would lie on the floor on the nights of heavy bombardment, turning the terrifying sounds overhead into a grim game—guessing whether the shrieking noise was a bomb or a shell from the naval guns. At a very young age, the children in the town had learned to distinguish the different sounds of war—not just bombs and shells, but also the thud and whistle of anti-aircraft fire, the back-and-forth exchange of machine guns as the army advanced and Tamil fighters responded, the crack of incendiaries as they landed, the shock waves from high-explosive bombs, preceded by a seismic wave, and when the firing finally ceased, the haunting screams of the wounded filling the silence. Schools in areas closed during the bombing raids and for days thereafter.

The next two years continued in this fashion, with bombings and air raids punctuated by intermittent silence. It was these periods of silence that were most troubling, as no one knew when the next wave of attacks would begin.

The Internecine War

In late April 1987, Tamil people were shocked and distressed when one of the Tamil militant groups, the LTTE, turned against another, TELO), precipitating an internecine war. Within weeks, the clash ended with TELO disarmed and several of its senior leaders, including its head Sri Sabaratnam, dead. The people, who had seen the militants as their defence against the Sri Lankan army, were dismayed.

The LTTE claimed that they were only targeting criminal elements
But this justification rang hollow.[42]

---

[42] According to Sumantra Bose, author of *States, Nations, Sovereignty: Sri Lanka, India, and the Tamil Eelam Movement,* Indian diplomats involved in Sri Lanka policy admitted to backing TELO to undermine the independent and less pliable LTTE. TELO, described as politically unsophisticated with a large criminal element, was seen as the perfect proxy for India's intelligence agency, Research Analysis Wing (RAW). The LTTE sought to disarm TELO believing that its association with RAW threatened their cause. Because of TELO's loose recruitment policy, its ranks included some criminal elements who were responsible for anti-social acts. While many Tamils disapproved of TELO's behaviour, they also could not condone the infighting among Tamil groups. The LTTE, reliant on Indian support, was unable to publicly expose RAW's role, as doing so would have jeopardised their much-needed Indian backing against the Sri Lankan regime.

"Operation Liberation"

The Sri Lankan state, emboldened by this clash, saw it as an opportune moment to mount a massive offensive called Operation Liberation. Their main goal was to 'liberate' the Northern Tamil district. Point Pedro was the most important town in the district.

In May 1987, when Operation Liberation began, Roy was seventeen. He remembered it as a time when bombs rained down incessantly. The family hid in their bunker. Over the past two years, Tamils had learned that survival required more than just lying on the floor and hoping for the best—defences needed to be built. Now, most homes had a bunker. Roy could hear heavy explosions and the sounds of homes, including bunkers, being destroyed. The only thought running through the minds of those in the bunker was, "Could ours be next?"

The previous year, the LTTE had managed to confine the Sri Lankan army to its barracks. Apart from periodic shelling from its bases, the army had been unable to move out. But now, the army was on the offensive, with five thousand men breaking out of their bases to take on the LTTE, which they believed had been weakened during the internecine war. It took the army five days to capture Point Pedro.

The bombings ceased following its capture June 1. The town was now a graveyard for both the living and the dead.

Taken Prisoner

On emerging from the bunker, hungry and exhausted, Roy heard the sound of boots long before he saw the soldiers. A large group of uniformed Sri Lankan soldiers, led by their captain, Udugama, approached, bearing a Sri Lankan flag. One of the first tasks the army undertook after 'liberating' Point Pedro was to separate able-bodied young Tamils from their families. They rounded up about three thousand of them, some from Point Pedro and others from neighbouring villages. Udugama seized Roy's skinny arm and dragged him to join a forced march across a field that the Tamil Tigers had mined in an attempt to stop the army's advance. Roy quickly realized that Udugama was using the captives to clear the minefield. It was the longest march of his life, and some didn't make it.

The march across the minefield was just the first of many death-defying moments Roy would experience in the next two months. Soon after, shackled in groups of ten, Roy was loaded onto an old cargo ship and confined to a dark hold with no lights and little air. During the gruelling six-day journey, Roy and his fellow captives endured hunger, thirst, and lack of sleep, all while being forced to relieve themselves in the same confined space. One of his fellow inmates, who had lost consciousness, was unceremoniously thrown overboard by two soldiers. Having survived the minefield, Roy was unwilling to face death again as he fought against the fatigue, knowing he had to stay vigilant.

Upon arriving in the southern Sri Lankan city of Galle, Roy and his fellow captives were frog-marched to the massive Boosa Prison, where Roy would spend the next two months. His captors' primary demand was that he becomes an informant. Roy knew that few of his fellow prisoners were Tamil militants. Yet he refused to become a snitch, despite witnessing people being beaten, sexually assaulted, and some so brutally attacked that they bled from their ears and lost their ability to see or hear. Roy recalls a moment when huddled among his broken fellow inmates with blood seeping between his fingers, when he was suddenly overcome by a sense of clarity and perfect calm. Though the beatings persisted, Roy would return to these moments from time to time—they became a refuge, helping him maintain his sanity.

Escape from Sri Lanka

In a lucky break, Roy managed to contact a Sinhala friend of his father, which proved to be a turning point in his escape.

Roy endured two months of torture before being rescued by "Uncle" Fernando, the Sinhalese family friend and colonel in the Sri Lankan army. When Roy was finally reunited with his father—a man he deeply admired—he was taken aback by his father's sad words: "There is no future for you in this country. I want to send you away." Reluctantly, Roy complied as his father helped him flee to Canada on 18 April 1988. Just two days after Roy's departure, his father was killed by the Indian army, supposedly on a peacekeeping mission.

Within days of arriving in Canada as a young refugee, Roy was confronted with the devastating news of his father's untimely and tragic death. He had to endure the harsh weather, with temperatures plunging to zero and begin building a new life in a foreign land with an unfamiliar culture. The challenges were formidable for anyone, let alone an eighteen-year-old who had survived Sri Lanka's brutal torture chambers and lost a parent —all within just two months.

"Whatever You Do, Do It Well"

Roy never forgot his father's parting words of advice: "In Canada, you will have opportunities that I never had. Don't squander them." And almost as an afterthought, his father added something profound: "I have asked many things of you. Now, I ask one more. I ask that you live." His father's death instilled in Roy a deep conviction: to honour his father, he had to live not just for himself, but for the man who had sacrificed so much for him.

With his father gone, Roy's mother was now living alone in a place where the same army that had killed his father remained active. He knew he had to get her out. To do so, he needed money, which meant finding work. At the same time, he felt a deep obligation to honour his father's wishes by educating himself. Roy began working and studying part-time, taking a factory job and saving money by walking to work. But despite his efforts, he earned just enough to keep body and soul together and wasn't able to do anything more.

Realizing he needed more income, Roy made the difficult decision to drop out of school and took on another job, cleaning office buildings in downtown Toronto. There, he had his first glimpse of Bay Street, Canada's equivalent to Wall Street. The money was still insufficient, so he took on yet another job, this time as a security guard.

One day, Roy made a bold decision: he quit all of his jobs, determined to find work in an office—a "proper job." As fate would have it, he secured a position as a mailroom clerk, a role that had initially been denied to him due to his lack of "Canadian experience." Undeterred, Roy took the initiative to contact the employer directly, and it paid off. This mailroom job would become a turning point in his life.

He quickly moved into administration, working hard while keeping his father's oft-repeated mantra in mind: "There is dignity in work." Another phrase from his father, in Tamil, also guided him: "*Seivana thiruntha chei*" (whatever you do, do it well). The organization was thriving, and Roy was learning more and more about the business of fund management. But it wasn't just the technical skills he was honing; he also picked up the art of public speaking from the CEO and founder, Robert McRae. In Bill Holland, a senior executive in the organisation, Roy found a mentor who further shaped his career. Soon, Roy also passed his high school exams having pursued his education at night school.

Roy was determined not to remain a lamb—he wanted to become a lion.

Haunted by the Past

Despite his professional progress, Roy's nightmares continued to haunt him. In these dreams, he would see his father, dead in their home; a woman with an eye blown out of its socket; and other horrific scenes from his traumatic past. The nightmares were accompanied by the rattle of gunfire and the stench of death. Sometimes, Roy would lose his sense of time and place. One day, while walking down Yonge Street, he heard a helicopter overhead. In an instant, he was mentally transported back to Point Pedro, once again a terrified 15-year-old. Confused and scared, he found himself crouching under the awning of a nearby building. It took him a moment to reorient himself and realise he was still in Toronto.

Even as Roy grappled with his nightmares, his concern for his homeland remained ever-present. The ongoing war and its atrocities weighed heavily on his mind. Roy found some solace in managing to get his mother out of the hell his homeland had become, but life dealt him another blow when she was diagnosed with schizophrenia. There was no accounting for the toll the war and the loss of her husband had taken on her.

On a deeper level, he recognized that the anger which sometimes threatened to derail his life stemmed from trauma and post-traumatic stress, and he sought to address it. During moments of doubt, when he felt overwhelmed and on the brink of giving up, Roy would remind himself that these challenges were minor compared to the hardships he had endured in Boosa prison and the harrowing journey in the hold of a cargo ship, chained and helpless.

A Canadian Career

Meanwhile, Roy's career, which had been progressing well, came to a sudden halt when his ambition outpaced his patience. He was forced to resign, but seized the opportunity to continue his studies full-time, encouraged by Sue, his wife-to-be at the time. Roy soon returned to his old company and quickly regained his footing. Ever focused on self-improvement and aware of his limitations, Roy diligently worked on refining his accent and honing his presentation skills.

Fortune smiled upon Roy when CI Financials, the company where he held shares and worked, rose to prominence. Thanks to the astute leadership of its new CEO and Roy's mentor, Bill Holland, the company successfully emerged as a prominent asset management company in Canada. This achievement not only marked a significant milestone for the firm but also improved Roy's financial situation considerably.

Concern for His People

In a bold commando raid on July 23, 2001, the Tamil Tigers infiltrated Sri Lanka's major airbase in Katunayake, destroying several of the nation's warplanes. Roy felt a surge of jubilation—those very machines had once rained death upon his hometown. The attack carried added significance as it coincided with the anniversary of Black July, the brutal pogrom that had claimed the lives of over three thousand Tamils and escalated a low-intensity militancy into a full-scale armed conflict. The operation was executed by fourteen "Black Tigers", an elite group of commandos on a suicide mission. While LTTE suicide bombers typically targeted military and economic sites rather than civilians, this did not always spare innocent lives. This particular attack was different as there were no civilian casualties. The event took on an even more personal note when Roy learned that one of the commandos involved was his former classmate from Hartley College, Ravishankar, known by his nom de guerre, Charles.

Roy's jubilant reaction mirrored that of many in the Tamil diaspora, including those who seemed focused solely on settling down and facing the challenges of life as new migrants. Yet, despite the anger he felt toward the Sri Lankan government, Roy harboured no hatred for the Sinhalese people. He had forged deep friendships with many Sinhalese, and he would always remember Uncle Fernando, who, despite losing his son to the war, had helped Roy escape from prison.

Roy would come to understand the full significance of this attack in the months that followed. The commando raid had sent a powerful message to Sri Lanka and its supporters: the Tamil Tigers were not a force that could be easily defeated. The operation compelled the Sri Lankan state to the negotiating table, ultimately leading to a ceasefire.

Many months later, Roy learned of another attack—this time by Al-Qaeda, using planes to bring down the Twin Towers of the World Trade Center. He had complicated feelings about the actions of both Al-Qaeda and the LTTE. The LTTE had targeted Sri Lanka's Air Force and had not killed civilians, whereas Al-Qaeda had deliberately attacked civilians. Still, he worried that the world might begin to view the LTTE in the same light as Al-Qaeda, especially since the Tamil cause was still largely unknown in the West at that time.

This soul-searching caused Roy to come to a momentous decision; he wanted to be a voice in the West to shape the narrative of the Tamil struggle for freedom. He started with opinion blogs, and engaging readers with letters to the editor. He wanted the world to know the truth, not allow it to be drummed out by the effective propaganda of the Sri Lankan state.

Return to Sri Lanka

The ceasefire, born from the Sri Lankan state's realization that it could not defeat the LTTE, brought an end to hostilities. Roy contemplated a return to his homeland, at least for a visit. As the Singapore Airlines flight descended toward Sri Lanka's Katunayake Airport, Roy felt a wave of nausea. He knew all too well the Sri Lankan government's reputation for brutality. Stories of journalists, dissidents, and Tamils suspected of being Tamil Tigers or sympathizers who were kidnapped by white vans and never heard from again. Roy had spoken out against the Sri Lankan regime in the past, criticizing its penchant for rewriting history, and he knew that some of his statements were well-known.

Roy's visit to the North, the land he once called home, was a journey through a landscape scarred by war and a heart heavy with emotion.

The climate, once familiar and invigorating, now felt oppressive, with the heat bearing down on him like a relentless burden. Nothing could have prepared him for the sheer scale of devastation that lay before him. The once-majestic coconut palms of the Vanni stood decapitated by artillery shells, their severed trunks a silent testament to the violence that had ravaged the land. In Kilinochchi, the town was a shadow of its former self—crumbling buildings, unpaved roads that sent plumes of dust and sand into the air with every passing vehicle, and fields littered with mines.

Meeting amputees, Roy was overwhelmed by a flood of emotions: profound sadness, seething anger, and an acute sense of guilt. How was it that his fellow Tamils were left to suffer in such a state, while he lived in the comfort of luxury far away? But it was in the eyes of the war-orphaned children that Roy saw the deepest cruelty inflicted upon his people.

When he finally reached Point Pedro, a wave of conflicting emotions surged within him. There was a fleeting pleasure in seeing familiar sights— the old lighthouse, his school—but the pain of witnessing the scars of war on these once-beloved landmarks was undeniable. The most personal moment came when Roy visited his old family home, now owned by someone else. The new owner, gracious and understanding, allowed him to visit the very spot where his father had been killed. Standing there, Roy felt nothing—no tears, no immediate grief. He was numb, the weight of it all too much to process at once. It would hit him later; in ways he couldn't yet foresee. That visit, though painful, was in some ways therapeutic. It brought him a measure of closure, and he knew, as he left, that he would not return to Sri Lanka anytime soon.

Personal and Professional

Despite the sense of closure, Roy knew that he was still haunted by the demons of his past. The trauma he had endured as a teenager had left deep scars that were not easily healed. Yet, he was determined to confront these lingering shadows, supported by his wife, Sue, whose steadfast presence helped him navigate the complexities of his inner turmoil.

In 2005, Roy became a father, a moment of profound joy and relief for him. The memory of the torture he had endured in Sri Lanka —particularly the horrific prodding of his genitals with electric rods—had always left him with a gnawing fear that he might have been permanently damaged. But the birth of his child dispelled that fear, bringing with it a renewed sense of hope and a deep, quiet gratitude.

He continued to be a voice for his people and now mentors emerging young leaders in the asset management industry. In 2020, Roy was named one of Canada's fifty best executives by Report on Business, an honour bestowed upon those who led their companies through the challenges of COVID19.

Bearing Witness

In 2022, Roy embarked on writing his memoirs, driven by a desire for his son, Aaron, to understand the hardships and lessons his father had faced. What began as a personal account soon expanded into a broader mission: to tell his story as a reflection of the collective experience of Sri Lanka's Tamil people, who were forced to flee and forge new lives in foreign lands. Roy sought to help the second generation of uprooted Tamils grasp the depth of trauma endured by their parents and address the lingering intergenerational trauma.

He also wished to express gratitude to the host nations that had offered refuge to the Tamils, providing them with the freedom and dignity that Sri Lanka had denied. The culmination of this effort was his book, *Prisoner #1056: How I Survived War and Found Peace*. At Boosa, detainees were reduced to just a number—a dehumanizing tactic employed by the authorities. The book was endorsed by Canada's 18th Prime Minister the late Right Honourable Brian Mulroney. It was fitting because his immigration policy had allowed Roy to enter Canada.

The Proud Canadian

Roy is no longer recognizable as the skinny, confused teenager who once stood at Toronto Airport. At fifty-six, he is a well-built, confident man, radiating a vitality that belies his years. His toned physique reflects a commitment to regular workouts, while his poised demeanour exudes the self-assurance of someone who has faced and overcome immense challenges. Retired from his role as Vice Chairman at CI Financial, Canada's largest independent asset management company, Roy is now the author of a best-selling book.

In May 2025, Roy Ratnavel and his wife, Sue, donated $1 million to the Scarborough Health Network (SHN) Foundation to support inpatient mental health services at Birchmount Hospital.

Today, Roy considers himself an "accidental Sri Lankan by birth, an unapologetic Tamil by heritage, and a proud Canadian by choice." Comfortable in his skin, his hardships in a Sri Lankan prison and overcoming challenges in Canada have profoundly shaped him.

Reflections

His journey—from a lost and frightened boy to a revered leader—stands as a testament to the power of perseverance, rooted in the unyielding belief that one's past does not define their future but fuels their purpose. For Roy, that purpose includes a deep commitment to giving back to the community that shaped him, ensuring others have the support and opportunities he once fought hard to find.

SOCIAL ACTIVISTS

Shaun Christie-David: The Privilege of Escape, the Responsibility to Act

Recognised on the National Stage

When Australian cricket captain Pat Cummins[43] set out to understand leadership, he identified ten individuals who embodied the quality he admired most: resilience. Among them were former Prime Minister Julia Gillard, legendary fast bowler Dennis Lillee, and John Bertrand, who led Australia to a historic victory in the 1983 America's Cup against all odds, also on that list was Shaun Christie-David—the son of Sri Lankan Tamil migrants.

Shaun's inspiring journey has captured national attention. In May 2024, he was featured on *Australian Story*, the flagship program of the Australian Broadcasting Corporation (ABC), renowned for its compelling human narratives. In the same year, Richard Fidler—host of ABC National Radio's *Conversations* program—described his interview with Shaun as one of the most memorable in his two decades of broadcasting. Shaun's influence also reached international audiences through Episode 540 of the Impact Boom podcast, released on February 3, 2025. The podcast highlights authentic stories of social entrepreneurs and changemakers who harness business as a force for good.

A Family's Journey Across Continents

Shaun, the youngest of three brothers, was born in Australia in 1986. One of his older brothers was born in Sri Lanka, and the other in Saudi Arabia, where their father, Clement, worked as a mechanical engineer. In the 1970s, Shaun's parents had moved to Saudi Arabia to take advantage of the economic opportunities offered by the oil-rich kingdom.

During their time there, civil war erupted in Sri Lanka between the state and the Tamil people. As Tamils, facing rising persecution, the Christie-David family no longer saw Sri Lanka as a safe place to return to. Yet, Saudi Arabia was never intended to be a permanent home, nor was it ideal

---

[43] Pat Cummins, *Tested*, Australia HarperCollinsPublishers, 2024, p147-171

for raising a young family. Fortunately, they had relatives in Australia who were willing to sponsor their migration. With hope for a safer and more stable future, the family resettled in Sydney.

Growing Up in Sydney's Western Suburbs

Growing up in Sydney's western suburbs, Shaun Christie-David lived a life much like his peers. His father, Clement—whose mechanical engineering qualifications were not recognised in Australia—set up a mobile mechanic business, working long hours in all weather conditions. His mother, Shiranie, found work in childcare. At school, Shaun encountered racial prejudice but took it in stride.

The Lure of Corporate Power

A formative moment came during a visit to Sydney's Central Business District, where he observed corporate executives in sharp business suits striding confidently through the city, exuding wealth and power. He was captivated. These were the people who seemed to matter—and he wanted to be one of them. He wanted to be a suit.

Motivated, he studied hard and eventually landed a position at a leading bank. He often jokes that his hyphenated Anglo name—Shaun Christie-David[44] —was what got him the interview. But despite the impressive salary and perks, Shaun found the work unfulfilling. While intellectually stimulating, the environment around him felt joyless. More troubling was the racism—subtle, pervasive, and harder to brush off than what he had faced in school. It was often casual, but cutting. At work, he was the only brown man—Tamil—and his colleagues nicknamed him "Tamil Tiger."

Power and Prejudice in the Corporate World

In his youth, prejudice had been easier to dismiss. In the corporate world, it felt darker—power laced with prejudice. Two incidents crystallised this for him. The first was during a hiring process, when Shaun was reviewing a résumé. His manager noticed the applicant had an Indian

---

[44] It is not uncommon for various Tamil communities in Sri Lanka to have adopted Western names, often as a way to identify themselves as Christians. Russel Arnold, the Sri Lankan cricketer, was also a Tamil with an Anglo name—one his ancestors took on when they converted from Hinduism to Christianity.

name and had gone to school in one of Sydney's outer western suburbs. Without hesitation, the manager said, "Wrong side of the bridge, wrong last name."

The second moment of reckoning came on the day Barack Obama was elected U.S. President. Shaun was on a call with a multimillionaire client in Perth. "Right, so I call this dude," he recalls, "and the first words out of his mouth were, 'Can you believe they voted a N in America as president?'" Shaun realised that, to the man on the other end of the line, he was simply "Shaun Christie-David with the very, very white voice." There was no filter, no hesitation—just a casual expression of racism. That moment hit hard. It confirmed what Shaun had long suspected: this world wasn't for him anymore.

Moments of Reckoning

Reflecting on this during an interview with Richard Fidler on ABC's *Conversations* program, Shaun conceded that he had likely known it subconsciously for some time. He had already felt the disillusionment—the joyless corporate environment, the relentless pursuit of money, the shifting definitions of success. "I'm not that cynical," he told Fidler. "I'm not in that world mentally and emotionally. Yeah, it was a combination of so many things."

Survivor's Guilt

Sometime after the war ended in Sri Lanka, Shaun's family travelled there to reconnect with relatives they hadn't seen in years. It was during this visit that Shaun came to understand what his mother had often meant when she spoke of his "luck and privilege." He met boys, barely fifteen, working in a tailoring shop—making suits that seemed like bargains to him but were worth a fortune to them. They looked at him with a kind of awe.

Shaun recalls the moment clearly: "It hit me hard. I thought, I'm no different from you. The only thing that separates us is that my parents got out." He now recognizes that moment in Colombo as his first visceral experience of survivor's guilt.

Toward Meaningful Work

Shaun returned to work, but the feeling that he was meant to do something more meaningful never left him. He spent time in the UK, working on a project with the National Health Service (NHS), before returning to Australia two years later. Back home, he collaborated with Norman Swan, renowned Australian broadcaster and creator of ABC Radio National's long-running *Health Report*, on a project aimed at improving patient health literacy. Together, they developed a network of television screens to be placed in GP consulting rooms, providing patients with valuable health information before their appointments.

During this time, Shaun—who felt a deep sympathy for the inequity faced by Indigenous Australians—also helped establish the Aboriginal Health Television Network. Shaun was motivated by a desire to showcase indigenous health professionals and inspire younger generations to pursue careers in healthcare. The aim was clear from the outset: to eventually hand over full ownership and operation to Indigenous Australians. Once that goal was achieved, Shaun stepped away.

The Birth of Colombo Social

Shaun's next venture was inspired by his love for food—specifically, Sri Lankan cuisine. While he knew of several places in Sydney serving excellent Sri Lankan food, most were modest, no-frills establishments offering hearty meals at low prices. Shaun envisioned something different: a fine dining experience that celebrated the richness of Sri Lankan flavours. But his vision extended beyond the food—he wanted to create opportunities by employing refugees and asylum seekers.

When he approached the banks for funding, they weren't interested. Shaun was disheartened. Years later in an interview with Australian cricket captain Pat Cummins, he confessed "I've never cried in front of my parents before, but one day I started bawling. I had done so much work and was so convinced it would work." It was then that his father, Clement, stepped in—emptying his superannuation savings to support his son's dream.

That leap of faith paid off. Colombo Social opened its doors to great success, and Shaun was able to repay his parents. But just as the business was finding its feet, the COVID-19 pandemic struck.

Responding to COVID-19

This was when Shaun's resilience truly came to the fore—the same quality that later caught the attention of Australia's cricket captain. Many of Shaun's employees were asylum seekers, ineligible for government assistance. Shaun supported them from his own funds. He also turned Colombo Social's kitchen into a community lifeline, providing free meals to people in need. During Covid along with some partners the restaurant delivered meals to the vulnerable.

Three months in, Shaun restructured Colombo Social into a social enterprise called Plate it Forward—aligning the business with its deeper mission. Today, it operates as a hybrid model: its commercial arm supporting its charitable initiatives. It continues to employ refugees, asylum seekers, and others facing barriers to employment, including people who have struggled with addictions—staying true to Shaun's belief that food can nourish both the body and the soul.

Expanding the Vision: Kabul, Kyiv, and Kolkata Social

But Shaun didn't stop there. Other wars had forced new waves of asylum seekers to Australia—and they too needed support. Building on the success of Colombo Social, Shaun expanded his vision through Plate It Forward, launching ventures Kabul Social, Kyiv Social, and the most recent, Kolkata Social. Each of these restaurants employs and empowers refugees and asylum seekers from diverse backgrounds. Together, these initiatives have created job opportunities and career pathways for over 250 people from marginalized communities, and have provided more than 660,000 meals to those experiencing food insecurity. These numbers continue to grow, alongside Shaun's expanding network of social enterprises.

Another of his initiatives, Second Chance Kitchen, is a Plate It Forward program supporting young people in the incarceration system. It connects them with mentors who teach practical cooking skills—dishes they can recreate and build a future with once they're out.

Recognition and Awards

His leadership has earned widespread recognition, including the 2024 NSW Governor's Humanitarian Award, the 2023 Not-for-Profit CEO of the Year, and the 2021 Australian Human Rights Commission's Community Human Rights Champion Award.

A Legacy of Values

Listening to Shaun, it becomes clear that his mother, Shiranie, played a pivotal role in shaping his values. She often warned him about the dangers of falling into the "money trap," reminding him that "money is a necessary evil." She instilled in him a strong work ethic, but perhaps most importantly, a deep understanding that privilege comes with responsibility—the responsibility to support those who haven't had the same opportunities.

While Shaun's parents instilled in him values that would help him lead a meaningful life, they also sought to protect him by not dwelling on the circumstances that had led them to seek a better life in Australia. As a result, Shaun grew up with only a vague understanding of their displacement. He pieced together fragments of the story from the occasional newspaper article or overheard conversation, but his awareness remained limited. Reflecting on this, he remarked, "I don't think anyone in Australia understood the breadth and depth of what was going on."[45]

Future Directions

Shaun's vision for the future is to continue expanding his efforts to empower the disempowered and help create pathways to a better life. One such initiative involves building a kitchen at a high school in the Batticaloa district of Sri Lanka, designed to provide meals for over 400 students.

While the Sri Lankan government's National Schools Meal Programme supports primary school children, high school students are excluded from this assistance. Shaun's project seeks to fill this gap—albeit on a modest scale—by ensuring that older students, too, have access to nutritious meals that support their learning and wellbeing.

Reflections

Shaun Christie-David's story is one of resilience, purpose, and a refusal to accept the status quo. From the corporate towers of Sydney's CBD to

---

[45] In conversation with this writer during a zoom conference on 17 July 2025.
The irony was that the conflict in Sri Lanka—the civil war—has been an extensively researched topic across multiple academic disciplines. Scholars from fields including political science, anthropology, history, psychology, economics, and international relations have produced a broad range of studies, analyses, and commentaries addressing various dimensions of the conflict.

the community kitchens of Colombo Social, he has carved a path that blends personal conviction with social responsibility. For him, privilege is not something to be protected, but something to be used in service of others. Through his work with refugees, asylum seekers, and vulnerable communities, he has reimagined success in modern Australia—not as personal advancement, but as the ability to uplift others.

Max Jeganathan: The Politics of Grace

Speaking to Power

On 24 November 2024, as Priyan Max Jeganathan stood in the Great Hall of Parliament House—its towering ceilings and polished glass amplifying a rare stillness—he commanded the room's attention with quiet conviction. Before a gathering of lawmakers, he stepped forward and declared, "All of our stories have great adversity and struggles that we are dealing with. All of our stories have things – grace in action – things that we can be grateful for." His unmistakably Australian accent carried a weight born of memory and exile—not just as a former political adviser or lawyer, but as someone who had, in infancy, narrowly escaped death during one of Sri Lanka's darkest hours. Seven months later, on 19 July 2025, he would carry that same unyielding message to a very different audience, addressing the *Confident Faith Conference* at the Oxford Union, where leather and dark wood replaced glass and marble. Across continents and contexts, his call never wavered: not to power, but to grace.

The Weight of Memory

Max's message of grace, offered from podiums in Canberra and Oxford, was not born of abstract principle. It was forged in fire—*literally*. Long before he stood beneath the vaulted ceiling of the Oxford Union or the polished halls of Parliament House, Max was a baby cradled in panic as his parents fled for their lives through the burning streets of Colombo. His earliest story is not one he remembers, but one that lives within him—retold with reverence, as if its memory belongs to all who have been forced to flee, survive, and rebuild.

A Life Spared[46]

Max, or Priyan as his parents called him, was just a baby when violence

---

[46] The first-person narrative here is an extract from the article, *A refugee's story of racism and redemption* and input provided by Max Jeganathan.
found in https://thirst.sg/a-refugees-story-of-racism-and-redemption/

arrived at his family's doorstep. It was July 1983—when anti-Tamil violence swept across Sri Lanka with terrifying speed and brutality. This was nothing new, since Sri Lanka (then Ceylon) became independent of British rule in 1948, bouts of anti-Tamil violence had become common. Black July was the worst and for Max's parents, that night would mark the beginning of a life forever changed.

"My dad grabbed me and ran into the bathroom at the back of the house," recalling what his parents had told him much later to explain their presence in the 'Lucky Country'. "My mum was stuck in the front when a gang burst through the door."

Max, less than a year old, began to cry—alerting the intruders to their hiding place. "They were high on drugs, and they had all sorts of equipment. They started pounding on the bathroom door—a flimsy, old wooden door with a tiny latch."

"There was no reason it should have held. Everything—physics, logic, experience—suggested the door would give way. But it didn't. "They banged and banged," Max says, "and somehow, the latch held. Eventually, they gave up. As they left, they shouted, 'We'll come back and burn the house down.'"

There was no time to gather belongings. Max's parents grabbed him, a nappy bag, and ran into the bushes beside their home. There, a young girl from a neighbouring household approached. What she said next remains seared in family memory.

"She told my parents they may not survive the night. Give us your baby. We'll take care of him. He'll be safe."

Faced with an impossible choice, Max's parents handed over their infant son—believing it could be the last time they would see him. From the bushes, they watched as their home was set ablaze, everything they owned reduced to ash.

Somehow, all three survived. Max was taken to safety. His parents remained hidden through the night. The next morning, Max's uncle, who was a police officer and a fluent speaker of the Sinhalese language, found Max and reunited him with his parents.

"By the grace of God, we were reunited," Max says. "We lost everything, but we survived."

It was a night that would shape not only Max's life but his eventual understanding of faith, justice, and what it means to begin again—uprooted, but not broken.

From Refuge to Renewal

Resettled in Australia, the Jeganathan family began again with very little. Like many Tamil refugees, they carried the trauma of loss, but also the determination to rebuild. For Max, growing up in suburban Australia—in Melbourne, then Perth meant learning to navigate multiple worlds: the expectations of a new country, the heritage of a displaced community, and the unspoken weight of his people. survival.

Max's parents worked hard and tirelessly. In their early days as Australians, they would hunt for furniture on nature strips during hard-rubbish collection. Over time, Max's father – a textile engineer – and his mother, an executive at the Department of Veterans' Affairs – would advance in their careers. The family moved around, with a shifting economy, new opportunities, and a firm faith - as their guides.

Max proudly recalls a childhood drenched in love, stability, opportunity, and surrounded by friends, cousins, uncles and aunties. Max proudly attributes his childhood to his parents, his Amma and Appa – boldly acknowledging their love, faith and courage during his speech at Parliament in November 2024.

From the Eastern suburbs of Melbourne to the southern foreshore of the Swan River in Perth, the Jeganathans built friendships, served in churches, travelled overseas, enjoyed their family, and modelled the joys of becoming true Australians, while remaining thoroughly Tamil. In high school, Max played bass guitar for both a rock band, and also for fundraiser concerts to raise money for Sri Lankan Tamil refugees. From Metallica to Bollywood, his upbringing was emblematic of integrated multiculturalism.

Finding Grace

In his teenage years, as Max began to understand the full scale of what had happened in Sri Lanka—not just to his family, but to thousands of Tamils who were killed, raped, displaced or silenced—Max began to feel the pull of bitterness. He saw the silence of the international community, the impunity of those responsible, and the way history was selectively remembered. These wounds, inherited and lived, were deep. As a teenager, Max had become a Christian, embracing for himself the faith of his parents, and now wrestling with the task of forgiveness alongside the need for healing.

In his university years, while studying law and politics at ANU in

Canberra, Max became more fluent in the language of justice. But that language alone did not bring healing.

Education and opportunities came quickly. Max excelled academically and would go on to complete degrees in law and political sciences at the Australian National University (ANU). Max was admitted to the bar and practised law for three years. He then served as a political and policy adviser in the Rudd-Gillard Governments, followed by time as a senior adviser to the then Opposition Leader Bill Shorten. By his late twenties, as a political adviser in Canberra, Max was working at the centre of power in his adopted country. Yet even there, surrounded by parliamentary process and policy debates, the deeper questions remained: this included dealing with inherited trauma without being consumed by it.

It was during this period, in what he describes as a time of "internal restlessness",[47] Max began to explore his faith more deeply—not simply as a family tradition living truth with the transformative resources for confronting the past and redeeming the future. Through the Christian message. Max found grace and a new season beckoned.

A Ministry of the Mind and Heart

After 8 years in professional politics, Max felt the pull of deeper questions. His love for the law and politics did not waiver. However – newly married – Max and his wife Fiona resigned from their jobs, spent time volunteering in Cambodia, backpacked through Europe, and arrived in Oxford in the UK where Fiona took up a senior role in international development, and Max began postgraduate study.

. Though he came from a family of strong Christian faith, Max sought an academic foundation that was intellectually rigorous and theologically sound. Oxford would become his new young family's first home, and the setting for both his intellectual sharpening and the genesis of his public speaking and writing career. He spent two years at the University of Oxford and graduated with postgraduate qualifications in theology, specialising in ethics and moral reasoning.

Max spent the next five years as a Christian apologist and speaker, based

---

[47] In an interview given to *Salt & Light*, a Christin publication, Max articulated the source of this 'internal restlessness' in his inclination to "hate injustice more than I love justice!" https://saltandlight.sg/news/i-saw-the-need-to-forgive-but-i-wasnt-willing-to-let-injustice-go-rzims-max-jeganathans-journey-to-reconciliation/?

in Singapore and speaking primarily across the Asia-Pacific, but also Europe, the United Kingdom and the United States.

He and his young family relocated to Sydney, Australia in 2023, where he took up a role as Senior Research Fellow for with the *Centre for Public Christianity (CPX)* — speaking and writing life, faith, culture, meaning and ethics through writing for public newspapers, podcasting and public speaking.

His experience in law and politics and his training in theology and philosophy have given him an intellectual foundation that coupled with his faith , enables Max to offer deep insights on life's biggest questions. Max has debated atheists, taught students and spoken at universities, churches, political institutions and businesses - including Goldman Sachs, Lego, Samsung and Amazon. His writing has appeared in outlets including *The Sydney Morning Herald*, ABC's *Religion & Ethics Report*, *The Guardian* and *The Canberra Times*. His first book *The Freedom Trap* was released by Acorn Press in March 2025.

Reflections

In a time of deepening polarisation, Max stands as a public thinker who does not shout, but invites. His story—like that of so many uprooted Tamils—is not simply one of survival, but of transformation. From the ashes of Black July to the chambers of Parliament and the podiums of Oxford, Max Jeganathan's life bears witness to a truth often forgotten in politics and public debate: that even amidst division and loss, it is grace that restores, and grace that endures.

What sets Max apart is not only his intellect or eloquence, but his ability to hold pain and hope together within a frame of redemption. He speaks not as one who has escaped suffering, but as one who has gone through it—scarred, but not hardened. In his public reflections, there is no bitterness, only a quiet moral clarity rooted in faith, grace and lived experience. And in an era, hungry for outrage but resistant to humility, his life offers a compelling alternative: a voice shaped not by vengeance, but by vision.

Ambalavaner 'Siva' Sivanandan: Fighting Race and Class

Baptism of Fire: Fleeing Violence in Ceylon

In 1958, Sri Lanka—then Ceylon—erupted into its first wave of brutal anti-Tamil violence. Ambalavaner Sivanandan (known to friends and family as Siva), a 35-year-old Tamil, found himself at the heart of this horror.

At the time, press censorship was so extreme that, according to respected Sinhalese journalist Tarzie Vittachi,[48] it rivalled that of Nazi-occupied Europe during World War II.[49] As a result, the atrocities remained hidden from the outside world—until Vittachi himself exposed them.

Amid the chaos, Siva, to save his family from a marauding Sinhalese mob, disguised himself as a policeman and wielded a gun—unloaded, but menacing enough to ensure their escape. His family survived unharmed.

He had witnessed unspeakable cruelty: people burned alive, friends brutally murdered, and even his nephew among the dead. The trauma of those horrific moments would haunt him for the rest of his life. Realizing he could no longer raise a family in a country descending into hatred and violence, Siva made the life-altering decision to leave Ceylon. He arrived in Britain shortly thereafter, seeking to start anew. The decision was doubly painful for Siva, who, defying his family's wishes, had married a Sinhalese woman. Now, he was forced to flee the land of his birth, driven out by a state that had chosen to exploit Sinhala chauvinism for political gain—shattering the bonds he once believed could unite them.

---

[48] Tarzie Vittachi was a Sri Lankan journalist whose book on the anti-Tamil violence of 1958 won him the Magsaysay Prize in 1959. From 1960 to 1965 he was Asian director of the International Press Institute, an organization of editors devoted to promoting the freedom of the press. He was, at the same time, a correspondent for *The Economist*, the BBC and *The Sunday Times of London* and wrote a column for *Newsweek*.

[49] Tarzie Vittachi, *Emergency '58*, Andre Deutsch, London, 1958, Cover

A New Storm: Arrival in a Racially Divided Britain

When Siva arrived in London, he found himself stepping into yet another storm of racial violence—the Notting Hill riots. This time, the victims were Caribbean migrants, attacked by gangs of white youths. Fresh from the trauma of anti-Tamil violence in Sri Lanka, these new experiences compounded his personal and political awakening. As he would later describe it, a "double baptism of fire",[50] setting the stage for his lifelong commitment to confronting racism. It was during this period that he began to write.

From Tea Boy to Librarian: Confronting British Racism

In Britain, Siva encountered a different form of racism—less overtly violent but deeply systemic. He faced great difficulty finding work. Despite holding a degree in economics and having served as a bank manager, his qualifications and experience were disregarded, overshadowed by the unspoken assumption that someone like him was unsuitable for managerial positions. Undeterred, he took a position as a "tea boy" in a library and, trained himself to become a librarian. Siva took a job in Middlesex libraries and worked variously in public libraries, for the Colonial Office library. In 1964 was appointed chief librarian at the Institute of Race Relations (IRR) in central London.

Siva's appointment at the Institute of Race Relations (IRR) would profoundly reshape the understanding of race relations in Britain. When he joined, the IRR operated as an elite academic institution that approached the study of race relations in a detached, neutral, and scientific manner. Its funding came from influential organizations such as the Ford Foundation, Rockefeller Foundation, and Shell, and it largely continued to function as it had during its earlier days as a department of the Royal Institute of International Affairs (Chatham House).

At the time, the IRR focused primarily on analysing racial dynamics in newly independent nations of the Global South, often in ways that aligned with Western global interests. One such study was *Ceylon: A Divided Nation*, authored by B.H. Farmer and published by Oxford University Press in

---

[50] A Sivanandan, *Communities of Resistance: Writings on Black Struggles for Socialism*, Verso, London cited by Paul Gordon in Soul *Writing: the existential/personal vein in Sivanandan's Work*, Race & Class, Vol 41, 1/2 p68

1960. This report examined the anti-Tamil violence of 1958 in Sri Lanka (then Ceylon).

Revolutionising the IRR: From Research to Resistance

Siva, the newly appointed librarian at the IRR, embarked on a complete and transformative overhaul of its library. Under his guidance, the library evolved into a political hub that examined the intersections of race, colonialism, independence movements, and the emergence of neo-colonialism. This new approach, reflected in the library's collection, resonated with the Institute's staff and members.

Siva also forged connections with the American civil rights movement, visiting the United States in 1968, where he met, among others, members of the Black Panther Party. His activism extended internationally, and he played a key role in shaping the World Council of Churches' radical Programme to Combat Racism in 1969.

Taking Over the IRR: A Battle for Institutional Change

However, the IRR's Management Board remained disconnected from the growing realization among staff and members that racism in Britain was not merely an immigration issue but a product of a fundamentally racist society. This ideological rift came to a head in 1972, with Siva playing a pivotal role in the ensuing struggle. The confrontation led to the resignation of the Board, marking a significant turning point for the Institute.

Following this shift, Siva was appointed Director of the IRR, a position he used to steer the organization towards addressing systemic racism. In 1974, he also became editor of its magazine, Race, which was renamed Race & Class, solidifying his leadership and the Institute's broader focus.

Under Siva's leadership, the IRR underwent a profound transformation, becoming unrecognizable from its previous incarnation. Gone was the detached, academic approach of analysing situations, publishing findings, and maintaining strict neutrality. In its place emerged an IRR that not only analysed but also actively took positions aligned with its staunch anti-racism stance, focusing on action-oriented advocacy.

Race & Class: A Platform for Radical Thought

Race & Class, under Siva's editorship, was no longer a traditional academic journal; instead, it became a platform for well-researched arguments and incisive opinions that exposed the deep-seated racism underpinning British society. The influence of Siva's early exposure to Marxism in Ceylon was evident in the journal's articles, which critically examined the intersections of race, class, and systemic injustice.

The transformation of the IRR under Siva's leadership was aptly encapsulated by Hazel Walters in the July-December 1999 issue of *Race & Class*, describing it as the "transformation of the Institute itself from serving the policy-makers to serving the policed." It was fitting that this observation appeared in the Introduction to that particular issue, which was dedicated to exploring and celebrating Siva's unique contributions on the occasion of his 75th birthday. The decision to devote the issue to him, made by the journal's editorial working committee, was itself a profound tribute from his peers and colleagues.

A Marxist Lens: Linking Race, Class, and Empire

Siva's actions were fuelled by a deep sense of righteous anger and a steadfast commitment to his Marxist beliefs. He viewed Marxism as the only framework capable of offering solutions through its very analysis, describing it as "the only mode of (social) investigation in which the solution is imminent in the analysis."[51] In this essay *Globalism and the Left*, Siva underscored the need for socialist ideology to guide revolutions by painting a vivid picture of the socio-economic despair driving mass uprisings:

> *The farmers have no land, the workers have no work, the young have no future, the people have no food. The state belongs to the rich, the rich belong to international capital, the intelligentsia aspire to both. Only religion offers hope; only rebellion, release. Hence, when the insurrection comes, it is not class but mass—sometimes religious, sometimes secular, often both, but always against the state and its imperial masters.*
>
> *But there is no socialist ideology to give direction, no organic intellectuals to plan strategies. Hence, the revolutions end up by bringing another version of the same, the second time as farce.*

For Siva, racism was not an isolated social ill but deeply intertwined

---

[51] A Sivanandan, "Globalism and the Left", *Race &Class* (Vol 40, 2/3 1988/99),7

with the capitalist mode of production.[52] This perspective shaped much of his work, including his critique of global geopolitics. For instance, in a 1976 special issue of *Race & Class*,[53] he boldly highlighted the reluctance of Arab leaders to support the Palestinian cause, pointing out that these rulers had found natural allies in their Israeli counterparts, perceiving the revolutionary nationalism of the Palestinians as a threat to their power.

Siva's foresight extended to the impact of the digital revolution. Long before most Marxist thinkers grasped its implications, he recognised the shift from industrial to informational capitalism as epochal in nature. His prophetic understanding of this transformation would take another decade to gain broader acknowledgement within Marxist circles.

Words that Endure

Siva had a remarkable ability to distil profound insights into concise, memorable quotes that have endured as powerful tools for conveying complex ideas. These sharp, pithy statements not only capture the essence of his thinking but have also been widely adopted by others as succinct expressions of compelling arguments.

Here are some of his most impactful quotes.[54]

"We are here because you were there"

The quote "We are here because you were there" succinctly captured Siva's incisive analysis of migration and its inextricable link to colonial history.

In an era where anti-migration and anti-refugee rhetoric dominated, Siva's words challenged explanations of immigration, such as the neutral "push and pull factors" often cited in academic discourse. Instead, he emphasised a dialectical understanding: the presence of post-war migrants from the Global South in Britain was directly tied to the destruction wrought by British colonialism in their home countries—economically, culturally, and politically.

Decades later, Siva's observation continued to resonate with new

---

[52] Paul Gordon, Soul Writing: the existential/personal vein in Sivanandan's Work, *Race &Class*, (Vol 41,1/2,1999) p59.
[53] A Sivanandan, editorial, *Race &Class* (Vol XVII no ,3, Winter 1976)
[54] To be found in, Archives Key Saying in **https://asivanandan.com/key_sayings/** and in "Ambalavaner Sivanandan Obituary", *The Guadian*, 7 February 2018.

generations of non-white Britons who invoked his words to highlight the enduring legacy of empire. This included Sanjay Patel, an LSE Fellow in Human Rights, whose book on post-war migration to the UK, *We're Here Because You Were There: Immigration and the End of Empire*[55], explicitly referenced the quote. Likewise, Reni Eddo-Lodge cited Siva's words in her bestselling book on racism in Britain, *Why I'm No Longer Talking to White People About Race*,[56] reaffirming its ongoing relevance in contemporary discourse.

"The personal is not political, the political is personal"

"The personal is not political, the political is personal" reflected Siva's insistence on focusing the fight against racism on its systemic and structural roots rather than on individual attitudes or behaviours. By this, he meant that racism is not just about personal prejudice or bias but is deeply embedded in institutions, laws, and societal systems that shape people's lives and opportunities.

"The violence of the violated"

"The violence of the violated" encapsulated Siva's belief that acts of violence by the oppressed do not arise from inherent malice or a thirst for revenge but are a direct response to the systemic violence imposed upon them. This systemic violence—rooted in racism, colonialism, or institutionalized injustice—inflicts profound damage on the psyche, leaving individuals and communities feeling powerless and without choice.

Siva's insight resonates with Nelson Mandela's observation: "A freedom fighter learns the hard way that it is the oppressor who defines the nature of the struggle, and the oppressed is often left no recourse but to use methods that mirror those of the oppressor. At a point, one can only fight fire with fire."

"Who you are is what you do"

Siva's quote, "Who you are is what you do," reflected his critique of identity politics that focuses solely on personal identity without engaging in collective action for broader social transformation. He believed that

---

[55] Verso, 2021
[56] Bloomsbury, 2018

identity is not simply defined by innate characteristics such as gender, race, or ethnicity but by how individuals engage with the world and contribute to creating a more just society. For Siva, identity could only be affirmed through action and participation in collective struggles against oppression. It is through such actions, rather than self-centred identity politics, that individuals truly define themselves and drive meaningful change.

"If those who have do not give, those who haven't must take"

This quote by Siva underscores the inevitability of resistance and redistribution in the face of systemic inequality. It highlights his belief that societal structures that hoard resources, wealth, and power without addressing the needs of the underprivileged ultimately create conditions for rebellion. In effect it suggests that when those in positions of privilege and wealth refuse to share or address the injustices that sustain their advantage, they leave the marginalized with no option but to demand or take what is necessary for survival. It reflects Siva's understanding of social justice: addressing inequality is not merely an act of charity but a moral and political necessity to avoid conflict and ensure equity.

Siva on Sri Lanka

While Siva's activism primarily focused on the racism underpinning British society, he remained deeply attuned to the ways racism was promoted and exploited in his country of birth, Sri Lanka. Having experienced it firsthand during the anti-Tamil pogrom of 1958, Siva was compelled to act when violence erupted again in July 1983, during Black July. He took it upon himself to expose the systemic racism fuelling the atrocities.

The Summer 1984 issue of *Race & Class* was devoted to the theme "Sri Lanka: Racism and the Authoritarian State." In his powerful editorial opening, Siva stated:

"Ever since independence, successive Sri Lankan governments have done everything in their power, from state-sponsored racism to state-sponsored pogroms, to render Tamil people a separate people, and inferior—and then cried out against that separatism when Tamils embraced it to carve out their own dignity and future."

The issue featured contributions from Tamil and Sinhalese Sri Lankans, as well as a compelling article by Nancy Murray, a member of the *Race & Class* editorial committee, titled "The State Against the Tamils."

Together these pieces provided a searing indictment of the Sri Lankan state's role in perpetuating racism and violence against the Tamil people.

Essayist and Novelist

Siva's essays have been published in three influential collections: *A Different Hunger* (1982), *Communities of Resistance* (1990), and *Catching History on the Wing* (2008). While the publications covered a range of subjects, they were unified by the central themes of racism and imperialism

In 1997, Siva published his epic novel, *When Memory Dies*, a sweeping narrative spanning nearly a century and told through the perspectives of three generations of a Tamil family. Masterfully examining the colonial and postcolonial history of Sri Lanka, the novel offered a poignant portrayal of the experiences of marginalized and subordinated people. By brilliantly connecting the broader forces of colonialism and postcolonial politics to the intimate, lived realities of its characters, the novel provided a profound and compelling perspective. Unsurprisingly, it was widely celebrated and won the 1998 Commonwealth Writers' Prize for Best First Book, cementing Siva's legacy as both a literary and political thinker.

Reflections

Siva died in 2018 at the age of 94, just five years after his retirement as the Director of IRR, a post that he held for 40 years. *The Guardian*'s obituary on 7 February 2018 noted "He was a tireless and eloquent voice explaining the connections between race, class, imperialism and colonialism."

Siva's life and work serve as a testament to the power of intellectual rigour, moral courage, and unwavering commitment to justice. Forced to flee his homeland of Sri Lanka after witnessing unimaginable violence, he transformed his displacement into a source of strength and purpose. The trauma of his exile never diminished his resolve; instead, it deepened his understanding of systemic oppression and shaped his lifelong fight against racism and colonialism.

From his groundbreaking leadership at the Institute of Race Relations to his incisive essays and his literary masterpiece *When Memory Dies*, Siva bridged the personal and the political, illuminating the interconnectedness of struggles across the globe. His work was driven by a profound empathy for the marginalized and a relentless determination to challenge structures of power and inequality.

Siva's resilience in the face of adversity, his ability to turn personal loss into collective empowerment, and his call to action—rooted in solidarity, resistance, and the pursuit of justice—remain as relevant today as ever. His legacy is not merely an inheritance but a challenge: to speak truth to power, to amplify the voices of the oppressed, and to ensure that the struggle for justice continues with the same fervour, clarity, and hope that defined his life.

Danny Sriskandarajah: Power to the People.

A Global Voice for Change

On his first day at school in Papua New Guinea, a teacher stumbled over the name *Dhananjayan* and simply dubbed him "Danny." That improvised nickname stuck—and followed him across continents, as he rose from the child of Tamil refugees to one of the most respected and dynamic leaders in the global non-profit sector.

Today, Dhananjayan "Danny" Sriskandarajah is known not just for his name, but for breaking barriers. He made history as the youngest and first non-British Director General of the Royal Commonwealth Society. He went on to lead CIVICUS, a global alliance of civil society organisations, and later served as Chief Executive of Oxfam GB, guiding it through one of the most turbulent chapters in its history.

In January 2024, Danny took the helm of the New Economics Foundation (NEF), a British think tank long known for challenging economic orthodoxy. His appointment underscored a lifelong commitment to tackling inequality, amplifying civic voices, and reimagining systems of power.

As *The Guardian* observed in July 2024, Danny is "a political radical, forged in the fire of childhood exile from Sri Lanka and his family's fight from their new home in Australia for the persecuted Tamils left behind."

From Karainagar to the World

Danny's journey began in the tumultuous backdrop of Sri Lanka's ethnic conflict. At just one year old, his parents—university lecturers—left the island to pursue postgraduate studies abroad, a necessary step to secure their academic careers. During their absence, Danny remained in Sri Lanka under the care of his grandparents on the northern island of Karainagar. The arrangement, intended to be temporary, reflected the family's hope for a brighter future despite the growing storm of political and ethnic unrest around them.

However, the escalating persecution of Tamils and the growing violence in the country upended those plans. Tragedy struck when Danny's uncle was killed during a wave of anti-Tamil violence, making it clear that returning to Sri Lanka was no longer safe. In response, Danny's father, who had completed his doctorate at the University of Sydney, secured a teaching position in Papua New Guinea. With his mother also finishing her studies, the family was finally reunited, and Danny—now six years old—joined his parents to embark on a transformative new chapter in their lives.

A New Life in Australia

Having spent five formative years apart from his parents, Danny faced the challenge of adjusting to an entirely unfamiliar environment when he reunited with them. Raised by his grandmother, he had called her *Amma* (mother in Tamil). He referred to his mother as *Mootha Marumakal*—Tamil for "eldest daughter-in-law," echoing how his grandparents addressed her. Now, he had to reorient himself to calling his mother *Amma* and forging a closer bond with her. Learning English was just one of many hurdles.

Hawkesbury Agricultural College in Sydney offered Danny's father a position, prompting the family to move to Australia in early 1986

Settling in Richmond, a small town on the outskirts of Sydney, Danny found himself one of only two ethnic minority children at his new primary school—the other being an adopted child of white parents. The experience was unfamiliar and, at times, bewildering. He vividly recalls a curious little girl rubbing the skin on his arm, seemingly to check if the brown colour would come off. Without any preconceived notions of racism, Danny viewed these moments as quirky and intriguing, a reflection of his natural adaptability and openness to the new world around him.

In 1988, at thirteen, Danny became an Australian citizen—a moment etched deeply in his memory. For his family, who had been displaced and exiled by the war in Sri Lanka, this milestone was both a triumph and a bittersweet reminder of their journey. As Tamils, they had endured the indignities of being treated as second-class citizens in their homeland. Now, in Australia, they embraced the full rights and privileges of a vibrant democracy. No longer a persecuted minority, they felt welcomed into Australia's multicultural experiment.

Sydney's growing Tamil diaspora offered a stark contrast to their experiences in Sri Lanka, brimming with dance recitals, music concerts, drama performances, and religious ceremonies. For the Sriskandarajah family, Australia truly lived up to its reputation as the "lucky country," encouraging them to celebrate their heritage while embracing the many opportunities this new chapter of life had to offer.

Roots and Responsibility

During his teenage years, Danny's home life was deeply intertwined with the anxieties of the Tamil diaspora over the plight of their community in Sri Lanka. The escalating conflict there, overlooked by much of the world, seemed destined to become a forgotten war. With Tamils in Sri Lanka unable to speak out, the responsibility fell heavily on those in the diaspora. Danny's parents, along with their community, threw themselves into activism, and Danny eagerly joined their efforts.

The family wrote letters to politicians, held rallies outside the Australian parliament, and worked tirelessly to garner media attention for the Tamil cause. Danny's cousin was involved in setting up a Tamil community radio station. Danny helped and was involved in fundraising events to support refugees. Danny even wrote a letter to the Dalai Lama urging him to call for peace in Sri Lanka—and he was awestruck when he received a reply.

This activism became an all-encompassing part of their lives. Weekends, for most of Danny's friends, were filled with carefree fun, but for him, they usually involved attending Tamil events with his parents. The work, while demanding, left a profound impact on Danny. Decades later, he would reflect on how these experiences, and the example set by his parents, nurtured a deep sense of activism that has shaped his personal and professional path.

Danny recognized the privilege of having escaped the war that continued to ravage his homeland. Yet this privilege came with a responsibility—to advocate for those who could not. He felt obligated to speak out against injustice and give voice to the silenced. And, perhaps most importantly, he felt empowered: he had the means to make a difference.

Becoming Tamil Australian

Like many children of the Tamil diaspora, Danny's early experiences of integrating into mainstream Australia were deeply influenced by his time at James Ruse Agricultural High School in Carlingford, New South Wales, a selective school for gifted students. He thrived in this environment, excelling both academically and socially. Active in athletics and earning the prestigious role of school captain, these formative years played a pivotal role in shaping his identity. It was during this time that Danny embraced his heritage, proudly identifying as a Tamil Australian.

The Quest for Justice

In the late 1990's while at the University of Sydney, he co-organised[57] a forum titled *Neethi Forum*, meaning justice in Tamil, to raise awareness about the history of Sri Lanka's conflict and the challenges of achieving peace with justice. The forum held at the university brought together students, academics, and activists to explore the roots of the war and emphasise the importance of equitable solutions.

The Rhodes Scholar

Danny spent four transformative years at the University of Sydney, where he completed an Economics Honours degree. In 1998, his academic and leadership achievements earned him a Rhodes Scholarship, making him the first Asian Australian immigrant to receive this prestigious award. Reflecting on his selection interview, Danny recalls being asked how he, as a young man of colour, felt about accepting a scholarship tied to the controversial legacy of Cecil Rhodes. He answered that the best use of such a legacy was to further his education and activism, channelling the resources toward meaningful change. Interestingly, Danny credits former Prime Minister Tony Abbott, then a backbencher serving on the selection committee, as one of his advocates, despite their contrasting political views.

At Oxford, Danny pursued an M.Phil. and later a D.Phil. in International Development, focusing his research on inequalities and ethnic conflict in Sri Lanka. Initially, he planned to return to Australia after completing his M.Phil. and join the Department of Foreign Affairs.

However, during his time at Oxford, Danny met Suzanne Lambert, a fellow Rhodes Scholar from Trinidad and Tobago, and the two fell in love. Faced with a choice between returning to Canberra to work for the John Howard government or staying in Oxford to undertake a doctorate and remain with Suzanne, Danny chose the latter, committing to both his academic pursuits and their relationship.

A Not-for-Profit Journey

Between completing his doctoral studies and becoming CEO of the New Economics Foundation in January 2024, Danny worked for many

---

[57] The other partner was the Australasian Federation of Tamil Associations (AFTA)

organisations, including the Institute for Public Policy Research (IPPR); Royal Commonwealth Society; CIVICUS and Oxfam GB.

Laying the Foundations: Migration and Public Policy at IPPR

At IPPR Danny served as Director of Research for three years, during which he researched several aspects of migration including the finding that migration offered one of the ways to improve prospects for countries and individuals.

A Radical Turn at the Royal Commonwealth Society

In his early 30s, Danny was approached for the role of Director General at the Royal Commonwealth Society (RCS), an institution founded in the mid-1800s as the British Colonial Institute. Though unfamiliar with the RCS, Danny was intrigued by its evolution into a progressive force for the modern Commonwealth, including hosting Nelson Mandela's first London press conference in 1991. Despite his youth and lack of CEO experience, Danny's fresh perspective aligned with the RCS's desire for a radical departure from tradition. He embraced the challenge, becoming the first non-British and first person of colour to lead the Society in its 140-year history. Danny's tenure was defined by the Commonwealth Conversation, a landmark consultation engaging citizens and policymakers across the Commonwealth to redefine its purpose for the 21st century. This culminated in the 2009 report *Commonwealth?* critically examining the institution's relevance. Key figures like former Australian Prime Minister Malcolm Fraser provided insights, including his candid remark: "The problem with the Commonwealth, mate, is that it's stuffed if Britain tries to own it, and it's stuffed if Britain tries to disown it."

Danny's leadership over three years revitalised the RCS, steering it toward greater inclusivity and modern relevance.

Championing Global Civil Society: Leading CIVICUS

In 2013, Danny became the Secretary-General & CEO of CIVICUS, a South Africa-based global alliance of civil society organisations and activists working to strengthen citizen action and civil society throughout the world. As CEO Danny attended Obama's 2013," Stand with Civil Society" initiative.

During his six years as Secretary General of CIVICUS, Danny led groundbreaking efforts to safeguard global civic freedoms. He responded to President Obama's 2013 Stand with Civil Society challenge by identifying urgent threats to civic space and launching the CIVICUS Monitor, a tool that tracks and categorizes countries from "closed" to "open" in real time. Danny exposed systematic threats, such as oppressive laws and violent crackdowns in nations like Russia and Uganda, amplified the voices of activists like Saudi women's rights advocate Nassima al-Sada and Honduran environmentalist Berta Cáceres, and held established democracies like the UK, USA and India accountable for eroding civic freedoms, underscoring that threats to civil society are a global concern.

Through his work at CIVICUS, Danny helped illuminate the systematic global assault on civic space and championed the power of ordinary citizens to organize and mobilize for change despite mounting challenges.

Steering Oxfam GB Through Crisis and Reform

In 2019, Danny joined Oxfam GB as its CEO, stepping into the role during a time of crisis for the organisation, which had been rocked by a horrific scandal involving Oxfam GB staff paying for sex with survivors of the 2010 Haiti earthquake, some of whom were believed to be children. This scandal led to the resignation of Oxfam GB's previous CEO, Mark Goldring. Danny's appointment was a strategic move to help Oxfam GB recover from the damage caused by the scandal. He was welcomed by many within the aid sector as a strong advocate for the "global south" and a progressive thinker on development issues. However, it was clear from the outset that Danny faced a significant challenge. The scandal had severely damaged Oxfam GB's reputation, causing a loss of private donors and putting the organization's future at risk.

Upon taking the helm as CEO of Oxfam GB, Danny made it his top priority to rebuild trust and reform the organization in the wake of a scandal that had severely tarnished its reputation. His leadership focused on safeguarding vulnerable communities, aligning Oxfam's humanitarian mission with ethical practices at every level. Central to this effort was the implementation of robust policies that embodied the principle of "do no harm," acknowledging that any harm caused in the course of humanitarian work undermines the very essence of Oxfam's purpose.

Demonstrating a hands-on approach, Danny visited challenging regions such as the Democratic Republic of Congo and Yemen, where the risk of power abuse is heightened by instability and resource scarcity. These visits highlighted his commitment to ensuring that Oxfam operates responsibly, even in the most complex and hostile environments. Recognizing that ethical dilemmas are inherent in humanitarian work; Danny navigated the delicate balance between continuing Oxfam's vital services and addressing misconduct. He understood that withdrawing aid due to wrongdoing could deprive communities of essential support, so he prioritized safeguarding measures and worked to minimize abuses of power.

Through transparency, hands-on leadership, and a steadfast commitment to reform, Danny steered Oxfam toward delivering impactful humanitarian work with the utmost integrity.

At the end of 2023, Danny stepped down as CEO of Oxfam GB after five transformative years at its helm. During his tenure, he re-established Oxfam's reputation, guided the organization through several complex and challenging humanitarian crises, and adeptly navigated the unprecedented challenges posed by the COVID-19 pandemic.

Speaking Truth to Power: A Global Advocate

Danny was also a vocal advocate for justice and human rights, using his platform to address global injustices. Notably, during the crisis in Gaza, he took a principled stand, condemning Israel's actions as "collective punishment." He highlighted the weaponisation of food in conflict and boldly called out political leaders for their lack of moral courage, underscoring the urgency of addressing such violations with integrity and resolve.[58]

Danny's accusation of Britain's political leaders' lack of moral courage was particularly striking, given that he made it while seated alongside Sir Jacob Rees-Mogg MP, a quintessential representative of the conservative British political establishment.

As one of his final acts as Oxfam GB CEO, Danny urged the British government to reclaim its global leadership in development. In a powerful Guardian article, on 14 December 2023, he called for an end to aid cuts and the misuse of funds for political ends, advocating instead for aid focused on rebuilding communities and strengthening public health systems. Danny proposed a bold, solidarity-driven development framework to tackle interconnected crises like climate change, inequality, and migration. He championed innovative funding, such as taxing

---

[58] *BBC Question Time*, 16 November 2023

polluters and addressing wealth inequality, and called for reparations for historical injustices, including slavery, to promote racial justice and equitable partnerships. Danny's vision extended beyond traditional aid, advocating systemic reform and global collaboration. His appeal to the Labour Party was clear: seize the opportunity to lead with compassion and integrity, restoring Britain's status as a force for good in the world.

Reimagining Economics: A New Chapter at NEF

Danny's career at NEF began in 2024, the Foundation's 40th year of operations. His vision for the organisation as he outlined in a podcast[59] on 22 July 2024, central to his vison for NEF is the rejection of orthodox economics which are incapable of addressing modern challenges. This vision is built on the belief that economies are human constructs, and as such, they can and must be reshaped to foster equity, sustainability, and resilience against the challenges of the 21st century.

Power to the People

Also in 2024, Danny's book *Power to the People* was published by Headline Press. The book addresses the power of active citizen engagement to reshape society and address growing global challenges.

He explores why traditional institutions, including governments and global organizations, are increasingly out of touch with the needs of ordinary people, resulting in widespread voter apathy and distrust in leadership.

In the first half of the book, he examines issues like inequality, climate change, and the inadequacies of institutions like the IMF and World Bank, illustrating how they often fail to meet modern challenges. He argues that these institutions are outdated, and reform is essential to bring about fairer, more inclusive governance. The second half of the book offers solutions, focusing on empowering communities through methods like citizen assemblies, co-operative models, and digital activism. Danny advocates for "people-powered" approaches, showcasing real-life examples of grassroots successes. He calls for structural changes that include public ownership of social media spaces, democratizing share ownership, and creating a

---

[59] Do One Better with Alberto Lidji in Philanthropy, Sustainability and Social Entrepreneurship.https://uk-podcasts.co.uk/podcast/the-do-one-better-podcast/danny-sriskandarajah-ceo-of-the-new-economics-foun

"people's chamber" at the United Nations to give more voice to global citizens.

Overall, *Power to the People* is both a critique of current governance and a hopeful manifesto, urging people to reclaim their power and work collaboratively for meaningful, democratic change

Reflections

Danny's life story is a powerful testament to resilience, adaptability, and global leadership shaped by personal experience and displacement. Born in Sri Lanka and uprooted by conflict, he lived in Papua New Guinea, Australia, South Africa, and the United Kingdom—an odyssey that shaped his identity as a true internationalist. Despite this global journey, Danny considers Australia central to who he is. Arriving during a period when the Australian Labor government was actively embracing multiculturalism, he found a society that valued inclusivity and diversity. These values left a lasting imprint. As he told SBS Radio in 2019, "I still call Australia home," even after more than two decades living in Britain as a citizen.

His formative years in Australia instilled in him a deep commitment to fairness, egalitarianism, and social justice—principles that have guided his professional path. As former CEO of Oxfam GB and current leader of the New Economics Foundation, Danny has championed bold initiatives to tackle poverty, inequality, and climate change. He is known for challenging economic orthodoxy, advocating for systemic reform, and promoting economies that serve both people and the planet. His leadership style reflects his personal journey: grounded, principled, and globally conscious.

Danny's story is more than one of career achievement; it is a reflection of how displacement, multiculturalism, and global citizenship can forge a transformative leader. His continued dedication to justice and sustainability serves as an inspiration to those seeking to build a more equitable world.

EDUCATORS AND SCIENTISTS

C J Eliezer: Scholar, Advocate, and Global Educator

A Brilliant Mind Returns Home

In 1948, Christie Jayaratnam (Jayam) Eliezer, a Cambridge prize-winner, Isaac Newton Scholar, and recipient of the Award for Original Work in Mathematics from the American National Academy of Sciences, turned down the opportunity to continue at Cambridge University to accept a professorship in mathematics at the University of Ceylon. His decision was met with jubilation in his homeland, as Eliezer, ever the patriot, intended to build his academic career in the land of his birth. Many hoped that he would be the university's next Vice-Chancellor.

Eliezer was eminently qualified, having served as Professor of Mathematics and Dean of Science at the university between 1949 and 1959. He was the author of the 'Eliezer Theorem,' formulated in 1943 while at Cambridge, and had a career that included studying and teaching at prestigious institutions such as Cambridge, Princeton, and Chicago. His mentor, Nobel laureate in Physics Paul Dirac, described Eliezer as "the most brilliant mathematician the East has produced in this age."[60] Additionally, he was a barrister, called to the Middle Temple in London in 1949. Eliezer was undoubtedly one of the country's most gifted academics.

Standing Up Against Discrimination

This, however, was not to be. Eliezer had become vocal in his criticism of the political developments in the country, particularly the 1956 law that declared Sinhala the sole official language of Ceylon (as the country was known until 1972)—a law that profoundly impacted the country's Tamil population.

Many of Eliezer's Sinhala friends and acquaintances were equally alarmed by the discriminatory law and its consequences. Among them were Rev. Celestine Fernando, an Anglican priest, and Sir Richard Aluwihare, the highly respected Inspector General of Police. Both had

---

[60] Ranee Elizer, *Conquering Scientist*, Ranee Eliezer, 2012, p10

expressed their concerns: the former alerting Eliezer to the dangers, and the latter supporting his stance.

Vice-Chancellor Sir Nicholas Attygalle was among the law's strongest advocates, attempting to extend its reach by removing Tamil as a medium of instruction at the university. In this endeavour, Attygalle had the backing of several influential members of the University Council, including former Prime Minister Dudley Senanayake, H. V. Perera QC, and N. S. Weerasoorya QC.[61] Undeterred, Eliezer appealed directly to the Prime Minister—the architect of the law—seeking clarification that it applied only to government administration, not education. This clarification displeased Attygalle. In this tense environment, it was little surprise that when Eliezer requested a year's leave to help establish the Department of Mathematics at the University of Malaysia, university authorities should seize the opportunity to deny his request, pressuring him to resign.

Forced Out

Earlier, the university had granted leave to two Sinhala academics—Malalasekera, to pursue a diplomatic career in Moscow, and Amerasinghe, to take on a teaching assignment in Singapore. Denying Eliezer's request was calculated to embarrass him and force his resignation. Furthermore, it ensured that Eliezer, a highly qualified Tamil candidate, would not be in the running for the university's next Vice-Chancellor.

Eliezer's departure sparked widespread criticism. The *Ceylon Observer* (16 June 1959), in an article titled "Quietly Fades the Don," observed that "Eliezer would have made a good Vice-Chancellor." It then went onto add cryptically that the "matter was handled in the fourth dimension" and questioned Eliezer's situation further, asking whether he was a "victim of higher algebra," suggesting powerful, unseen forces were at play.

It was difficult to conceal the fact that Eliezer's departure had been politically orchestrated.

There are of course reasons to believe that Eliezer might have left the country regardless, as just a year earlier, in 1958, Ceylon had been engulfed in one of its early anti-Tamil pogroms, during which hundreds of Tamils were hunted down and killed. Eliezer would not have wanted his young

---

[61] Eliezer CJ "Discrimination in Education in Sri Lanka in the Last 50 Years" in S Sivanayagam (ed), *50 Years of Decay*, International Tamil Foundation, London,1997, pp 5-18,

family to remain in a country which was becoming extremely dangerous for Tamil people.

A New Chapter in Malaya

Eliezer, who at the age of 23 earned a first-class Mathematics Tripos from Christ's College and completed his PhD five years later in 1946, accepted an offer from the University of Malaya. In 1959, he became the Head of the Department of Mathematics. Originally intended as a short-term assignment, the university—proud to have a world-renowned mathematician on its staff—extended Eliezer's tenure. During his nine years at the university, he served as Dean of the Faculty of Science from 1959 to 1963 and later as Deputy Principal and Vice-Chancellor for another three years. He left the university in 1968.

In Malaya, Eliezer reconnected with Father Xavier Thaninayagam, a Catholic priest and fellow academic from his days at the University of Ceylon. Father Thaninayagam had joined the University of Malaya as a Professor in Indian Studies, and Eliezer was a Professor of Mathematics. Their renewed friendship flourished at the University of Malaya and was strengthened by regular rounds of golf at the Royal Selangor Golf Club.

Rekindling a Love for Tamil

Thaninayagam was primarily a linguist, whose natural flair for languages was cultivated during his training as a monk in Rome. He could fluently read and speak about a dozen languages, including French, German, Italian, Spanish, and Portuguese. At Annamalai University, in India, he specialized in Tamil and later earned a Ph.D. in Education from London. His broad academic training allowed him to bring a modern, multidisciplinary approach to Tamil language, literature, and culture. His friendship with Thaninayagam rekindled Eliezer's interest in the Tamil language, particularly its antiquity and uniqueness.

It was, therefore, no surprise that Eliezer was deeply moved by the writings of Kaniyan Pungundranar, a Tamil poet and philosopher from the 6th century BCE. Eliezer, a 20th-century educator, frequently recited the 2,500-year-old poem's opening line in Tamil: "*Yaathum oore; Yaavarun Kelir,*" which translates to, "The world is my town, and its people, my kinsmen." The poem conveyed far more than this sentiment. It encapsulated an entire worldview—one that resonated profoundly with

Eliezer.

> "The world is my town and its people my kinsmen
> Good and evil come not from others.
> Pain and respite emanate from within;
> Neither death is new nor life.
> We rejoice in felicity terming it a balmy breeze
> and patiently bear adversity
> The wise deem life a rudderless boat
> borne along rapids,
> even as lightning and rain strike down from darkened skies
> The boat moves steered by fate
> Needless then, this praise of the rich
> More so the insult of the poor" [62]

Meanwhile, Thaninayagam, who believed in the uniqueness of the Tamil language and its associated culture, felt that this needed dedicated research. He founded the International Association of Tamil Research (IATR) to advance studies into the Tamil language. In 1966, the IATR held its first conference in Kuala Lumpur, Malaysia's[63] capital, with strong support from the University of Malaysia and the Malaysian government—unsurprising, given that Tamil was one of the four major languages spoken in the country. Professor Eliezer and his wife, Rani, played a pivotal role in organizing the conference, and managing much of the logistical work.

At the conference, Eliezer also presented a paper on a subject close to his heart: mathematics. His paper, presented during the session "Social History: Society of the Modern Period," focused on the life and work of the mathematician Srinivasa Ramanujan.

Ramanujan, a Tamil from South India, is considered among the greatest mathematicians in history. Despite having almost no formal training in pure mathematics, Ramanujan made significant contributions to mathematical analysis, number theory, infinite series, and to solving problems that were once considered unsolvable.

Eliezer's paper also highlighted his connection to the legacy of Ramanujan, as G.H. Hardy, Ramanujan's collaborator, had been Eliezer's professor at Cambridge. In his paper, Eliezer noted how Tamil society's admiration for those with mathematical talent was rooted in its cultural heritage, which celebrated the knowledge of mathematics. He quoted two Tamil sayings to illustrate this.

---

[62] https://ilakea.blogspot.com/2015/01/translation-yadum-oore-yavarum-kelir.html
[63] On 15 September 1963, Malaya changed its name to Malaysia.

The first, attributed to the Tamil poetess Avvaiyar [64] declared, "Numbers and letters—these are the twin eyes of the mind." The second, by the philosopher Tiruvaluvar,[65] emphasized, "the importance of numbers (quantitative knowledge) as fundamental to human life, comparing them to the eyes that guide and support us." The first is to be found in *Kondrai Vendhan*[66] and the second in the *Tirukural*,[67] thought to have been written between 1st Century BC and 6th Century AD.

A Global Ethos

Eliezer, a practising Christian, was open-minded and often borrowed from other traditions to express his life philosophy. One of his favourite quotes was from Hillel the Elder, a Talmudic sage from 2,000 years ago: *"If I am not for myself, who am I? If I am for myself alone, who am I? If not now—when?"*

This quote encapsulated the brilliant academic's worldview, especially in his advocacy for the rights of the Tamil people. Eliezer believed that while we must stand up for ourselves, we equally must stand up for others. And importantly, we must not delay in fulfilling these responsibilities.

Another guiding quote for Eliezer stance came from the *Saivite*[68] scriptures. In Tamil, it read: *"Naam Yaarkum Kudi Yellom, Namanai Anjom"*,[69] which translates to "We are not subject to anyone, we do not fear death." This defiant declaration was one he often shared, both privately and publicly, to inspire fellow Tamils advocating for Tamil independence. It was a message of resilience and resistance, aimed directly at the oppressive policies of the Sri Lankan state.

---

[64] Balasubramani Palaniyandi, The Wisdom Words of Ancient Tamil Sages (Workbook): Avvaiyar's Kondrai Vendhan (Quotes from Ancient Tamil Authors), Kindle, Amazon.
[65] Tiruvalluvar (1st century BC or 6th century AD, India) was a Tamil poet-saint known as the author of the Tirukkural ("Sacred Couplets"), considered a masterpiece of human thought, compared in India and abroad to the Bible, John Milton's Paradise Lost, and the works of Plato. https://www.britannica.com/biography/Tiruvalluvar
[66] Balasubramani Palaniyandi, The Wisdom Words of Ancient Tamil Sages (Workbook): Avvaiyar's Kondrai Vendhan (Quotes from Ancient Tamil Authors), Kindle, Amazon.
[67] https://www.britannica.com/biography/Tiruvalluvar
[68] Saivite scriptures include the poems and sayings of the 63 Tamil saints, identified as Nayanmar, who lived during the sixth and eighth centuries and were devotees of Siva, one of the principal deities of Hinduism.
[69] This quote is attributed to Thirunavukkarasu, one of the 63 Nayanmar (Saivite Saints), who defied the king's order summoning him.

A New Life in Australia

In 1968, Eliezer moved to Australia, just two years after the country had removed discriminatory barriers against non-white applicants for citizenship. Although it would take another five years to fully dismantle the "White Australia Policy," individuals like Eliezer with brilliant academic credentials, were welcomed. That year, Eliezer was appointed the inaugural Professor of Applied Mathematics at La Trobe University. He remained with the university for the next 15 years, serving as Dean of the School of Physical Sciences (1969–71 and 1982–83) and as Deputy Vice-Chancellor for a period. Upon his retirement in 1983, he was appointed Emeritus Professor at La Trobe.

Australia became Eliezer's home for the remainder of his life, where he endeared himself to students and colleagues at La Trobe and beyond. His warmth and keen sense of humour played no small part in this. A story, later shared by his wife Rani, provides a glimpse into his playful character.

A Man of Wit, Warmth, and Humility

One of the rare moments of extravagance for the Professor was his cherished Valiant, a large car that he had shipped from America to Kuala Lumpur and later to Melbourne, where he converted it from left-hand to right-hand drive. The limited-edition model boasted advanced features for its time, such as push-button gears and headlights that remained on for a minute after the engine was switched off—innovations not yet common in other cars. One day, Eliezer parked the Valiant at the university, locked it, and strolled off to his office. A staff member stopped him, saying, "Professor, you've left your lights on." Calmly counting the seconds, Eliezer turned around and theatrically "blew" the lights out, as they automatically switched off. He would later recount, with a twinkle in his eye, how the woman stood there for another two minutes, mouth agape in disbelief.

That same blend of playfulness and brilliance extended into his home life. His youngest child, Tamara, was born in Australia in 1969. Jayam Eliezer doted on his children, leaving his wife, Rani, to be the disciplinarian. Despite his many achievements, Eliezer remained humble—so much so that his children only learned of his academic collaboration with Albert Einstein after his passing.

Building a Tamil Community Down Under

In Australia, Eliezer immersed himself in academic life, family, and broader civic engagement. He was particularly drawn to Australia's commitment to multiculturalism and worked hard to promote and support an inclusive approach. His interests were wide-ranging and included bridge and golf (he helped establish the Yarra Valley Country Club so he could indulge his passion without travelling too far), the study of evolution from a Christian perspective (he authored a book titled *Evolution or What?* [70]), and music (he learned to play the violin after retirement). However, his enduring focus was the welfare of the Tamil people—both those arriving in Australia in increasing numbers and those facing hardship in their homeland.

By the late 1970s, Australia's Tamil community had grown considerably, largely comprising Sri Lankan professionals—doctors, engineers, and accountants—seeking safety and stability. As conditions in Sri Lanka grew increasingly difficult, and even dangerous, for raising families, many, like Professor Eliezer a decade earlier, found their way to Australia through a familiar path. This often involved leaving Sri Lanka to take up positions in former British colonies before eventually settling in Australia. These colonies welcomed Sri Lankan-trained professionals, whose education closely followed the British system.

In 1978, Professor Eliezer helped establish the Ceylon Tamil Association as a social platform to foster kinship among new Tamil immigrants and assist them in adapting to their new environment. By naming the association after 'Ceylon,' the island's former name, and deliberately avoiding 'Sri Lanka'—the Sinhala term enshrined in the 1972 Republican constitution consolidating majoritarian rule—there was an unmistakable political message of defiance.

Over time, the association changed its name to the Eelam Tamil Association, adopting the Tamil name for the island. Later, it was renamed the Victoria Tamil Association, reflecting a more local flavour. While the association's primary objective remained social, its members were deeply concerned about the political developments in Sri Lanka. 1983 turned out to be a significant year for the association because this was the year of Black July—an event that transformed the conflict in Sri Lanka from low-

---

[70] Christie J Eliezer, *Evolution Creation or What?* New Delhi, ISPK, 1996

intensity militancy into a full-scale war and caused thousands of Tamils to flee to Australia.

In the same year, Christie Jeyem Eliezer—"Jeyem" to his friends—turned 65, ready to embrace a well-earned retirement after a remarkable 46-year career spanning six countries and four continents. Yet, as the small man with pepper-and-salt hair and a twinkle in his eye stood on the podium to deliver his valedictory address, he appeared much younger than the typical age for retirement. Reflecting on his journey, he shared, with a touch of whimsy, an early notion he'd once entertained: that every five years he should change his place of work and every twenty years his profession. He admitted, with a smile, that things hadn't exactly unfolded that way. More significantly, Eliezer emphasized that it was at La Trobe where his initial professional loyalties—mathematics and universities—had matured into lifelong passions.

However, retirement for Eliezer took an unexpected turn. The escalating conflict in Sri Lanka overshadowed any plans he might have had, forcing him to shelve them. The situation back home, with its increasing threat to the Tamil people, urgently demanded international attention, and Eliezer knew he could not stand aside while his community faced such peril.

The Ceylon Tamil Association of which he was President at that time was committed to the social welfare of those Tamils who were transitioning to a new country, it required a dedicated organisation to engage with the Australian Government on political matters.

In 1984, the Australasian Federation of Tamil Associations (AFTA), was established to do just that. AFTA's founding chairman, Professor Eliezer, recognized the need for a unified Tamil voice to make political engagement with the Australian Government and the wider community effective. Thus, AFTA became an umbrella body, bringing together representatives from Tamil associations across Australian states and New Zealand. AFTA was explicitly political, and dedicated to raising awareness about the situation in Sri Lanka from a Tamil perspective.

Under Eliezer's leadership, AFTA's efforts to promote this counter-narrative gained significant traction. The organization maintained regular contact with the Sri Lankan desk of Australia's Department of Foreign Affairs, and Australian politicians began raising concerns about Sri Lanka's actions in parliament. Meanwhile, Australian newspapers started publishing opinion pieces by Tamil activists, amplifying AFTA's powerful challenge to the Sri Lankan government's portrayal of the conflict.

In 1996, in recognition of his commitment to multiculturalism

Professor Eliezer was awarded the Order of Australia. In 1997, in recognition of Eliezer's success in advocating for the Tamil cause and his unwavering commitment to the self-determination of the Tamil people, the LTTE conferred upon him the title of *Mamanithar*. In awarding this honour, LTTE leader Pirapaharan wrote to Eliezer, stating that the title *Mamanithar* was "the highest national honour of Tamil Eelam, in recognition of your patriotic service to the cause of national freedom."

These developments inevitably drew the attention and scrutiny of the Sri Lankan regime.

Vilified for Speaking the Truth

In 1999, the Tamil perspective found a platform on *Dateline*, Australia's award-winning international documentary series. However, in October 2000, the same *Dateline* program aired a documentary that could only be described as a hatchet job. To be more precise, it was a failed hatchet job. It sought to depict Eliezer as a 'terrorist sympathiser' and AFTA as a 'terrorist front'. Many viewers suspected the Sri Lankan state's influence behind this failed hatchet job.

Sri Lankan doctor and Sinhalese advocate for the Tamil cause, Brian Senvewiratne summed it best: "It is incredible that a program as one-sided as this should have been aired."

Then drawing from various newspaper articles published in the wake of the controversy, caused by the program, Senvewiratne summarized the episode as follows[71]:

On October 4, 2000, Australia's Special Broadcasting Service (SBS) aired a Dateline program about how the Tamil Tigers raised funds to support their war in Sri Lanka. It was the most expensive program Dateline had ever produced, costing Australian taxpayers around $100,000, with filming done in Britain, Sri Lanka, Israel, Canada, and Zimbabwe. The program was directed by Graham Davis, who had joined SBS two years prior after leaving Channel 7's "Witness" program following a legal dispute. Davis had developed a reputation for explosive temper tantrums.

During filming in London, his cameraman walked off the job after a confrontation, forcing Davis to finish with freelance crews. In one of his notorious tirades, Davis loudly shouted profanities in the open-plan news and current affairs office of SBS, with his outbursts heard as far as the office of the Director of Television, Peter Cavanagh. Angie Kenyon, the SBS Harassment Officer, also heard the outburst. When Kenyon objected,

---

[71] https://tamilnation.org/forum/brian/001102sbs

she was told to "F--- off." After filing a formal complaint, Davis was suspended just 13 days before the program was due to air, with neither the storyline written nor the footage edited.

The program's Executive Producer, Mike Carey, scrambled to salvage the project, asking at least two other Dateline journalists to write the story. Understandably, they refused, citing their lack of knowledge on the subject. Carey was ultimately forced to write the script himself. The final broadcast was a mishmash, with Carey providing voiceovers while Davis conducted the interviews. One experienced current affairs journalist described the result as "a dog's breakfast." An expensive "dog's breakfast" at that."

The documentary aimed to link AFTA's Chairman, Professor Eliezer, to the LTTE—casting him as a terrorist sympathizer to intimidate both him and AFTA and silence the Tamil perspective. Rather than retreat, Eliezer met the accusation head-on, refusing to disown his admiration for the LTTE and taking the bull by the horns. The interview unfolded as follows:

Reporter: Are you an agent for the LTTE?

Prof. C.J. Eliezer: Certainly not.

Reporter: How would you describe, then, your relationship with the LTTE?

Prof. C.J. Eliezer: As an admirer, as an emotional admirer of the LTTE.

Reporter: A sympathizer?

Prof. C.J. Eliezer: Sympathizer, yes.

Reporter: Somebody who gives the LTTE advice?

Prof. C.J. Eliezer: I have not given them any advice.

Reporter: Somebody who provides the LTTE with support when asked?

Prof. C.J. Eliezer: Well, they haven't asked me for anything, but irrespective of that, they'll find my pronouncements at meetings and things, they'll find them useful.

Reporter: Useful in terms of furthering their cause?

Prof. C.J. Eliezer: Yes, because they're all committed to the idea of liberation, and as they are, I am, and we do it in different ways.

(Interview with SBS Television, 4 October 2000, Australia)

Just a day before the program was set to air, SBS reached out to AFTA's Secretary, whose interview responses had already been selectively edited, requesting the name of another spokesperson to further expand on the Tamil perspective. The urgency of the request hinted that the broadcaster was trying to mitigate potential backlash. Although the new spokesperson provided a counterbalance to some of the bias, the program remained slanted, revealing that the broadcaster had allowed its coverage to be compromised.

In 2001, five months after the devastating SBS program, which sought to discredit him Eliezer died.

Reflections

Professor Christie Eliezer's life was marked by unwavering dedication to both academic excellence and the pursuit of justice for his people.

From his early brilliance in mathematics to his later role as a unifying voice for the Tamil diaspora, Eliezer demonstrated a rare combination of intellect, courage, and integrity. His advocacy reflected both deep personal conviction and a nuanced understanding of the wider political and social context. As the founding chairman of AFTA, he provided an articulate and measured counter-narrative to the Sri Lankan state's portrayal of the conflict, helping to shape international perspectives on the Tamil struggle.

Despite attempts to discredit him, Eliezer remained resolute, guided by the principles that had defined his life. His legacy as a scholar, advocate, and leader continues to resonate within the Tamil community and beyond, leaving an indelible mark on both academia and the global fight for self-determination. The title of *Mamanithar*, bestowed upon him by the LTTE, symbolized not only the high esteem in which he was held but also the profound impact he had on the Tamil cause.

In every sphere he touched—whether in the classroom or on the global stage—Christie Eliezer exemplified the power of intellect and conviction in the service of a greater cause.

The high regard in which Eliezer was held became evident on 21 November 2022—more than two decades after his passing—when the School of Computing, Engineering and Mathematical Sciences, in collaboration with La Trobe Asia (established to lead the university's engagement with Asia), inaugurated the Christie Eliezer Memorial Lecture.

Suresh Canagarajah: Reimagining the English Language

Escape from Jaffna

One day in October 1995, Suresh Canagarajah—cradling his infant daughter in one arm and gripping a small bag with the other—stepped onto a Red Cross boat in pitch darkness. Behind him lay Jaffna, the city he had loved, taught in, and hoped to hold onto. Now it was under siege by the Sri Lankan army, and like many others, he was forced to leave everything behind.

From Displacement to Distinction

That journey marked the beginning of a new chapter. After arriving in the United States later that year, Suresh rebuilt his life and academic career. Today, he is the Evan Pugh University Professor of Applied Linguistics, English, and Asian Studies at Pennsylvania State University—the university's highest academic honour, awarded to only a few distinguished scholars. A prolific writer, he has authored seven books, edited several more, and published widely in leading academic journals.

Early Life and Education in Jaffna

Born in 1957 in Jaffna, the northern peninsula of Sri Lanka, Suresh, is the eldest of four siblings.[72] His parents were both teachers, and he completed his secondary education at St. John's College, a formerly missionary school. As a student there, he was involved in various creative arts, including drama, creative writing, music, and elocution.

Most of Suresh's life in Sri Lanka was centred in Jaffna, the historical capital of ancient Tamil kingdoms, except for the four years he spent as an undergraduate at the University of Kelaniya in the south.

---

[72] One of his siblings, Nishan Canagarajah (born 1966) is the current president and vice-chancellor of the University of Leicester

A Calling Reconsidered: From Priesthood to Teaching

Before deciding to pursue university studies, Suresh approached the Anglican Church's Archdeacon Gnanaprasam with the intention of studying theology. After successfully passing an entrance test, the Archdeacon encouraged him to first attend university, highlighting the importance of having educated clergy in the church and assuring him that a position in the priesthood would remain open for him in the future.

Upon completing his degree, Suresh realized that he no longer wished to become a priest and felt he could better serve as a teacher. Suresh returned to Jaffna to begin his teaching career.

The Burning of Jaffna Library and Black July

In June 1981, he witnessed anti-Tamil violence in Jaffna for the first time when the predominantly Sinhalese Buddhist police force orchestrated a wave of looting and arson, including the burning of the Jaffna Public Library, which housed over 97,000 books, as well as the destruction of the home of a Tamil member of parliament, newspaper offices, a printing press, and numerous shops. According to a 2024 account by Sinhalese journalist Nandana Weeraratne[73] —information he had been prevented from exposing for decades—these operations were overseen by four cabinet ministers at that time: Ranil Wickramasinghe, Gamini Dissanayake, Cyril Mathew, and Festus Perera. Of these, Ranil Wickramasinghe—later both Prime Minister and President of Sri Lanka—was the only one still living at the time of Weeraratne's exposé

Two years later, in July 1983, Black July—a state-orchestrated wave of violence—erupted, claiming the lives of over 3,000 Tamils in the South and displacing tens of thousands to the northern peninsula. At this time, while teaching at the University of Jaffna, Suresh was also working part-time as Assistant Editor for *Saturday Review*, an English-language weekly that reported news from the Tamil homeland to the rest of the island. Following Black July, the publication faced strict censorship and was eventually banned, forcing its editor, Sivanayagam, to seek refuge in India in September 1983.

---

[73] https://www.youtube.com/watch?v=QBr5B6A7AdI

Academic Pursuits Abroad: From Jaffna to Texas

With *Saturday Review* now defunct, Suresh focused fully on his role as a lecturer at the University of Jaffna. However, to secure tenure, he needed a higher degree, leading him to the United States, where he completed his PhD in Applied Linguistics at the University of Texas at Austin. In 1990, he returned to Jaffna, ready to resume his academic career in his homeland.

Life Under Siege: Teaching During Wartime

Suresh's life soon became interwoven with political turmoil, ethnic violence, and military campaigns as the conflict between the Sri Lankan state and the Tamil people escalated into a full-scale war—a culmination of years of anti-Tamil policies punctuated by bouts of violence. Even as an infant, Suresh experienced this unrest firsthand, as he and his parents boarded the last flight back to Jaffna after a visit to relatives in Colombo, narrowly escaping the anti-Tamil violence of 1958. This event led the esteemed Sinhala journalist Tarzie Vittachi to question in his book, *Emergency '58*, whether the Sinhalese and Tamils had reached "the parting of the ways."

Sures's teaching career in Jaffna, along with his family life, was profoundly shaped by the war. To protect his family from frequent aerial attacks and shelling, he—like many others—dug a bunker in the backyard. In the rare lulls between attacks, he would go searching for food, as essentials were often hoarded amid the scarcity. The university's operations were constantly disrupted by bombings and power cuts; with Jaffna's power stations destroyed, the city had no electricity.

Theatre as Resistance: Political Drama in a War Zone

During this challenging time, students and teachers would gather in the evenings at the home of A.J. Canagaratna, a distinguished Tamil writer and scholar, to discuss politics, current events, literature, and the arts. From these gatherings grew a desire to stage plays that would engage audiences in critical reflection on issues of justice and inequality. Many students, already experienced in Tamil theatre, collaborated with Suresh and colleagues from the English Language Teaching Unit (ELTU) to produce these plays in English.

The selected plays carried powerful social and political messages that resonated deeply with the audience, as they reflected the Tamil community's current situation. *The Accused*, a Palestinian play, portrayed an outspoken character falsely accused of treason; another, *The Trial of Dedan Kimathi*, a Kenyan play, recounted the trial and execution of a freedom fighter. For Tamils, these narratives held special significance, as they, too, felt like an occupied and colonized people. After centuries of colonial rule by the Portuguese, Dutch, and British, they now faced what they perceived as a new form of cultural and political colonization under Sinhala-Buddhist hegemony, enforced by a military presence.

The gatherings also sparked difficult conversations about how Tamil militants suppressed overt criticism, fearing dissent could be weaponised by their adversaries to undermine their cause. In this tense atmosphere, these plays not only offered a space for expression but also encouraged a critical dialogue on freedom, resilience, and the complexities of justice.

"Operation *Riviresa*" and Forced Exodus

Suresh's life as an academic at the University of Jaffna was upended by the Sri Lankan army's launch of Operation *Riviresa* in October 1995, an aggressive campaign to seize the Jaffna Peninsula. As the military advanced, most of Jaffna's inhabitants fled—some seeking refuge on the northern mainland, others attempting a perilous escape by sea to Colombo, while those unable to leave braced for the impending violence. Suresh, with his wife and two infant daughters, narrowly escaped with the assistance of the International Committee of the Red Cross (ICRC), managing to board a boat bound for Colombo before the mass exodus. Although the army eventually captured the peninsula, they entered a ghost city, its people scattered and its vibrancy drained.

A New Chapter: Emigration to the United States

Shortly after reaching Colombo, Suresh and his family emigrated to the United States, where he was appointed as a Tenure Track Assistant Professor of English at Baruch College, City University of New York.

Reimagining English in the Tamil Context

Suresh's lifelong interest in multilingualism began with his schooling and early teaching career in Sri Lanka. During British rule, English was the preferred medium of education, but after independence in 1948, instruction shifted to the local vernacular, Tamil in the North and East, and Sinhalese in the rest of the island. English language and literature continued as a subject in some urban schools for the middle class, though most people spoke a localized form of Sri Lankan English. Suresh was educated in Tamil, with English taught as a second language.

When Suresh began teaching English to students in Jaffna whose native language was Tamil, he gained valuable insights into how English was being reshaped by students' own linguistic, cultural, and personal values. He observed that these students, rather than merely adopting English, transformed it—enriching the language in ways that reflected their unique identities. Suresh saw how this adaptation subtly resisted the colonial and imperial perceptions of English, broadening its relevance as a global means of communication.

Resisting Linguistic Imperialism: A Groundbreaking Work

These insights culminated in his book, *Resisting Linguistic Imperialism* in English Teaching, published by Oxford University Press in 1999. The book details how teachers and students in peripheral communities adapted English to their contexts, subtly resisting the linguistic imperialism embedded in traditional English instruction. The book won the Year 2000 Mina Shaughnessy Award from the Modern Language Association of America. It was shortlisted for the Year 2000 Best Book Award by the British Association of Applied Linguistics.

A Geopolitics of Academic Writing: Challenging Western Norms

Suresh's next book, *A Geopolitics of Academic Writing*, published by the University of Pittsburgh Press in 2002, reflected his research and experiences from his time at the University of Jaffna between 1990 and 1994.

In this work, he argued that when academics from the Global South, influenced by their indigenous cultural and intellectual traditions, expressed their ideas in local forms of English, mainstream journals often rejected their work. This rejection was based on an implicit bias that articles that adopted alternate styles and language norms somehow rendered the subject matter less valid.

Insights from a Diverse Classroom

While teaching at the City University of New York, Suresh expanded his research to explore how the diverse linguistic backgrounds of his students created new synergies for literacy development. His classroom ethnographies revealed that, far from being a liability, students' multilingualism provided them with valuable skills and perspectives for constructively navigating diversity. This work culminated in an award-winning article published in the *Journal of Second Language Writing*.

Academic Recognition and the Kirby Professorship

In 2007, Suresh became William and Catherine Kirby Professor of Applied Linguistics and English at Pennsylvania State University. This role allowed Suresh to expand his interdisciplinary work in sociolinguistics, literacy, rhetoric, and education, while continuing to publish widely accepted research. He continued to publish his research which was widely accepted.

A committed social activist, Suresh carried forward the advocacy he began in his youth as Assistant Editor of the *Saturday Review*, a publication that actively supported the Tamil cause. As an academic in the United States, he continued this activism on behalf of multilingual scholars and students. From 2005 to 2010, he served as editor of TESOL Quarterly, the international Teachers of English flagship journal to Speakers of Other Languages (TESOL) association.

Faith, Illness, and Resilience

In 2014, Suresh was diagnosed with a rare and aggressive form of appendiceal cancer, requiring extensive surgery followed by gruelling cycles of chemotherapy. These treatments left him with lasting physical challenges, including neuropathy in his hands and feet and spinal stenosis, which made walking, climbing, and maintaining balance difficult.

Despite these hardships, Suresh found strength in his Christian faith, viewing his struggle as part of a greater plan beyond his understanding. That year, his Christmas message to family and friends reflected this faith and hope, drawing poignant parallels to the Christmas story. He highlighted Mary's faith in carrying a child outside of marriage, trusting it as part of a divine plan; Joseph's belief that their unconventional marriage and the mystery of the child's birth had a purpose; the shepherds' hope amid poverty; and the wise men's vision of a promised future.

Suresh naturally turned to the Christian faith he had nurtured since youth—faith strong enough to once inspire him toward priesthood. Suresh recognizes that his Christian faith, deeply interwoven into his personal and professional life, is unconventional within the predominantly secular academic community. Nevertheless, this faith has profoundly shaped his work, prompting him to explore and write increasingly about its influence on his scholarly pursuits.

Having entered remission, Suresh shared the insights cancer had given him in a 2018 lecture to mark the award of the Distinguished Scholarship and Service Award by the American Association of Applied Linguistics, where he spoke with resilience and humour. He recounted how people speculated about his cancer's origins, attributing it to lifestyle or genetics, leading him to self-reflect on these assumptions. He also found humour in the unsolicited emails offering burial options and insurance—ironic reminders of mortality—as he defied such expectations by surviving.

Embracing Embodied Knowledge in Scholarship

Determined to continue working from his hospital bed, he revised an academic paper on a small computer provided by his institution—a tool that helped him adapt to his physical limitations. Remarkably, he continued teaching and committee work, scheduling chemo on Thursdays and using audio-only Zoom sessions to mask his hospital setting, thereby maintaining his professional presence and identity. Reflecting on the role of objects and environment in his life, Suresh described his laptop and iPad as "prosthetics" that expanded his abilities, even from a hospital bed. This period of work earned recognition, including an award-winning article completed while undergoing treatment. This journey illuminated how the body's limitations could deepen one's research.

Engaging with the concept of "embodied knowledge," Suresh drew on perspectives from disability and postcolonial scholars, recognizing how vulnerability and pain could enrich intellectual pursuits and deepen relationships. His experiences underscored that true resilience often emerges from embracing, rather than concealing, vulnerability.

Language of Incompetence: The Power of Vulnerability

In *Language of Incompetence* (2022), Suresh reflects on the insights he gained following his cancer diagnosis and the physical challenges that came with it. He offers a unique South Asian interpretation of Christianity—emphasizing acceptance and framing it as a faith for the "wretched of the earth."

Giving Back

Suresh's endowed professorship includes an annual $27,000 discretionary fund. Suresh views this as an opportunity to foster academic development and mentorship for scholars from the Global South. He has initiated several projects to support young academics, particularly from under-resourced regions.

One major initiative focuses on Jaffna, where he has organized an annual conference and mentoring institute at the University of Jaffna. The program aims to bridge the gap in knowledge and academic preparation for students aspiring to study abroad. With colleagues from New Zealand and England, Suresh aims to establish Jaffna as a regional hub for scholarship, drawing participants from India, Pakistan, and beyond.

In addition, Suresh uses his funds to support international scholars at his university by sponsoring their travel and participation in week-long workshops, where they engage with senior academics to discuss research and teaching interests. He has extended similar initiatives to other regions, such as Tunisia, which he sees as a gateway to supporting African scholars.

Through these efforts, Suresh demonstrates his commitment to empowering marginalised academic communities and fostering international scholarly collaboration.

Advocacy Beyond Academia

Suresh's influence extended well beyond academia. From 2015 to 2019, he served as a member of the Pennsylvania Governor's Advisory Commission on Asian-Pacific American Affairs (GACAPAA), where he established a pro-bono program to help immigrant community members who were voluntarily teaching heritage languages develop professional teaching skills. To further support these community educators, he founded AAPLES (Asian and Asian Pacific Language Education Schools), creating a network for heritage language teachers across the state. In 2020, Governor Tom Wolf appointed Suresh to the Pennsylvania State Law Enforcement Citizen Advisory Commission, where he advised state police on potential areas of miscommunication with minority communities.

Reflections

Suresh's journey—from teaching in war-torn Jaffna to becoming an acclaimed academic in the United States—reflects a life grounded in resilience, curiosity, and a deep commitment to justice. Amid bombings and shortages, he fostered dialogue through literature and theatre, encouraging students to voice their struggles. These early experiences shaped his later work challenging linguistic imperialism and advocating for marginalized communities to claim English on their own terms.

In the U.S., he championed the Global South within academia, reframing multilingualism as a strength that enriches identity and fosters resistance. His scholarship has influenced language teaching worldwide, emphasizing inclusivity and pluralism.

Despite personal trials, including a cancer diagnosis, Suresh drew strength from his Christian faith, meeting adversity with both grace and humour. His continued support for immigrant educators and advocacy on minority issues reflected a lifelong commitment to uplift others.

His love for Jaffna remained constant—evident in his return there after graduation, his decision to stay through much of the war, and his investment in its academic future. Through it all, Suresh's life has been a bridge between cultures, a testament to the power of belief, knowledge, and service to community.

Elagu Elaguppillai: Science, Service, and Entrepreneurship[74]

A Pioneer

When Velupillai "Elagu" Elaguppillai arrived in Canada in 1967, the Sri Lankan Tamil community in the country numbered just a few dozen. In the years that followed, Canada welcomed Tamils fleeing persecution, especially after Black July—the state-sponsored anti-Tamil pogrom of July 1983 that uprooted much of Sri Lanka's Tamil population. What began as a small presence gradually transformed into one of the most vibrant diasporas in the country. By 2021, Tamil Canadians numbered approximately 240,000, representing about 0.7 percent of the national population.

Elagu's Legacy

Elagu's personal journey mirrors the evolution of this diaspora. While he earned deep respect within the Tamil Canadian community—organizing cultural events, mentoring newcomers, and serving on civic and arts boards—his influence extended well beyond. As Senior Scientific Advisor at the Canadian Nuclear Safety Commission, he played a pivotal role in shaping national nuclear policy. His academic appointments at the University of Toronto and Carleton University advanced education in physics and radiation protection. In 1998, he bridged the worlds of science and business by founding *Innopharm* Inc., a biopharmaceutical company based in Markham, Ontario. Across all these fields, Elagu demonstrated a rare blend of dedication, innovation, and public service—building bridges between science, business, and community, and helping lay the foundations for a thriving Tamil presence in Canada.

---

[74] Much of this chapter is based on the autobiography by Velupillai Elagupillai, *Anuvaith Thulaithu* Colombo: Velupillai Elagupillai, 2022), and on information from verified online sources.

Humble Beginnings in Rural Sri Lanka

Elagu was born on 7 September 1941 in Kakayin Seman, a small farming hamlet nestled in the village of Avaragal, about ten miles from Jaffna, the capital of Sri Lanka's Northern Province. He came from humble beginnings—his family, like most in the area, lived off the land, part of the rural peasant community that shaped much of the region's identity. Curiously, his birth certificate records his date of birth as 31 October 1941, a discrepancy that arose because his father, occupied with the demands of daily life, failed to inform the village Registrar of Births in time. Left without exact information, the Registrar simply guessed the date.

Elagu began his education at the local school, Sri Somaskanda Tamil Vidyalayam. Like many children from rural, working-class families, he went to school barefoot. During the hot summer months, crossing tarred roads became painful as the melting tar burned his feet. To protect him, his father crafted makeshift shoes from the bark of the Palmyra tree, which grew in abundance across the Jaffna Peninsula. In the absence of a hat or umbrella, young Elagu would use pieces of old jute sacks for shade—simple but resourceful solutions born of necessity.

Born into a modest farming family, Elagu grew up with limited means but abundant determination. His parents, though impoverished, were unwavering in their commitment to ensure that Elagu and his four siblings were fed, clothed, and educated. Elagu vividly remembered instances when his mother would forgo her own meals to provide for the family. One poignant memory stood out: his mother selling the saree she had purchased to celebrate Deepavali—a festival deeply significant to Tamil Hindus, symbolizing joy, new beginnings, and purification. For her, the well-being of her family took precedence over personal celebrations.

While helping his father cultivate leased land, Elagu still excelled in his studies. His father, deeply rooted in the agrarian lifestyle, envisioned Elagu continuing the farming tradition. However, his mother, Vallipillai, was resolute in her belief that education was the key to transcending their impoverished circumstances. She often recounted stories of historical figures who achieved greatness through diligence and perseverance, instilling in Elagu the conviction that hard work and learning were pathways to a better life. Inspired by her unwavering support and guidance, Elagu consistently ranked at the top of his class throughout his primary and secondary education.

A Mother's Faith and the Power of Aspiration

Elagu's mother held a deep belief in astrology, a tradition woven into the fabric of rural Tamil life. Each year, a respected astrologer from the nearby village of Achchuveli would visit their community, often stopping by their home for tea. On one such occasion, while examining Elagu's horoscope, the astrologer, made a striking prediction: the alignment of the stars indicated that Elagu was destined to become a world-renowned scientist. For his mother, this prophecy was more than mere words—it was a celestial affirmation of her unwavering faith in her son's potential. For Elagu, it became a source of inspiration, further fuelling his dedication to his studies and his dreams.

Struggles and Success in Schooling

In 1957, Elagu achieved a remarkable milestone—he became the only student from Sri Somaskanda Tamil Vidyalayam to pass the Senior School Certificate (SSC) examinations in the Science stream. Despite the astrologer's prophecy of a future in science, Elagu's own aspirations at the time leaned more towards becoming an engineer. Even this goal required overcoming major obstacles. Admission to university required fluency in English, as higher education was conducted entirely in the language—a challenge compounded by the fact that no student from his school had ever entered university.

Undeterred, Elagu set himself a rigorous daily goal: to learn ten new English words each day. He even considered transferring to Jaffna Hindu College, a prestigious institution located ten miles away, but the cost of boarding made it unattainable for his family. Recognizing both his potential and his circumstances, the principal of Sri Somaskanda Tamil Vidyalayam stepped in. He encouraged Elagu to persevere, expressing confidence that he could become the school's first university entrant. He arranged for Elagu to use the school building after hours for study and ensured he received meals.

Encouraged by his principal and his mother's faith, Elagu redoubled his efforts—balancing farm work with intense academic focus. His perseverance bore fruit when he made history as the first student from Sri Somaskanda Tamil Vidyalayam to gain admission to university.

The Long Road to University

But Elagu's journey to higher education was far from over. Gaining admission to the Faculty of Engineering at the University of Ceylon required not only academic merit but also attendance at a viva—an oral examination conducted in Colombo. The journey itself posed a financial hurdle. On the day of his scheduled travel, his parents had no funds for the journey. As fate would have it, a neighbouring farmer needed his land ploughed urgently and was willing to pay for the task. Elagu seized the opportunity, ploughing the field under the light of the moon and finishing the work by dawn. Without pause, he boarded the train to Colombo that very morning.

The interview, conducted in English, proved daunting due to Elagu's limited fluency. Fortunately, two of the panel members agreed to proceed in Tamil, easing the exchange. Yet, despite his determination and capability, his insufficient command of English cost him a place in the Engineering program. Instead, he was offered admission to pursue a Bachelor of Science degree—a path he accepted with resilience and quiet resolve.

Academic Excellence and Early Career

Elagu's unwavering commitment to his studies culminated in his graduation with First Class Honours in Science from the University of Ceylon, Colombo. His exceptional academic performance earned him the Gold Medal for the best performance in the entire science faculty in 1964. In recognition of his academic success, the university appointed him as a lecturer, opening doors to further opportunities.

A Scholarship to Canada

In 1967, Elagu was awarded the prestigious Canadian Commonwealth Scholarship, which enabled him to pursue advanced studies in Physics at the University of Toronto. There, he obtained his M.Sc. and Ph.D. degrees in nuclear physics in 1968 and 1970, respectively.

Teaching Across Continents

Following his academic achievements in Canada, Elagu embarked on a distinguished international teaching career.

In 1970, he served as a visiting lecturer in physics at the University of Penang in Malaysia and subsequently at the University of Zambia, sharing his expertise and inspiring students across continents. By 1974, he returned to Canada to join the University of Toronto, further solidifying his role in academia. In 1992, he joined Carleton University, where he developed and taught a graduate course in Radiation Protection, reflecting his commitment to education.

Scientific Contributions

Beyond teaching, Elagu contributed significantly to scientific research and policy. On completing his three-year term in Zambia, he joined the United Nations International Atomic Energy Agency (IAEA) as a Nuclear Research Program Officer. In this role he was responsible for the UN - funded nuclear research program in Eastern Africa. For five months in 1986–1987, Elagu contributed to the Chernobyl cleanup program. From 1992 to 1996, he served as a Canadian expert on the United Nations Scientific Committee on the Effects of Atomic Radiation (UNSCEAR), and he was a member of an expert panel convened by the International Atomic Energy Agency (IAEA) focusing on nuclear science education in high schools and universities.

Principles Over Position: Standing Up to CSIS

In 1997, Elagu' made the difficult decision to step away from his work at the Canadian Atomic Energy Commission after the Canadian Security Intelligence Service (CSIS) refused to renew his security clearance. Although he had held this clearance without issue since 1975, it was abruptly revoked in 1996. The reason for this change was clear: Elagu's unwavering and outspoken support for the Tamil freedom struggle in Sri Lanka. As he later reflected, "My active participation in the Sri Lankan conflict resolution, open support for the Tamil freedom struggle, and active lobbying of Canadian politicians, foreign diplomats, and national and international human rights groups, annoyed the mighty Canadian security Intelligence Service (CSIS) on several occasions. CSIS had advised me to quit Tamil issues, but I steadfastly refused—a decision I took with pride and dignity for my people."[75]

---

[75] Velupillai Elagupillai, *Anuvaith Thulaithu*, Colombo, Velupillai Elagupillai, 2022, p255

Building New Institutions

The very next day, Elagu joined the Institute for Research on Environment and Economy (IREE) at the University of Ottawa as a scientific advisor. That same year, he co-founded the International Centre for Low Dose Radiation Research (ICLDRR), securing substantial research funding from nuclear agencies in the United States, France, Japan, and Germany.

Entrepreneurship

In 1998, Elagu ventured into the business sector by founding *Innopharm* Inc., a biopharmaceutical company based in Markham, Ontario. This marked a bold transition for a nuclear scientist into the realm of pharmaceuticals as an entrepreneur. Serving as its founding president and chief operating officer, Elagu led the company until its sale to the Delaware-based American firm, Contact Pharmaceutical, in 2005.

In 2001, he expanded his influence in the pharmaceutical field by becoming the chairman of the editorial advisory board of Pharmaceutical Canada magazine, based in Markham. True to his enduring commitment to education, Elagu co-founded the Academy of Applied Pharmaceutical Sciences (AAPS), a postgraduate pharmaceutical college in Toronto, in 2004. The institution is registered as a private career college under the Private Career Colleges Act, 2005, and is recognized by the Government of Ontario.

Elagu's scientific achievements brought him into contact with many influential Canadians—among them David Kilgour, then Deputy Speaker of the House of Commons, who became a close friend. At Kilgour's suggestion, Elagu joined the Liberal Party in 1994 and soon took on an active role. In his 2022 Tamil-language autobiography *Anuvaith Thualaithu*, (Piercing the Atom) he explains that his move into entrepreneurship was driven not by profit but by a strategic vision shared by his political allies: for Canada's Tamil community to shape federal policy on Sri Lanka, it needed economic as well as cultural strength.

Politics and Advocacy for the Tamil Cause

In the wake of the state-orchestrated pogrom of Black July in 1983, Elagu played a pivotal role in making formal representations to the Honourable John Roberts, then Canada's Minister of Immigration.

Through persistent lobbying and clear appeals to Canada's humanitarian traditions, Elagu was instrumental in opening Canadian doors to Tamil families fleeing violence, helping to secure safe passage and new beginnings for those uprooted by the conflict.

Elagu's membership in the Liberal Party opened doors to senior political figures, including Prime Minister Jean Chrétien, whom he also approached to highlight the plight of Sri Lankan Tamils. In September 1999, Elagu accompanied, David Kilgour, Deputy Speaker of the Canadian Parliament to Washington to enlist former President Jimmy Carter as a neutral mediator. Carter agreed—but only if both parties issued a formal invitation. While the LTTE promptly signalled its consent, the Sri Lankan government, after a two-month delay, declined via its High Commissioner in Ottawa.

Elagu actively encouraged Tamil Canadians to engage in politics. His efforts bore fruit in 2011 when Rathika Sitsabaiesan became a Member of Parliament, and again in 2025 when Gary Anandasangaree was appointed Minister of Justice and Attorney General under Prime Minister Mark Carney.

Reflections

Elagu's life story is one of unwavering determination, boundless curiosity, and compassionate leadership. From rural Sri Lanka to the forefront of Canadian academia and policy, he bridged worlds—advancing nuclear science, educating future generations, and driving pharmaceutical innovation. Equally vital has been his devotion to community: guiding newcomers, advocating for Tamil refugees, and fostering cross-cultural understanding. Elagu has shown the way for Canada's Tamil community—uprooted from the land of their birth—to honour their heritage, stand in solidarity with those still affected by conflict, and flourish as loyal, contributing citizens of their adopted country. In every role—scientist, educator, entrepreneur, and civic leader—Elagu has embodied the ideals of service and integrity, leaving an enduring legacy that continues to inspire.

Brindha Shivalingam: Leading the Way in Brain Surgery

Fleeing War, Finding Her Calling

When Brindha Shivalingam stood at the threshold of her career in neurosurgery, she had already overcome more than most of her peers would ever face. Forced to flee Sri Lanka as a child during the violent upheaval of Black July, she arrived in Australia with memories of loss, separation, and survival. Decades later, she would become one of the few women to lead a neurosurgical department in the region—she brought not only surgical skill but also a lived understanding of resilience, compassion, and perseverance.

Surgeon and Researcher

Associate Professor Brindha Shivalingam is the Director of Neurosurgery at Chris O'Brien Lifehouse in Sydney. Her surgical practice focuses on glioma surgery, skull base tumours, and the treatment of complex brain conditions. She conducts research on gliomas and brain metastases from melanoma and is affiliated with multiple organizations promoting cancer research and neurosurgical excellence.

She is also actively involved in research on gliomas and melanoma.

Flight From Sri Lanka

Brindha's family fled Sri Lanka during the anti-Tamil violence of Black July in 1983—an experience shared by many Tamil families.

In her interview with ABC Radio National's *Conversations* (aired July 2022), Brindha spoke candidly about her childhood memories of Black July, when anti-Tamil riots erupted, marking the beginning of Sri Lanka's long and brutal civil war.

As a young girl growing up in Colombo, she had lived in a neighbourhood where Tamil and Sinhalese families coexisted peacefully—until that peace was shattered by the sudden outbreak of violence.

She described the confusion and fear that swept through the community as mobs began targeting Tamil homes, businesses, and individuals.

Her family was eventually forced into hiding as the violence escalated. She witnessed firsthand the destruction and chaos of those days—experiences that left a deep and lasting impact on her. Ultimately, it compelled her family to flee Sri Lanka and seek refuge in Australia—a move that would profoundly shape her life and career

In her interview with Richard Fiddler of ABC's *Conversations*, she reflected on the emotional aftermath of fleeing Sri Lanka. "There was a lot of depression about being torn away from what I thought was home," she recalled. The sudden loss of familiar routines—dance classes, the man who cut down coconuts, the family garden, and the nearby beach—was deeply unsettling. But what cut deepest was leaving behind loved ones. "We'd left behind my auntie and my cousins. They were like a second mother and siblings to me." The experience, she said, felt as though her family had been "ripped in two"—a rupture that left a lasting emotional imprint and shaped her early understanding of loss, identity, and dislocation.

Transition to Life in Australia

Despite the trauma of fleeing Sri Lanka, Brindha's transition to life in Australia was relatively smooth. Unlike many refugees who face significant challenges adapting to a new culture and language, she was fortunate to already speak English and to be familiar with aspects of Australian culture. Having arrived from Sri Lanka—a country that was a British colony for over 150 years and where English is widely spoken—Brindha found it easier to adjust to her new environment.

She remembers her time at Mercy College Chatswood as welcoming and positive.

The school's multicultural environment meant that she never encountered racism there, nor later at medical school, where nearly half the students were of Southeast Asian and South Asian backgrounds. Growing up in Sydney, she never experienced any behaviour that could even vaguely be construed as racist.

If there were subtle forms of racism present, she says she simply did not perceive them. Reflecting on this, she suggests it may be because of her early experiences in Sri Lanka, where she had faced overt and violent forms of racism. "I felt accepted in Australia," she explains. "I guess, when you've been through that sort of blatant racism—where your house is burnt down because you're Tamil, you're kicked out of the country because you're Tamil—it doesn't get worse than that, apart from genocide. That was my understanding of racism. So, anything subtle, I actually don't see."

Brindha later came to understand that the racism in Sri Lanka was, in part, fuelled by the school textbooks used by Sinhala children, which propagated ultra-chauvinist views. However, when she shared this observation with a journalist in Sydney, her comment was misrepresented. The resulting report falsely claimed that it was Tamil textbooks that promoted racist views—an ironic distortion of her original point![76]

Passion for Science and the Drive to Cure AIDS

From a young age, Brindha displayed a deep fascination with science, a passion that took root during her early teenage years. By the time she was in Year Eight or Nine, her curiosity had been captured by the global AIDS epidemic. She recalls being acutely aware of the virus and the devastation it caused, particularly its insidious ability to attack and dismantle the immune system.

At just 14 or 15 years old, Brindha was already immersing herself in scientific literature, driven by a determination to understand the virus at a molecular level. She spent hours reading and learning, captivated by both the science behind HIV and the human toll of the disease. Her fascination wasn't detached or purely academic—it was personal and purposeful. As she puts it, "I was definitely hoping to find a cure."[77]

She completed her high school education at Mercy College Chatswood and entered the University of Sydney Medical School in 1990.

Breaking Barriers

That passion eventually led her to medical school, where she realised that her true calling wasn't confined to a laboratory. "Once I was in med

---

[76] Jaqueline Maley "This Top Neurosurgeon Learnt Everything She Could About the Human Brain. Then She Had a Stroke", *Sydney Morning Herald*, 1 March 2024, https://www.smh.com.au/national/this-top-neurosurgeon-learnt-everything-she-could-about-the-human-brain-then-she-had-a-stroke-20240227-p5f89a.html

[77] *The Beauty of the Brain*
https://www.abc.net.au/listen/programs/conversations/brindha-shivalingam-neurosurgeon-brain-surgery-sri-lanka/103872136

school, though, I knew I had to be a doctor."[78] Yet entering the medical profession came with its own set of challenges. Medicine—and surgery in particular—was still very much a man's world. "99% of the people studying—and all the surgeons at the time—were men,"[79] she remembers. That didn't deter her. Despite the scepticism of some of her older male peers, who questioned her ability to juggle a demanding career with personal aspirations, Brindha forged ahead. One even told her bluntly that if she wanted to be a mother, she shouldn't be a surgeon.

Brindha refused to let others define her limits. At 25, she was pregnant with her first child and fully committed to both motherhood and medicine. "I've never been happier to prove someone wrong,"[80] she says. She went on to have her second child four years later—all while continuing her medical training and embracing a career that blended clinical practice with a deep-rooted interest in research.

Speaking on 6 March 2014, she noted, "These days, I'm still in the minority, as women only make up 9% of neurosurgeons in Australia, New Zealand, and Singapore." Yet even then, the challenges had never dulled her commitment. "I work hard, but I'm driven by an unwavering passion, and, without a doubt, I love my work as much as I ever did."

Brindha's Career

After graduating from medical school, Brindha completed her junior medical years at Royal North Shore Hospital and went on to undertake advanced neurosurgical training at Prince of Wales, St Vincent's, and Royal Prince Alfred Hospitals in Sydney. She also spent a year at the University of Sydney focusing on research and neuropathology, and in 2006, she earned her FRACS (Fellow of the Royal Australasian College of Surgeons) diploma.

In 2007, she further specialised in brain tumour and skull base surgery during a fellowship in Cambridge, UK. A decade later, in 2017, she was appointed Director of Neurosurgery at Chris O'Brien Lifehouse in Sydney. A strong advocate for innovation, Brindha has embraced advanced surgical technologies, including intraoperative MRI and minimally invasive

---

[78] *Dr Brindha Shivalingam, 42, 'I've gone from war to land of opportunity'*, Prevention, 6 March 2014: https://au.lifestyle.yahoo.com/dr-brindha-shivalingam-42-ive-235200810.html
[79] *Dr Brindha Shivalingam, 42, 'I've gone from war to land of opportunity'*, Prevention, 6 March 2014: https://au.lifestyle.yahoo.com/dr-brindha-shivalingam-42-ive-235200810.html
[80] https://au.lifestyle.yahoo.com/dr-brindha-shivalingam-42-ive-235200810.html

techniques. She remains optimistic about the future of brain cancer treatment, as new clinical trials and therapies continue to emerge.

Among her proudest accomplishments at the time was the founding of *Brainstorm* at Sydney's Royal Prince Alfred Hospital—a program focused on advancing brain cancer research. "It's still early days," she said then, "but I'm hoping to make a real difference and have never felt more optimistic about the future." Her words, spoken over a decade ago, continue to resonate—testament to a career driven by purpose, vision, and an enduring belief in the value of her work."[81]

A Surgeon Becomes the Patient

In 2019, Brindha's perspective as a surgeon was profoundly deepened when she suffered a series of strokes shortly after performing surgery. The experience gave her a unique understanding of the patient journey and further strengthened her empathy and dedication to her field.

Future Directions

Brindha acknowledges that while significant progress has been made over the past 25 years, the number of women entering neurosurgery remains low.

This trend, she observes, is not unique to her field but is evident across other professions such as law and engineering. Although women enter these fields in strong numbers at the university level, many begin to drop out as they progress in their careers. The real challenge, Brindha believes, is supporting young women to persist and advance through the professional ranks.

She points to the influence of entrenched gender roles as a key factor. "Even today," she reflects, "girls are raised to think that having a family and children comes first. For boys, it's your career that comes first." Brindha is determined to shift this mindset by encouraging young women to place their ambitions at the forefront. "It's about changing the perspective—helping young women see that it's okay for their career to be number one, and everything else can follow."

As a member of the neurosurgical training board, Brindha is actively working to reduce the structural barriers that hinder women's participation

---

[81] https://au.lifestyle.yahoo.com/dr-brindha-shivalingam-42-ive-235200810.html

and progression in the field. She advocates for policies that allow flexible training, part-time pathways, and time off during training—initiatives designed to make neurosurgery more accessible. Equally important, she emphasises, is the need to improve the culture within surgery, which has traditionally been male-dominated and, at times, unwelcoming to women. Creating a more inclusive and supportive environment, she believes, is essential to attracting and retaining more women in neurosurgery.

Reflections

Looking back, Brindha sees her journey—from a young girl fleeing conflict to a leader in neurosurgery—as one shaped by resilience, purpose, and an unwavering commitment to care. Each chapter of her life, from displacement and adaptation to surgical training and leadership, has deepened her understanding of what it means to serve others. Her experiences, both personal and professional, have instilled in her a profound respect for empathy, the courage to innovate, and an unshakable belief in the power of determination.

As a trailblazer in a field where women remain vastly underrepresented, she continues to champion excellence in patient care while using her platform to encourage and mentor the next generation of women in medicine. For Brindha, healing is not just a profession—it is a calling rooted in hope, purpose, and the will to make a difference.

Nadarajah Sreeharan: A Life in Service and Science

A Celebratory Reunion in Slough

On a cold winter evening in November 2024, more than 875 alumni of the University of Jaffna gathered at the Crystal Grand in Slough, United Kingdom, to celebrate a milestone event—the 50th anniversary of the University. The scale of the gathering was striking. That so many former students, now settled abroad, could come together in such numbers was a powerful reminder of both the Tamil diaspora's global reach and the profound displacement that had scattered them.

The Chief Guest for the evening was Professor Nadarajah Sreeharan. His presence felt both fitting and symbolic: as the founding Professor of Medicine and a key figure in establishing the University's Faculty of Medicine, he had laid the groundwork for generations of medical professionals. Six months later, in May 2025, in recognition of his enduring contributions, the University Council conferred on him the title of *Professor Emeritus*.

Return to Serve

Like many other uprooted Tamils, Sreeharan, chose to return to his homeland to serve his people. In April 2016, he resumed his connection with the University of Jaffna as an Honorary Visiting Professor.

Academic Foundations and Early Contributions

Sreeharan graduated with his medical degrees (MBBS and MD) from the University of Colombo in 1970, and went on to earn a PhD in cardiovascular medicine from the University of Leeds in 1978. Upon his return to Sri Lanka, he was appointed the Foundation Chair Professor of Medicine at the University of Jaffna. He was also tasked to be the Clinical Coordinator and was instrumental in establishing the professorial units at the Jaffna Teaching Hospital, helping transform it into a fully functioning teaching hospital.

Exile Amid Conflict

However, the escalating civil conflict in the Northern Province during the 1980s forced Sreeharan to flee Sri Lanka. As the war intensified, academic institutions in the North were repeatedly disrupted, and personal safety—particularly for Tamil professionals and academics—became increasingly precarious. Amid frequent university closures and military operations, many, including Sreeharan, were compelled to leave. His departure was part of a broader exodus of Tamil intellectuals and professionals during this turbulent period, as the environment became increasingly hostile to academic and medical work.

A Turn Toward Pharma

After leaving Sri Lanka, Sreeharan joined the University of Alberta in Canada as a Visiting Professor of Cardiology for a brief period before making a significant transition into the pharmaceutical industry.

Sreeharan's transition into the pharmaceutical industry was shaped by his early academic journey. While pursuing a PhD in cardiovascular physiology at the University of Leeds, his research was funded by Astra, making him an Astra Research Fellow. This exposure included involvement in clinical trials and visits to Astra's R&D facilities in Sweden, where he became deeply inspired by the development of new medicines. Faced with the choice between continuing in clinical practice or moving into industry-based research, Sree opted for the latter—a decision rooted in both professional curiosity and a desire to be at the cutting edge of science delivering patent-centric medicine.

Pioneering Research and Global Impact

This move led him to SmithKline Beecham, a reputable pharmaceutical company, which later merged with Glaxo Wellcome to form GlaxoSmithKline (GSK). Over the course of more than twenty years in the industry, Professor Sreeharan played a key role in the development of several major pharmaceutical products. These included the first non-ergot-selective dopamine agonist for Parkinson's disease, the first beta-blocker for congestive heart failure, an insulin sensitizer for type 2 diabetes, and a topoisomerase inhibitor for ovarian and small cell carcinoma.

Sreeharan served a period of approximately 13 years as European Medical Director during his career. His leadership contributed significantly to GSK's global reputation for innovation in drug development, particularly in the fields of neurology, cardiology, endocrinology, respiratory medicine, psychiatry, urology, and oncology.

In addition to his scientific and research contributions, Sreeharan played a pivotal role in the complex integration of medical and research divisions during the merger that led to the creation of GlaxoSmithKline (GSK). This experience marked a major turning point in his career, broadening his responsibilities beyond science to encompass high-level corporate strategy and organisational leadership. He regards this as one of the greatest challenges of his professional life—an experience that significantly deepened and refined his managerial and executive skills.

Leadership at Transcrip Partners

In 2008, he joined Transcrip Partners LLP as a Senior Partner. Transcrip, founded that same year, was established to meet the pharmaceutical industry's growing need for high-level, flexible drug development expertise at a time when many companies were reducing their in-house capacities. In this senior leadership role, as a board member, Sreeharan provided strategic, therapeutic, and operational guidance across the entire product lifecycle to clients in the pharmaceutical, biotech, and life sciences sectors.

Sreeharan remained with Transcrip Partners for several years, during which he also held a number of academic appointments—serving as Visiting Professor at institutions including King's College London, UITM University in Kuala Lumpur, Malaysia, and the University of Jaffna. He had previously held a similar role at the Postgraduate Medical School, University of Surrey. This concurrent engagement with both industry and academia gave Sreeharan a unique vantage point, allowing him to develop and refine key concepts such as Medical Governance and Patient Centricity.

Sreeharan is a Fellow of both the Royal College of Physicians and the American College of Physicians.

A Vision for the Future:

As he addressed the alumni of the University of Jaffna in November 2024—approaching his 78th year—Sreeharan reflected with nostalgia on the day he first travelled to Jaffna to assume the foundation chair in medicine. Looking back on that pivotal moment, he also cast his thoughts forward, asking what more could be done to advance the University of Jaffna and how its alumni might play a vital role in that journey.

Drawing on his experiences abroad, he observed that in many Western universities, alumni are a formal and influential force. At Oxford, for example, alumni even elect the Chancellor. While Sri Lanka may lack such institutional frameworks, he believed the alumni of the University of Jaffna had untapped potential and could accomplish much more by uniting to form a global association.

However, he cautioned that unity alone was not enough. Strategic planning, clear objectives, and genuine collaboration were essential for meaningful impact. Sreeharan urged alumni to identify a few focused initiatives—projects that would prioritize societal good, particularly the alleviation of suffering and the improvement of well-being among disadvantaged communities in Jaffna. At the same time, these efforts could help raise the university's profile on the global stage.

He reminded the gathering that giving back need not be limited to financial contributions. While money can be helpful, he warned that it may also create dependency. What was needed more, he argued, was the sharing of time, expertise, and—most importantly—compassion and love. He emphasized the deep value placed on gratitude in Tamil culture and reminded his fellow alumni of their moral debt to the university. To give back, he said, should be an act of genuine compassion, quoting Swami Chinmayananda: *"Giving without compassion is like building a temple without an idol."*

Sreeharan urged the diaspora to use their success and influence in host countries—not for personal prestige or power, but to meaningfully support the Tamil homeland. Above all, he emphasized humility and genuine partnership. He called on alumni to engage with those in Jaffna not as patrons or directors, but as collaborators. By fostering mutual respect and a shared sense of purpose, he believed that lasting and meaningful progress could be achieved.

Practising What He Preaches

What Sreeharan shared was never abstract theory—it stemmed from decades of direct, hands-on experience. His insights were rooted in a life of service, not only through his foundational work at the University of Jaffna but also through his sustained involvement with *Manitha Neyam*, a humanitarian organization founded in 1999. That same year, Sreeharan became one of the founding trustees of *Manitha Neyam*'s UK chapter, bringing both leadership and vision to its evolving mission.

Manitha Neyam founded by Kailasapillai[82] was born out of the chaos of war, originally focusing on the most vulnerable—children orphaned or displaced by conflict. It supported several orphanages across the war-affected Tamil homeland and provided vocational training to equip young people with the skills necessary for survival and self-reliance.

Following the end of the war, the organization shifted its focus from emergency relief to long-term recovery, emphasizing capacity-building, rehabilitation, and sustainable development. It was during this crucial transition that Sreeharan became more deeply engaged, leading several key initiatives and strengthening collaborations with local NGOs.

His efforts have included partnerships with the *Noolaham* Foundation and the Jaffna Public Library to preserve and digitize the cultural and intellectual heritage of Tamil-speaking communities; working with Social Economical and Environmental Developers (SEED) in Vavuniya to support livelihood training and empowerment for single women heading households in the post-war context; and collaborating with medical academics and recent graduates to promote drug-prevention initiatives grounded in values-based well-being.

Notably, Sreeharan also supported the *Meththa* Foundation in providing prosthetic limbs to war-affected individuals in the Vanni, culminating in the establishment of a Centre for Disability Rehabilitation in Kilinochchi. He has further helped build partnerships between *Manitha Neyam* and the US-based International Medical Health Organization (IMHO), facilitating projects in *Malayaham*, the Hill Country in Sri Lanka and home to Tamil people working in plantations.

Confronting the Past, Shaping the Future

Sreeharan is deeply aware of the enduring social impact of the war on

---

[82] Kailasapillai, the founder of *Manitha Neyam*, was a prominent Colombo-based businessman who suffered the tragic loss of nine family members when a car was set ablaze during the state-orchestrated pogrom of July 1983. Despite this profound personal tragedy, he held fast to his belief in the essential goodness of humanity. It was this conviction that inspired him to establish *Manitha Neyam*, with a vision "to ignite a universal passion and love for humanity that will steer future generations towards a world of peace, opportunity, and happiness."

Tamil communities in Sri Lanka. He has reflected on how trauma, displacement, and deep structural challenges continue to shape daily life in the Tamil homeland—from the increase in female-headed households to the breakdown of traditional support systems. He also recognizes the consequences of prolonged dependence on remittances from overseas relatives, noting how this has fostered a culture of dependency. For Sreeharan, this mindset is one of the lingering legacies of the 26-year war, and he believes it is an issue that urgently needs to be addressed.

At the same time, he remains hopeful. Sreeharan frequently speaks of the remarkable resilience of the Tamil people, especially the younger generation. He has been inspired by the emergence of young Tamils with a clear vision, strong purpose, and a deep commitment to shaping their own futures. In them, he sees not just a will to recover from the past, but a bold determination to rebuild with dignity, opportunity, and self-reliance.

Reflections

Sreeharan's life stands as a powerful testament to the enduring value of service grounded in knowledge, compassion, and humility. His journey—from his formative years in war-torn Sri Lanka to the global stage of pharmaceutical innovation—is marked not merely by personal success, but by a consistent and deeply rooted commitment to uplifting others.

As one of the pioneering figures behind the establishment of medical education in Jaffna, Sreeharan helped lay the foundation for generations of Tamil doctors and health professionals. His contribution went beyond infrastructure and curricula; it was about building capacity in a community grappling with conflict and limited opportunity. That same spirit of service carried him into the world of clinical research and drug development, where his work contributed to life-saving treatments that have impacted countless lives across continents.

But perhaps what sets Sreeharan apart most is his clarity of purpose. He has never viewed success as an individual pursuit or as an end in itself. Rather, he sees it as a responsibility—an opportunity to serve with integrity, to give back without condescension, and to empower others to lead. He often reminds the diaspora and young professionals that giving is not simply about money or influence, but about showing up—with empathy, humility, and a willingness to collaborate.

Even in his later years, Sreeharan remains an enduring source of inspiration. He continues to mentor, advise, and encourage initiatives that foster education, self-reliance, and dignity in the Tamil homeland and beyond. His legacy is not just found in the titles he held or the breakthroughs he contributed to, but in the quiet dignity with which he has lived—a life of service, generosity, and unwavering moral clarity.

Perhaps what best encapsulates Professor Sreeharan is this reflection by Dr. Shane Halpe, a Sinhalese medical practitioner who met him at the opening of the Disability Rehabilitation Centre in Kilinochchi in June 2025:

"I encountered not just a senior physician, but a true mentor—the kind who doesn't lecture, but gently invites you to think more deeply about your purpose."[83]

To honour him is to recognise that true leadership is not about status, but about impact. It is about remembering where we come from, remaining accountable to the communities that shaped us, and using our skills and knowledge to build a better future for others. In his story, we find a model of success defined not by accumulation, but by service.

---

[83] https://smhalpe.blogspot.com/2025/06/blog-post.html?m=1

Nadarajah Sri Sriskandarajah: A Quest for Justice and Sustainability

Early Imprints

In the predawn hours of a small Tamil village in Jaffna, six decades ago, in the early 1960's, a young boy helped local farmers weave coconut leaves under the gentle guidance of a Gandhian teacher. That boy was Nadarajah Sriskandarajah—known simply as "Sri."

A Life of Purpose and Conviction

Today, Sri is a professor emeritus at the Swedish University of Agricultural Sciences in Uppsala.

He finds himself navigating a world vastly different from what he had envisioned two decades ago. Instead of settling into what he once imagined as his 'retirement phase', Sri is more active than ever, working with renewed purpose and dedication.

His gentle demeanour, measured tone, and calm authority mark him as a seasoned academic. Leaving Sri Lanka in the 1970s to pursue a doctorate in veterinary science at the University of Sydney, Sri returned nearly half a century later—not as a veterinary scientist or a specialist in a specific discipline, but as an educator with a much broader, holistic perspective.

His approach to addressing modern challenges transcends disciplinary boundaries. With self-deprecating humour, Sri describes himself as "undisciplined." He finds the label "educator" problematic, noting that learning is organic and educators merely facilitate knowledge transfer. While he acknowledges that knowledge transfer is essential, Sri insists it must be grounded in an understanding of pre-existing realities. He argues that in the rush to embrace modern methods, humanity has neglected both the environment and the valuable insights offered by ancient wisdom.

Today, his primary focus is on a critical issue that resonates deeply with the people of the Jaffna Peninsula: managing dwindling water resources. He refers to this initiative as the development of governance frameworks to ensure water security.

Ever the activist, Sri plays a key role in these efforts, driven by a deeper conviction—the need for an approach to life that fosters global sustainability, not just environmentally, but in a broader sense rooted in coexistence and connectivity.

Formative Years: Gandhian Roots in Karainagar

It was Sri's early education at a school rooted in Gandhian teachings in Karainagar, his birthplace, that first opened his eyes to the wasteful consumerism and environmental degradation driven by modern capitalism. This formative experience significantly shaped his later convictions about sustainability and resource management.

Sri's exposure to Gandhian influence began at the age of five when he started attending the Wardha School in Karainagar, continuing there until he was 15. The Wardha School was established in the 1950s by educators in Jaffna influenced by Gandhian thought. Its establishment in Karainagar may have been inspired by Mahatma Gandhi's visit to Jaffna in 1927, during which he stopped in Karainagar. Unlike mainstream schools, the curriculum at Sri's Gandhian school was centred on the principle that education should develop the whole person within the context of their surroundings, language, and culture. This involved active participation in community life. Sri recalls helping local farmers during the harvest and weaving coconut leaves for various practical uses.

One teacher in particular, Sinnathamby Kanakanayagam, left a deep impression on him. Kanakanayagam was more than just a teacher—he was a yogi, scholar, and a man of deep principles, who practiced yoga and meditation. He embodied the role of a guru, held in high regard in Eastern culture. with a streak of activism when it came to doing the right thing.

Kanakanayagam found in Sri receptive to the ideas he sought to impart. Unfortunately, in 1960, the government passed legislation that led to the takeover of small and large private schools, including the Wardha School, which was absorbed into the state system. Sri describes this moment as the 'crashing down' of the island's educational system. Sri observed that the Wardha School was far ahead of its time. What was being taught there in the 1950s and 60s—developing the whole person, living in harmony with nature, and prioritizing sustainability—are now the very principles being championed by today's progressives as they confront the threats posed by modern civilization. Even the school's emphasis on mindful eating and conscious consumption resonates with the current movements advocating for sustainable living and environmental stewardship.

Educated within a Gandhian framework, Sri could perceive the power imbalance between the fishermen in his village and the buyers, even at a young age. While bargaining with the fishermen, he witnessed this firsthand as his mother often held the upper hand—an experience that revealed the broader dynamics of overfishing and waste. Deeply influenced by Gandhian principles of non-violence, Sri also embraced the *satyagraha* (non-violent resistance) protests organized by Tamil people across the north and east of Sri Lanka, the Tamil Homeland, in opposition to the government's discriminatory language policy that relegated the Tamil people to second-class status by making Sinhala the sole official language of the country.

Sri moved to the mainland to continue his education at a mainstream school and on completing high school, entered university where he completed an undergraduate degree in veterinary science and joined the same university as a lecturer.

Witness to Injustice: Growing Up Tamil in Sri Lanka

When Sri left for Australia to pursue his PhD, his intention was to return to the University of Ceylon. The decision to pursue a PhD stemmed from the university's requirement that lecturers obtain a postgraduate qualification—ideally a PhD—to secure their positions. However, events took an unexpected turn with the outbreak of Black July, the anti-Tamil violence that claimed the lives of 3,000 Tamil people in July 1983, making it impossible for Sri to return to Sri Lanka. Black July was just the latest in a series of anti-Tamil attacks that had occurred with alarming regularity since the 1950s.

Sri's first encounter with the anti-Tamil violence that would come to define Sri Lanka's political landscape, however, began in 1958, a quarter century before Black July. Reflecting on this experience at the 1996 *Peace with Justice* conference in Australia, he said, "My earliest image of the conflict was in 1958 when my father returned home in a refugee boat, alongside many others from the village, to recount their stories of survival and escape from the South."[84]

At that time, it was common for Tamil men from the north to work in the Sinhalese-majority south, often in government jobs, while their families remained in their villages. These men would send remittances home and

---

[84] N Sriskandarajah, "In Defence of Nationalism", *Peace with Justice*, Canberra, 1996

return to the north for holidays or family events. Because of these remittances, the Jaffna economy became known as a 'money order economy.' However, these men, living in shared accommodations or 'chummeries,' became easy targets during waves of anti-Tamil mob violence. Sri's father, who was working for the government at the time, was one of them.

In 1958, Sri's father along with other Tamil men and women were transported back to their homeland by sea in foreign cargo ships, at the request of the Sri Lankan government. This grim practice of transporting survivors by sea became a pattern over the next twenty-five years, as anti-Tamil violence erupted again and again.

By 1983, however, it was no longer foreign vessels but the Sri Lankan navy that carried Tamil survivors north. One naval officer, Ajith Boyagoda, tasked with transporting Tamils from refugee camps in the South to the North, made a poignant observation: "Never after this could I take issue with the idea of a Tamil homeland. If Tamil people were not safe in the South but were safe in the North, then that was their homeland—the government had conceded that."[85]

Growing up in Karainagar, it was impossible to be unaware of the oppressive presence of the Sri Lankan state and the impact it had on his experience of the Sinhalese people. As he further reflected in the course of his presentation at the 1996 conference, *Peace with Justice* Sri said: "My first exposure to Sinhala people was when I was very young in my village on the island of Karainagar—not because they lived among us, but because they were either the khaki-clad policemen stationed at a post on the beach near our home or the blue-and-white uniformed navy men who moved about carrying guns, even when transporting drinking water in tankers along the main street of my village."[86]

This was the case throughout the Jaffna Peninsula, where there were few Sinhala civilians. The only exceptions were the bakers, as all the bakeries were owned and operated by Sinhalese from the south, who enjoyed a cordial relationship with their Tamil customers and neighbours.

Later in life, as a student at Aquinas University College in Colombo and the University of Ceylon in Peradeniya, Sri met, mingled, and formed friendships with Sinhalese people. This was true for many middle-class Tamils and Sinhalese who spoke English. However, the events of Black

---

[85] Ajit Boyagoda, *A Long Watch*, Hurst & Company, London 2016

[86] N Sriskandarajah, "In Defence of Nationalism", *Peace with Justice*, Canberra, 1996

July not only cast a shadow over these relationships but also led individuals to keep their thoughts to themselves. In 1990, Tamil playwright Ernest Macintyre explored this phenomenon in his play *Rasanayagam's Last Riot*, staged in Sydney. He encapsulated it as follows: "Soon after the riots (an euphemistic reference to Black July), Colombo's mixed society of Westernized Tamils and Sinhalese tacitly settled on an arrangement that would enable it to continue functioning. Whatever was locked in their heads or embedded in their hearts, about which organizations and people were to be held responsible, they would not utter in public." Sri had a similar experience in July 1983, in the immediate aftermath of Black July, when he found himself in the company of both Sinhalese and Tamil academics attending a seminar in Japan. He recalled the unspoken agreement to avoid the subject was palpable.

The difficulties Sri faced in securing a scholarship from the Sri Lankan state made it clear that, despite friendships across ethnic divisions, the state had a deliberate policy of favouring Sinhalese academics. Sri's persistence did not yield results; he was rejected over 20 times. Ultimately, Sri secured a place at the University of Sydney in 1978—not because the Sri Lankan state relented, but because he met the specific criteria the university was seeking for a student to pursue a particular PhD program.

Life in Exile: Australia, Papua New Guinea, and the Quest for Sustainability

When Sri left for Sydney to pursue higher studies in Australia, his wife Sri Devi, an agricultural graduate left for New Zealand to pursue her studies, Sri's parents insisted that their infant son stay back with them. It was 1985 by the time the son, Dhananjayan was reunited with the family.

The family relocated to Papua New Guinea, where Sri joined the University of Papua New Guinea as a lecturer. In 1986, while working there, Sri learned about a new approach being developed at the Hawkesbury School of Agriculture in Australia. His long-standing concerns about the environmental impact of food production in Australia aligned perfectly with what Hawkesbury was addressing—how to make agriculture sustainable without causing long-term environmental damage. Intrigued, Sri expressed his interest, and Hawkesbury quickly recognized him as the ideal candidate. Thus, a relationship that began in 1986 flourished for the next 14 years, during which Hawkesbury became part of Western Sydney University.

This mutually beneficial relationship almost didn't happen, if not for the vigilance of Hawkesbury's Equal Employment Opportunity (EEO) Officer. Although Hawkesbury had offered Sri the position, there was a prolonged delay in the Australian immigration authorities issuing him a visa. One day, the EEO officer noticed that, while Sri's visa was still pending, an Englishman who had been offered a similar role around the same time had received his visa much earlier. Hawkesbury promptly alerted the Immigration Department, and within 24 hours, Sri's visa was approved. Sri credits this outcome to Australia's progressive EEO practices!

Advocacy and the Tamil Cause in Australia

During those 14 years, Sydney's Tamil population grew significantly. Thanks to an Australian government initiative, Tamils affected by Black July were allowed to migrate under a scheme known as the Special Humanitarian Program (SHP). They were soon joined by survivors of another calamity—the entry of the so-called Indian Peacekeeping Force (IPKF) into the Tamil homeland in Sri Lanka in July 1987. The IPKF had entered as part of the Indo-Lanka Accord, an agreement between the Sri Lankan and Indian governments. While the accord was publicly presented as a political solution to the conflict between the Tamil people and the Sri Lankan state, its real aim was to ensure Sri Lanka remained within India's sphere of influence. In exchange, the IPKF was tasked with disarming Tamil fighters, who had previously been armed by the Indian government. Realizing they had been used by India to pressure the Sri Lankan government, the Tamil fighters refused to disarm, knowing it would only strengthen the Sri Lankan state. The resulting conflict with the IPKF caused widespread destruction, forcing hundreds of Tamils to flee their homeland.

The growing Tamil diaspora enabled Tamils to appeal to the wider Australian community and government, seeking support for a political solution to the conflict their fellow Tamils faced with the Sri Lankan state. Sri became an active member of this advocacy effort. Initially, as a facilitator, he worked with various Tamil groups to help them become more effective in their advocacy, improve internal communication, and foster a spirit of teamwork. One of his very effective workshops involved helping Tamil activists reevaluate and re-envision their roles. Over time, he became more directly involved in the advocacy itself, often participating in seminars and conferences aimed at promoting the Tamil cause internationally.

In 1991, Sri, along with the Secretary of the Australasian Federation of Tamil Associations (AFTA), an umbrella organization for Tamil groups in the region, participated in an international conference held in Sacramento, U.S., titled *Tamil Eelam: A Nation Without a State*. In 1996, he presented a powerful paper, "In Defence of Nationalism", at the *Peace with Justice* conference in Canberra. Sri's engagement extended beyond political advocacy; he was deeply involved in cultural and artistic matters as well. In 1992, Sri played a pivotal role in organizing the 5th International Conference on Tamil Culture in Sydney.

Academic Diplomacy: Building Bridges in Scandinavia

Sri promoted Hawksbury's novel practices to other academic institutions. He found universities in Scandinavian countries to be especially receptive to these ideas. This led to a growing exchange of ideas, frequent visits, and collaborative teaching initiatives. As his engagement with institutions in that region deepened, fellow academics began to refer to him, with a touch of humour, as the "Scandinavian Ambassador."

In 2000, after having worked at Western Sydney University for 14 years, Sri decided to take a break and explore new opportunities. Europe, particularly Denmark, appealed to him as a place to work and experience a different culture. "Scandinavian Ambassador," Sri had little trouble securing a role at the University of Denmark.

For the next seven years in Denmark, Sri continued learning, teaching, and expanding his understanding of revolutionary agricultural methods, particularly those focused on sustainability. During this time, he also engaged extensively with the second generation of the Tamil diaspora. He quickly realized the serious challenges these young Tamils faced, caught between two contrasting cultures. Danish culture emphasized independence in all aspects of life, and the education system encouraged critical thinking and self-reliance. In contrast, many Tamil parents were traditional, and conservative, and expected their children to respect authority, defer to age, and comply without question.

Recognizing both the cultural expectations of the parents and the realities faced by the younger generation, Sri helped bridge the gap. He provided strategies to navigate these cultural tensions, fostering a deeper understanding between the two sides. He also noticed that many young Tamils were unaware of the causes and roots of the conflict that had displaced them, leaving them uncertain about the reasons for their presence in this corner of the globe. Sri helped them understand this too by providing them with a historical perspective on their displacement.

As in Australia, Sri played the role of a facilitator, working with Tamil activists in Denmark to promote the Tamil cause and helping them collaborate effectively within the wider Danish community.

Sri's work in Denmark's academic world earned him recognition from the Swedish University of Agricultural Sciences, which offered him a professorship. He held this position for a decade and is now professor emeritus with the Department of Urban and Rural Development at the Swedish University of Agricultural Sciences in Uppsala. His interests are deeply rooted in nature and natural resource management, reflecting his lifelong commitment to these issues.

Giving Back

Currently, Sri dedicates a significant amount of his time to the University of Jaffna, focusing on issues related to water security and governance. His interest in this area began in 1994 when he spent time at the same university, following an invitation from the late Vice Chancellor, *Mamanithar* Thurairajah.

The issue of water security is of great concern to the people of Jaffna, with many fearing that the peninsula may become uninhabitable due to unsustainable water usage. As a result, discussions around water security are often framed in alarmist terms. However, Sri takes a more balanced approach. He reminds people that past practices concerning water management were effective, allowing previous generations to thrive. He believes there is an opportunity to address the current water security challenges positively, and his message is one of hope rather than despair.

Reflections

In reflecting on the life and work of Professor Nadarajah Sri Sriskandarajah, it becomes clear that a unique blend of intellectual curiosity, activism, and a commitment to sustainability has defined his journey. From his early days in Karainagar, shaped by Gandhian values, to his role as a professor and advocate across three continents, Sri has consistently pushed disciplinary, geographic, or ideological boundaries. His holistic approach to education and problem-solving, grounded in ancient wisdom and modern knowledge, has made him a pioneer in addressing our time's pressing environmental and social challenges.

Sri's work on water security for the Jaffna Peninsula exemplifies his enduring mission: to bridge the gap between past practices and future possibilities, offering hope where others see despair. Whether facilitating the Tamil diaspora's advocacy efforts, mentoring young people to navigate the cultural tensions of migration, or leading initiatives in agricultural sustainability, Sri's influence has been profound and far-reaching.

As he continues to dedicate his expertise to the people of Jaffna and beyond, Sri embodies the spirit of a scholar-activist whose vision transcends borders. His legacy is not just one of academic achievement but of creating lasting frameworks for sustainable living and social justice—an ongoing mission for future generations to build upon.

POLITICIANS

Gary Anandasangaree: From Refugee to Canadian Cabinet Minister

From Exile to Office

On the morning of March 14, 2025, beneath the gilded ceilings of Rideau Hall, history was being quietly rewritten. Gary Anandasangaree—who had arrived in Canada as a ten-year-old refugee from war-torn Sri Lanka—stood poised to be sworn in as Canada's Minister of Justice and Attorney General. As he placed his hand on the oath book, the room held its breath. For Canada's Tamil community and for human rights advocates around the world, this was more than a ceremony; it was a powerful symbol of resilience, justice, and the extraordinary journey of a man who turned exile into leadership. His appointment also stood as a reaffirmation of Canada's commitment to multiculturalism—proof that its promise of opportunity and inclusion could extend even to those who once arrived seeking refuge from war.

Guardian of Public Safety

Two months later, in May 2025, Gary was appointed Canada's Minister of Public Safety in Prime Minister Mark Carney's government—an appointment that came at a time of growing global uncertainty. This new role followed his previous high-profile cabinet positions as Minister of Justice and Attorney General, and as Minister of Crown-Indigenous Relations, serving under both Carney and former Prime Minister Justin Trudeau. A lawyer, activist, and principled advocate, Gary has long been recognised as one of Canada's most steadfast voices for human rights, social justice, and democratic values.

A Childhood Marked by Protest

Gary's journey from refugee to federal cabinet minister began with a protest against a massacre taking place half way across the globe. In July 1983, at just ten years old, he stood on a street in Dublin beside his mother, clutching a placard and handing out leaflets exposing a brutal massacre unfolding in Sri Lanka.

That moment—far from the country he once called home—marked the beginning of a life defined by activism. After his parents separated in 1980, Gary and his mother Yogam had moved to Ireland, where they lived with relatives. Hoping one day to return to Sri Lanka, they planned a visit home in mid-1983. But the eruption of Black July—a violent anti-Tamil pogrom—changed everything. It made return impossible, forcing them instead to seek refuge in Canada. That early experience of injustice would shape Gary's worldview and fuel his enduring commitment to equity, justice, and public service.

A New Life in Canada

With their plans to return to Sri Lanka shattered, Gary and his mother, Yogam, sought refuge in Canada. They arrived on 31 August, 1983 to start life anew. It was a significant challenge. Shouldering the twin burdens of resettlement and single parenting, Yogam raised Gary in a new country. It was not easy. Those early hardships instilled in Gary a deep empathy for others facing adversity. Gary adapted quickly, dedicating himself to his education. After graduating from high school, he attended Carleton University in Ottawa, where he earned a BA (Honours) in Political Science in 1996. He later returned to Toronto, became a registered real estate agent, and worked in the real estate industry for several years.

During this period, he worked tirelessly to support refugee and other marginalised communities in Canada through public advocacy, education, mediation, direct intervention, and legal frameworks.

Law and Social Justice

His growing commitment to social justice led him to pursue legal studies at Osgoode Hall Law School at York University, where he obtained his LLB. He was called to the bar in 2006 and had already been recognized the previous year with the Osgoode Hall Law School "One to Watch" Gold Key Award.

After retiring from real estate, he founded his own law firm—Gary Anandasangaree and Associates—in Scarborough. His practice focused on corporate, commercial, business, real estate, and estate law, with particular attention to small and medium-sized businesses and investment transactions. Importantly, alongside this work, Gary maintained a robust pro bono human rights practice, advocating on issues such as barriers to education, free speech, and discrimination, particularly affecting students and marginalized communities.

Speaking Up for Rights at the UN

As an ardent champion of human rights, Gary regularly represented Lawyers' Rights Watch Canada (LRWC) at the United Nations Human Rights Council. Notably, he served as LRWC's delegate at the 15th Session of the Human Rights Council in Geneva from September 13 to 18, 2010, amplifying concerns related to legal rights and civil liberties on the international stage.

Building Community: Leadership and Service

Gary has involved himself in community welfare activities, He has served as Chair of the Canadian Tamil Youth Development Centre, President of the Canadian Tamils' Chamber of Commerce, and counsel to the Canadian Tamil Congress. He was also a board member of the Youth Challenge Fund, a member of the Toronto Police Chief's Advisory Board, and a member of the United Way Newcomers Grant Program.

In honour of his devotion to community service and local advocacy, Gary has received both the Queen Elizabeth II Golden Jubilee Medal and the Queen Elizabeth II Diamond Jubilee Medal. He has also been awarded the TREB Award and Henry Marshall Tory Award for Service.

Entering Politics: From Liberal Nominee to Parliament

Gary joined the Liberal Party before seeking the nomination for the newly created riding of Scarborough–Rouge Park ahead of the 2015 federal election. He was elected as a Liberal Member of Parliament on October 19, 2015. His reputation as a human rights lawyer and activist, along with his deep engagement in community issues, helped solidify his appeal among constituents. He was re-elected in 2019, 2021, and again in 2025—securing a fourth consecutive victory. In each election, he earned over 60% of the vote—a consistent mandate that signalled strong public trust, broad community support, and enduring confidence in his leadership.

The confidence Gary inspires was aptly captured by Steeves Bujold, partner at McCarthy Tétrault LLP in Montreal and past president of the Canadian Bar Association (CBA). Bujold first met Anandasangaree when he attended the CBA's presidential dinner on behalf of the Minister of Justice, and the impression was lasting. "I would describe him as someone deeply engaged—genuinely committed to the rule of law, the independence of the judiciary, and eager to connect with members of the legal community," Bujold reflected. "He was clearly interested in collaboration and in building strong relationships with the CBA."[87]

A Decade of Parliamentary Impact

Before his Cabinet appointments, Gary held several roles as Parliamentary Secretary, steadily building his profile within government. On July 23, 2023, he was appointed Minister of Crown–Indigenous Relations, followed by his role as Minister Responsible for the Canadian Development Agency on December 20, 2024. As previously noted, on March 14, 2025, he assumed one of the most senior roles in government when Prime Minister Mark Carney named him Minister of Justice and Attorney General of Canada and re-elected shortly thereafter in the May 2025 federal election.

Over his ten-year parliamentary career, Gary Anandasangaree has played a central role in advancing some of Canada's most important justice and reconciliation initiatives. As Minister of Crown–Indigenous Relations, he delivered a historic formal apology to the Dakota and Lakota First Nations in July 2024, acknowledging over 150 years of injustice and affirming their constitutional rights as Aboriginal peoples of Canada. He continued this work into 2025 by commemorating the 50th anniversary of Modern Treaties, underscoring their enduring significance for reconciliation and self-governance across the country.

In the realm of legislative reform, Gary was instrumental in the passage of Bill C-5, which repealed several mandatory minimum penalties from the Criminal Code. Through this, he addressed systemic racism in the justice system and championed fairness for Indigenous, Black, and other marginalized Canadians.

His leadership also extended to national reconciliation efforts, including the establishment of the National Council for Reconciliation—a permanent, independent body tasked with monitoring and reporting on

---

[87]https://nationalmagazine.ca/en-ca/articles/people/profiles/2025-369caeee0017d2d3b2ed4c00020a25f2/new-minister-of-justice-s-leadership-and-dedication-to-his-community-%E2%80%98unmatched

Canada's progress toward reconciliation, and ensuring transparency and public accountability.

Throughout his tenure, Gary has also used his platform for broader public advocacy. In the wake of the COVID-19 pandemic, he consistently spoke about the urgent need to address structural inequalities, calling for a more resilient, inclusive Canada—one that offers stronger support for its most vulnerable populations. Together, these contributions reflect a sustained and principled commitment to justice, equity, and systemic change.

A Defining Speech on Sri Lanka

Gary has delivered several speeches in Parliament—particularly on issues such as mandatory minimum sentences, Indigenous justice, and social supports. However, it was his address on Sri Lanka that emerged as his signature intervention, reflecting his longstanding commitment to human rights and international justice.

Delivered during a news conference on Parliament Hill in July 2022, this speech is widely considered his most impactful and widely recognized. In it, Gary called on Canada to impose sanctions on former Sri Lankan Presidents Gotabaya Rajapaksa and Mahinda Rajapaksa for their roles in alleged atrocities committed during the final stages of the Sri Lankan civil war.

He detailed the deaths of tens of thousands of civilians, the displacement of over 300,000 Tamils, the bombing of hospitals and no-fly zones, and the deliberate underreporting of population figures that led to starvation. He also condemned the disappearance of thousands—including surrendered combatants and children—and exposed the use of sexual violence and rape as weapons of war. Calling for international accountability, he urged Canada and other nations to exercise universal jurisdiction in prosecuting those responsible for atrocity crimes in Sri Lanka.

This speech stood out for its depth, specificity, and moral clarity, as Gary not only recounted the suffering of the Tamil people but also pressed for decisive Canadian and international action. He linked the ongoing pain of the Tamil community to the need for justice and accountability, and his call resonated with both survivors and human rights advocates. The speech was delivered on the anniversary of Black July, underscoring its historical and emotional significance for Tamils in Canada and around the world.

Family Legacy and Political Distance

Gary's father, V. Anandasangaree, was a prominent Sri Lankan Tamil politician. Although Gary and his mother were on their own during his early years, being identified as the son of V. Anandasangaree brought its own set of complexities.

These arose mainly because the elder Anandasangaree had taken a divergent political path from many of his peers in the Tamil United Liberation Front (TULF). He refused to join the Tamil National Alliance (TNA) when it was formed in 2001, in part because the TNA had adopted a more pro-Liberation Tigers of Tamil Eelam (LTTE) stance—one that V. Anandasangaree firmly opposed.

In its 2004 election manifesto, the TNA declared the LTTE as the "sole and authentic representatives of the Tamil people" and pledged full cooperation with the LTTE's armed struggle. Functioning as the political voice of Tamil nationalism during the final years of the civil war, the TNA frequently echoed LTTE positions in both Parliament and peace negotiations.

To many in the Tamil diaspora, this alignment appeared to strengthen the LTTE's hand in its negotiations with the Government of Sri Lanka. In contrast, Gary's father V. Anandasangaree's dissenting position was viewed by some as undermining Tamil unity and weakening the political leverage of the Tamil polity.

Gary Anandasangaree has countered this perception by consistently emphasizing that his political stance and advocacy work are independent from those of his father. Most importantly, he has demonstrated this by his vocal campaign against Sri Lankan government abuses and advocacy for international accountability at forums like the United Nations, actions that are distinct from his father's domestic political strategies.

Controversy and Criticism Over Gaza

Gary has also faced criticism from some members of the Tamil Canadian community for not being more vocal on the Israel–Palestine conflict.

At a Tamil Heritage Month event in January 2024, Gary Anandasangaree was confronted by some of his own constituents, who drew parallels between the Tamil massacre of 2009 and the ongoing crisis in Gaza. They questioned the value of remembrance if elected officials remain silent in the face of contemporary atrocities.

Despite petitions and public appeals—including calls for a ceasefire and for Canada to halt arms exports to Israel—Gary did not issue a public response, deepening a sense of betrayal among some long-time supporters. Critics pointed to a perceived moral inconsistency: while he had once been a vocal advocate for Tamils, he now appeared reluctant to condemn Israel or call for accountability in Parliament. The criticism intensified when he was named as a respondent in a lawsuit alleging Canada's complicity in the situation in Gaza, prompting many to ask whether he had abandoned the human rights principles that had once defined his career.

The Constraints of Office: Silence and Solidarity

Understanding Gary's stance on the Gaza issue requires consideration of the constraints imposed on him as a member of the Canadian Cabinet. As a Cabinet minister, he is bound by the principle of Cabinet solidarity and legal obligations that require him to uphold and publicly represent the government's official position. This significantly limits his ability to speak independently on contentious foreign policy matters.

Gary's long-standing record as a human rights advocate—particularly his unwavering support for Tamil justice—underscores his deep personal commitment to issues of equity and accountability. Yet, as a senior government official, he must navigate the difficult balance between personal conviction and institutional responsibility. While some interpret his silence on Gaza as a betrayal, others see it as emblematic of the complexities of governance, where influence is often exercised behind closed doors rather than through public dissent. In this context, Gary's approach appears shaped not by indifference, but by the practical realities and limitations of high office.

Given his pivotal role in securing Canada's recognition of the Tamil genocide in Sri Lanka, it is reasonable to view Gary's current position with empathy. His silence on Gaza is not easily dismissed, but it must be understood within the framework of Cabinet discipline—an obligation that can at times stand in tension with deeply held personal values.

Reflections

Gary Anandasangaree's journey—from a young boy handing out leaflets on a Dublin street to becoming Canada's Minister of Justice—is a testament to resilience and transformation. Rooted in his experience as a refugee and shaped by a lifelong commitment to human rights, he has brought a principled voice to critical issues of our time. High office brings constraints and difficult choices, yet his record shows consistent dedication to justice, accountability, and public service. His story reminds us that meaningful change begins with conviction—and that even within government, it is possible to carry forward a community's hopes and help build a more just, inclusive future.

Uma Kumaran: Redefining Representation and Resilience

A Voice in Westminster

When Uma Kumaran's parents fled Sri Lanka's civil war in the 1980s, it was Labour MP Jeremy Corbyn who helped them settle in Britain. They arrived with little more than uncertainty and the hope of safety. Forty years later, in July 2024, their daughter was elected as the first person of Tamil origin to the British Parliament. Representing the newly created constituency of Stratford and Bow, Uma stood not just as a Labour MP, but as the embodiment of courage, public service, and the long journey from displacement to democratic participation.

A Labour Landslide and the Rise of Diverse Voices

The Labour Party's resounding victory in the 2024 General Election was a historic turning point, destined to become a political legend. After 14 years of Conservative rule, Keir Starmer's Labour Party achieved a stunning transformation, overturning its devastating 2019 defeat to secure a landslide 174-seat majority. This victory marked a shift in governance and a profound redefinition of representation in British politics.

Hundreds of new faces entered the House of Commons, reflecting a dramatic increase in diversity. Labour's ranks now boast record numbers of women and ethnic minorities, with many firsts among their achievements. The party's groundbreaking progress is symbolised by figures like Rachel Reeves, Britain's first woman Chancellor of the Exchequer, and Angela Rayner, the new Deputy Prime Minister. Among these historic milestones is Uma Kumaran, the MP for Stratford and Bow, who at thirty-six became the first British parliamentarian of Sri Lankan Tamil descent.

From Refugee Roots to Parliamentary Power

Uma, embodies the triumph of resilience and representation. Reflecting on her election, she remarked,

"You feel the weight of history,"[88] her voice filled with emotion, she notes "I've seen an incredible outpouring of support from the Tamil diaspora"[89] acknowledging the significance of her achievement for an uprooted people.

Her victory carried profound significance, far beyond the Sri Lankan Tamil diaspora. Tamil Nadu's Chief Minister, M.K. Stalin, encapsulated this sentiment in his tweet: *"Hearty congratulations to @Uma_Kumaran on becoming the first-ever Member of Parliament for Stratford and Bow and the first-ever Tamil woman to join the UK Parliament. You bring great pride to the Tamil community."*

Sri Lanka's Claims

It was not only the Tamil community that celebrated Uma Kumaran's victory; paradoxically, Sri Lanka—the very country that had driven her parents and hundreds of thousands of other Tamils into exile—also claimed her as one of their own. LNW *(Lanka News Web)*, an online news outlet, ran bold headlines declaring, "Uma Kumaran of Sri Lankan Origin Elected to British Parliament in Historic Milestone"[90] glossing over the fact her parents had fled the Sri Lankan State-orchestrated pogrom of July 1983 (Black July) by glibly reporting that her parents "relocated to London during the 1980s amidst civil unrest."[91] Similarly, the *Daily Mirror* a leading Sri Lankan newspaper referred to her 'Sri Lankan' origin but omitted any mention of the tragic circumstances that led to her birth in the UK.

In her maiden speech on 5 September 2024, Uma Kumaran delivered a poignant truth about the intergenerational impact of displacement: "I was born here but by fate. I am the daughter of Tamil refugees and the child of a community that knows what it's like to endure prejudice and persecution."

Her parents, now proud British citizens, arrived over forty years ago—not in pursuit of opportunity, but fleeing for their very lives, leaving behind a prosperous past for an uncertain future. Yet, at just thirty-six, Uma Kumaran transformed that inherited trauma into a force for change. Her

---

[88] https://www.vogue.co.uk/article/women-labour-mps-vogue-interview
[89] https://www.vogue.co.uk/article/women-labour-mps-vogue-interview
[90] https://lankanewsweb.net/archives/58695/uma-kumaran-of-sri-lankan-origin-elected-to-british-parliament-in-historic-milestone/
[91] https://lankanewsweb.net/archives/58695/uma-kumaran-of-sri-lankan-origin-elected-to-british-parliament-in-historic-milestone/

election is not just a personal victory; it is a powerful testament to what is possible when the struggles of the past are met with a vision for a more just and equitable future.

Shaped by Struggle, Driven by Purpose

Uma holds a Master of Science degree in Public Policy, a Bachelor's degree in Politics and speaks four languages, English, Tamil, French, and German. Uma recognizes that many immigrant parents view politics as an unsuitable career. She hopes to change this perception by inspiring more individuals from Tamil backgrounds to pursue a path in politics.

That she would join the Labour Party was no surprise. It was a Labour Member of Parliament, Jeremy Corbyn, who helped her parents settle down, and she inherited family values from her grandfather, one of the first trade unionists in Jaffna, her ancestral home.

Uma Kumaran is deeply proud of her Tamil heritage and the British values she upholds. For her, these values are profoundly personal, reflecting the compassion and inclusivity her parents encountered when they arrived in the UK. Institutions like the NHS embody these principles, showcasing Britain as a place where people from all backgrounds come together to serve and support one another. It was because of these values that her parents were able to embrace British citizenship and rebuild their lives—a journey shaped by both struggle and hope. When her father suffered a heart attack, it was the National Health Service that saved his life—a poignant reminder, for Uma, of the care and unity that lie at the heart of British values.

Facing Threats, Finding Strength

In 2015, when she contested for a parliamentary seat, she faced a challenging campaign against Conservative Party candidate Bob Blackman, who had the backing of an organization called *Sewa Purvapaksha*.

She became this organisation's target for her party's support of the 2013 legislation to outlaw caste discrimination in the UK. It seemed until then Uma was making considerable progress. *The Guardian* of 12 April 2015 noted "In Tory-held Harrow East, on London's northern fringe, Labour has leapfrogged the Conservatives to a four-point lead in the latest Ashcroft poll. If the snapshot is correct, then the incumbent MP, Bob Blackman (who won the seat from Labour's Tony McNulty by more than

3,000 votes in 2010), looks set to lose his place in the Commons to Uma Kumaran, Labour's energetic 28-year-old candidate. The poll showed 47% of women backing the Labour candidate, compared with 38% for Blackman."

But, *Sewa Purvapaksha's* actions had muddied the waters to an extent that Uma Kumaran despite being a Hindu was seen as anti-Hindu and the significant Hindu population of the electorate was confused. Consequently, Uma lost.

Despite the loss, Uma continued with her dedication to public service and progressive change. She has worked for the NHS, served as an advisor to London Mayor Sadiq Khan, held the role of Deputy Director of Parliamentary Affairs for Labour leader Keir Starmer, and served as Director of Diplomatic Affairs for an international organization focused on climate change.

She did not contest the 2017 snap General Elections or the 2019 General Elections, intimidated by the actions of *Sewa Purvapaksha* in 2015. The actions had impacted her own family at that time and Uma could not with good conscience knowingly put them through a similar situation.

Uma's campaign to enter Parliament in 2024 was also dangerous and hostile. "Someone said they were going to rape me. I've had some horrible stuff,"[92] she recalls. On one occasion, a man driving past her mounted the curb with two children in the backseat, hurling abuse. "He said he hoped I'd die, suffer, and get raped,"[93] she recounts. Despite these traumatic experiences, Uma found a supportive environment in Parliament. Colleagues rallied around her during a particularly challenging time when her husband suffered an unexpected stroke. Their solidarity was evident when over 40 MPs attended her swearing-in ceremony, as she could not participate in the formal event due to her husband's illness.

A Sacred Oath and a Tamil Offering

Uma, a practising Hindu, took her oath of office by swearing on the Bhagavad Gita, the sacred text of Hindus. Later, she presented the Speaker of the House with a copy of the *Tiirukural*, an ancient Tamil text offering guiding verses on nearly every aspect of life, from professional to personal. She expressed her hope that a future MP of Tamil heritage might have the

---

[92] politicshome.com/news/article/new-labour-mp-uma-kumaran-on-abuse-in-politics
[93] politicshome.com/news/article/new-labour-mp-uma-kumaran-on-abuse-in-politics

opportunity to swear their oath on this profound text.

Tough Choices and Personal Integrity

In late November 2024, just a short time after entering Parliament, Uma faced a deeply complex decision: voting on a bill to allow terminally ill individuals to end their lives with medical assistance in England and Wales. After extensive consultations with her constituents and careful personal reflection, Uma chose to vote against the Terminally Ill Adults (End of Life) Bill. To the surprise of many, the bill passed by a wider margin than expected. Reflecting on the decision in a post on X, Uma described it as one of the hardest choices she had to make, citing concerns about inadequate safeguards and the potential for misuse.

Also in late November, Uma Kumaran expressed solidarity with Tamils worldwide as they remembered their war dead—those who lost their lives in the struggle for self-determination. She used the occasion to highlight the 2024 statement by the UN Human Rights Office, which urged the Sri Lankan government to uncover the fate and locations of tens of thousands of individuals subjected to enforced disappearances and to hold those responsible accountable. Uma also voiced her disappointment that Sri Lanka's new government had rejected the UN's call for international accountability. Her message resonated deeply with the Tamil diaspora, encapsulating their sentiments.

Uma supports Canada's recognition of May 18 as Tamil Genocide Remembrance Day and believes it should be a core goal of the All-Party Parliamentary Group on Tamils. She advocates for presenting a united front to the government to increase the chances of recognition and for seeking international court rulings on the genocide. She also called for the sanctioning Sri Lankan war criminals in the UK, similar to actions taken by Canada and the United States, and called for an assessment of sanctions against those accused of war crimes.

Uma Kumaran's stance on the ongoing conflict in Gaza is an area where she may diverge from her own government. On October 29, 2024, during parliamentary question time, she pressed Foreign Secretary David Lammy about the UK's potential to leverage its role as Chair of the UN Security Council to push for urgent humanitarian access, the protection of civilians, the release of hostages, and an end to the devastating conflict. Lammy's response was evasive, reflecting the complexity of the government's position.

Historically, Labour's stance on Israel and Gaza has been a source of contention. In October 2022, then-Leader of the Opposition and now Prime Minister Keir Starmer supported Israel's right to defend itself, including cutting water and power to Gaza, claiming it was in line with international law. However, Labour has since recalibrated its position. In July 2024, the UK resumed funding for the United Nations agency for Palestinian Refugees (UNRWA) and removed its formal objection to the International Criminal Court's authority to issue arrest warrants for Israeli Prime Minister Benjamin Netanyahu and Defence Minister Yoav Gallant. It also suspended some arms exports to Israel and, in October, voted in favour of a UN resolution demanding an "immediate, unconditional, and permanent" ceasefire.

Despite these shifts, there is growing pressure for Starmer's government to take further steps to hold Israel accountable under international law. If the government fails to make meaningful progress, it could become a contentious issue for Uma Kumaran and others who view the situation in Gaza as "genocidal" and advocate for a more immediate and decisive response.

Reflections

Uma Kumaran's journey to becoming the first British MP of Sri Lankan Tamil descent is a profound testament to resilience, purpose, and representation. Her historic victory has resonated far beyond her constituency, symbolizing the possibilities for marginalized communities to find their voice in the corridors of power. Uma's commitment to equity and justice is evident in her solidarity with Tamils worldwide, her advocacy for accountability in Sri Lanka, and her calls for compassion and humanitarian action in global crises like the conflict in Gaza.

Her actions reflect her deep connection to her Tamil heritage and British values, blending her unique perspective with a desire to create a more equitable world. Uma has shown that political leadership is not just about navigating the complexities of governance but also about giving a voice to the voiceless and fighting for principles that transcend borders. As she continues her work in Parliament, Uma's example will undoubtedly inspire future generations to challenge barriers, embrace their identities, and strive for a society that values inclusivity, justice, and compassion for all.

Samantha Ratnam: Championing Justice and Inclusion

Fleeing Sri Lanka: A Childhood Shaped by Conflict

At just six years old, in 1983, Samantha Ratnam's world was upended as she and her family fled Sri Lanka in the wake of Black July—a brutal, state-orchestrated pogrom targeting Tamils. As mobs tore through neighbourhoods, she and her twin sister hid, separated from their family in an aunt's house—a terrifying experience that left a lasting scar. Although their departure (which Samantha describes as a forced migration) came a few years later, it was deeply shaped by the aftermath of Black July.

That trauma opened her eyes to the devastating consequences of unchecked political power and ignited a lifelong conviction to confront injustice.

Samantha Ratnam's decision to enter politics in 2008 by joining the Greens was thus shaped by her early understanding of political power and its potential for positive change. Within a decade, she rose to lead the Victorian Greens, a testament to her commitment and resilience.

Samantha embraced the political arena to harness power as a force for justice rather than oppression.

Samantha realised the power of politics to change lives when she arrived in Melbourne in 1989. Thanks to sound political decisions, she received an excellent education, her mother accessed the medical care she needed, and—most importantly—the family felt included in society. It was a clear demonstration that politics mattered. So, it was no surprise that Samantha gravitated toward it. She seized her first opportunity to study the subject in Year 11 and later pursued an arts degree, majoring in Political Studies.

However, her intention was not to become a politician but rather to understand how political power shaped society.

Finding Belonging and Purpose in Australia

Growing up in Melbourne, Samantha experienced the profound duality of the migrant journey: a deep gratitude for the opportunities her family discovered in Australia, contrasted with the isolation and lingering grief of being uprooted from her ancestral home. Though she was young when her family was forced to flee, an unshakable yearning for the land they had left behind remained with her. While much of her time in Sri Lanka was spent in Colombo, her visits to the North—the Tamil homeland—held a unique and enduring significance, forging a connection that resonated deeply within her.

Returning to the Homeland and Social Work

It was, therefore, not surprising that in 2004, encouraged by the ceasefire between the Sri Lankan Government and the Tamil Tigers, Samantha seized the opportunity to return to her ancestral home. Now under Tamil administration—the de facto state of the Tamil people—she spent three months living there, training counsellors who were assisting the deeply traumatized and displaced. Samantha left Sri Lanka in 2005 as the ceasefire began to unravel. Acutely aware of the brutality with which the conflict ultimately ended, she reflects with sadness that some of the people she trained likely did not survive.

At that point, Samantha had transitioned into social work which felt like a natural step—a field deeply political in its own right, reminding her that the systems and structures we live within shape the choices and opportunities available to us.

As a social worker, Samantha worked closely with society's most marginalized and vulnerable populations—the homeless, refugees, and those in drug and alcohol rehabilitation programs. She came to understand that political decisions could mean the difference between someone having a roof over their head, feeling part of a community, or even life and death. She also recognized that outcomes fell short when political decisions failed to align with community needs and expectations.

Entering Politics: A Voice for the Marginalized

Unsurprisingly, this realization drove her to take the next step: she was elected as a councillor for the City of Moreland (now Merri-bek) in 2012 and became Mayor in 2015. In 2016, Samantha contested the federal seat of Willis, though she increased the Greens' vote, the seat remained with the Labor party. A year later Samantha, then working as a client services manager at the Asylum Seeker Resource Centre,
was preselected to succeed former state Greens leader Greg Barber as MP

for the northern metropolitan region, in Victoria's upper house. Soon after, she was elected unopposed as leader.

Her decision to enter politics as a candidate for the Greens felt natural; Samantha believed that addressing the country's major issues required a bold approach, and the Greens' core principles—ecological sustainability, grassroots democracy, social justice, and peace and non-violence—aligned perfectly with her values. Around 2007 having become very concerned about climate change and disappointed with Labor's policies on refugees or climate change, she joined the Greens on New Year's Eve 2008. Since then, her rise within the party has been meteoric, and she became its leader in ten years in 2018. Her political career had emerged as an extension of her social work, motivated by her growing awareness of systemic issues affecting communities.

During her tenure as party leader, Samantha collaborated closely with Greens MP Lidia Thorpe, a woman of Indigenous descent, to champion key legislation advancing First Nations rights. Together, they helped pass Treaty legislation and introduced measures to raise the age of criminal responsibility and reform unjust bail laws, aiming to alleviate the enduring impacts of dispossession faced by Australia's First Peoples. Then in a powerful speech on August 31, 2023, Samantha urged Australians to vote 'Yes' in the upcoming Voice to Parliament referendum, calling for justice and meaningful recognition of First Nations peoples in the constitution. Drawing on her own experience as a migrant from a colonized background, she underscored the ongoing harms of colonization and systemic injustice endured by First Nations communities. Samantha also appealed for solidarity from multicultural communities, emphasizing that the referendum offers an opportunity for Australia to listen, honour diverse voices, and build a foundation of truth, treaty, and equality for First Peoples.

Challenging Power: Advocacy, Identity, and Backlash

Samantha has never shied away from advocating for social justice and inclusiveness, even when it risks making her unpopular among the majority. In 2021, she took a stand on the issue of the Lord's Prayer in Parliament, arguing that, given Victoria's multicultural and multiethnic character, the practice of reciting the Lord's Prayer—a vestige of colonialism and British rule—should be replaced with a more inclusive approach. Predictably, the proposal was rejected by the majority, but

Samantha's commitment to diversity and inclusion remained unwavering.

Samantha believes that Australian politics will be healthier and more representative when people from culturally diverse communities actively participate. She expanded on this view during an interview with ABC Radio National's Patricia Karvelas in July 2024. When asked if the rise of the "Muslim vote" might impact her party's support in the federal elections, Samantha's response reflected her commitment to an inclusive, principled approach that goes beyond short-term gains. She emphasized her belief in a politics that embraces all communities, underscoring her dedication to a truly inclusive political landscape.

An issue that Samantha is passionate about is the fight against toxic racism, white supremacy and far-right nationalism. It was therefore not surprising that in October 2024 when Neo Nazis tried to disrupt refugee protesters' 100th night demonstrating outside the Department of Home Affairs in Docklands, Samantha should be one of the first politicians to strongly criticize these actions.

Samantha has strong objections to the Labor Party's approach to the housing crisis, particularly its inclination to handing over public land to private enterprises for housing development. She believes that this approach undermines the urgent need to address the housing crisis, which has pushed median house prices well over a million dollars. In her view, housing solutions must prioritize public interest over private profit.

Of course, like all members of the Greens, the issue most central to Samantha is climate change. Samantha's focus is to ensure the current energy requirements are met by renewable energy. She believes that this to be the most effective way to arrest climate change.

In September 2024, after nearly seven years of impactful leadership, Samantha Ratnam made the bold decision to step down as the Victorian leader of the Greens to contest a seat in Federal Parliament. She embraced the campaign with passion and purpose, undeterred by the risks of leaving a secure leadership role for the uncertainty of an election outcome. While she did not win, her candidacy marked a historic moment: had she been elected, Samantha would have become the first Greens member and the first woman to represent the seat of Wills since its creation in 1949.

Nonetheless, the results were impressive and spoke volumes about the strength of her campaign. Samantha secured 48.6% of the two-candidate-preferred vote, mounting one of the most formidable challenges the Greens have ever posed in the electorate.

Her opponent from the Labor Party retained the seat with 51.4%—a narrow margin during what became the best Labor victory in modern

Australian political history. Remarkably, it was also the first time since World War II that a sitting government increased its vote share after its first term.

Samantha's strong showing demonstrated that her message resonated deeply with voters and that change is on the horizon. Her campaign not only energized the Greens' base but also expanded it, confirming her place as a formidable figure in Australian politics with a growing national profile. Far from being a setback, the experience underscored her courage, her influence, and the growing appetite for inclusive, principled leadership in Australia's political landscape.

Support for the Palestinians and First Nation People and Other Persecuted People

Samantha has attended several pro-Palestinian protests following Hamas's October 7 attack on Israel and Israel's subsequent military response, with these demonstrations drawing large crowds in Melbourne. Her support for the Palestinian cause is seen as authentic. Having fled war-torn Sri Lanka for Canada in the late 1980s before settling in Melbourne, Samantha says she feels a kinship with Palestinians, as well as with migrants and First Nations people, shaped by shared experiences of displacement and oppression. "There are a whole bunch of people like me and my community, and the broader migrant community, who have experienced war, racism, colonization, and oppression," she says, "who see themselves in the oppression that Palestinian people are feeling."[94] Similarly, the Greens' longstanding policy of calling for formal recognition of the genocide of millions under the Ottoman Empire resonates deeply with her, given her own experience as a member of a persecuted community that has endured genocidal violence.

Family

Samantha's approach to politics is also deeply intellectual; she holds a PhD focused on young people and global citizenship. Pursuing this degree was perhaps also a nod to her parents' values, reflecting the Tamil community's strong emphasis on education. As Samantha often jokes, with

---

[94] https://www.theguardian.com/australia-news/2024/apr/20/a-test-in-wills-greens-hopeful-samantha-ratnams-federal-politics-gamble-will-pay-off

a brother who is a doctor and a sister who is a lawyer, the family pressure was off her, in any case. On a more serious note, Samantha is grateful for her family's unwavering support, understanding, and encouragement to pursue politics. She acknowledges that, without their help, she would have struggled to balance a demanding political career with raising a family.

Family played a central role in Samantha's life choices, including her parents' decision to settle in Australia after initially fleeing to Canada. As Samantha shared with *Indian Sun*: "It was not an easy decision to move countries, but moving to Australia from Canada was one of the easier moves. We really did not have close family in Canada. In Australia, on the other hand, we had that. My father's brother as well as my mother's brother lived here."[95]

For a time, it seemed that Samantha and her husband, Colin Jacobs, might not have a family of their own. After years of trying, they had resigned themselves to being childless and were considering foster care when Samantha learned she was pregnant at 42. Today, they have a daughter, whom they named Malala, after the Pakistani education activist Malala Yousafzai. Once again, family is vital in supporting Samantha and Colin, as they both have demanding careers—Samantha in politics and Colin as a postdoctoral astrophysicist at Swinburne University.

Confronting Extremism

Samantha's advocacy on sensitive issues has not been without controversy or personal attacks. Her support for the Kurdish community's struggle for self-determination has drawn significant criticism. Mark Burgess of The Australian Spectator has publicly denounced her stance on the rise of far-right extremism in Victoria. Such dismissive reactions from conservative politicians and journalists are not uncommon. Lydia Khalil, a Research Fellow at the Lowy Institute and Associate Research Fellow at Deakin University, explores this phenomenon in her book *Rise of the Extreme Right*. Khalil points out that conservatives often reject the term "far-right extremism," claiming that linking extremism with the "right" unfairly implicates conservative politics. This reluctance, particularly in countries like Australia, Canada, and the United States, has led to the term being avoided—a tendency researchers warn is dangerous. Far-right extremism, they argue, has now overtaken jihadism as the most significant

---

[95] https://www.theindiansun.com.au/2014/04/07/taking-stand/

security threat. Accurately labelling and addressing this phenomenon is essential for countering it; failing to do so risks enabling its proliferation. In this context, Samantha's willingness to call out far-right extremism for what it is remains both justified and vital.

Samantha faced criticism from far-right extremists for her stance against people critical of government approaches to the pandemic during the COVID-19 pandemic.

As a woman of colour, Samantha has endured significant abuse, much of it overtly racist and sexist, including calls to "go back to where you came from." In 2018, she faced particularly harsh treatment when Liberal MP Inga Peulich called her a "pig." Although not racially motivated, the comment was widely condemned as unparliamentary, underscoring the challenges Samantha faces in championing diversity and social justice.

Reflections

From her early experiences as a forced migrant to her current role as a leader, Samantha has consistently used her voice to champion the marginalized and advocate for a more inclusive, equitable Australia. Samantha understands the importance of belonging and the impact of navigating identity across cultures.

Samantha is acutely aware of how migration can transform lives and how it has fundamentally altered her family's opportunities, outlook, and identity. Indeed, Samantha entertains great hope in the power of transformation and change, even those changes that you were forced to make.

Samantha is deeply disappointed by today's Labor Party, which she sees as a stark departure from the compassionate leadership of Prime Minister Bob Hawke's era—a government that welcomed her family to Australia with openness and humanity. She is particularly alarmed by Labor's proposed bill, which includes measures she finds profoundly troubling: paying third countries to accept refugees, authorizing the confiscation of mobile phones in detention, re-imposing ankle bracelets, expanding the minister's power to overturn protection findings, and granting the government immunity from civil suits related to deportations.

The bill also allows refugees to be sent to third countries that are not signatories to the UN Refugee Convention, a move Samantha views as a betrayal of Australia's commitment to human rights and international obligations.

Her commitment to addressing issues like social justice, housing affordability, and political transparency demonstrates a steadfast belief that politics should serve the common good. As Samantha continues to push boundaries and challenge societal norms, she remains a reminder that true leadership is about staying rooted in one's values, no matter the obstacles. Despite being uprooted from her homeland, she has not only endured but thrived, turning adversity into a platform for lasting change.

CULINARY CHAMPIONS

Tasting Success: Culinary Superstars

Tamils from Sri Lanka have endeared themselves to their new countries in many ways through their resilience and contributions across various fields. This includes the universal language of food. Not just by introducing the rich and aromatic flavours of Tamil cuisine to the world, but a step further—mastering and redefining the culinary traditions of their host countries. From crafting award-winning pastries in Paris to winning competitions, these culinary trailblazers have not only embraced new cultures but have also earned acclaim at the highest levels, proving that food is both a bridge and a testament to their adaptability.

Brin Prathapan: MasterChef

MasterChef is a competitive British cooking television show created in 1990 and revived by the BBC in 2005. The revived format was sold internationally and adapted in several other countries. It is now produced in more than 50 countries and airs in over 200 territories; the winner of the competition is widely recognised in the culinary world. In many of these countries including the UK and Australia this competition has emerged to become the premier cooking show.

Essex-born, 29-Year-old Brin Prathapan, a veterinary surgeon was Britain's 2024 MasterChef by winning the 20th series of UK TV's biggest cooking competition. Brin attributes that crucial skills in surgery, such as multitasking and working at speed, greatly helped him during the competition.

Like thousands of Sri Lanka's Tamils Brin's father Gopal and mother Darley escaped Sri Lanka which was not a safe place for Tamils.

Speaking the day after his historic win Brin credited his parents, for inspiring his love of food and flavour, and said he felt lucky his Tamil culinary culture had such an integral role in his cooking.

In an interview with the *Tamil Guardian* on 23 May 2024, the then 29-year-old Brin spoke of the inspiration he drew from his Tamil background to create bold, creative combinations of flavours that led to him being awarded the coveted MasterChef trophy. He attributed his success to Tamil cooking in which "how every dish is there for a reason, how certain things do or don't go with certain things, and how flavours marry up."

Brin moved to Bristol to attend university, where he studied to become a vet. It is here that his culinary prowess really took off as he challenged himself to be creative with meals on a budget. According to Brin's fiancée Anna (whom he had since married) he does love his job but always been much more passionate about cooking. And that cooking was something that helped him get over a stressful day at work and feel really calm and relaxed.

Brin's winning performance at the finals was a three-course meal starting with fried capers, pickled chilli, pickled and charred shallots, orange and honey-glazed octopus with tempura mussels, herb tuilles dusted with scallop roe, an orange gel and samphire, on a romesco sauce. The main course was spiced venison loin, beef short-rib and pickled mushroom tartlet, celeriac and miso purée, salt-baked beetroot and pak choi, served with a gochujang and red wine sauce split with a herb oil. His dessert featured white chocolate and cardamom and saffron cremeux, with pistachio meringue shards, whisky-poached mango, raspberry gel, pistachio crumb and a mango, lime and chili sorbet.

Brin Pirathapan's journey not only celebrates personal achievement but also highlights the rich tapestry of flavours that emerge when diverse traditions converge. As Brin continues to explore new culinary horizons, his work stands as a testament to the enduring influence of heritage in shaping the future of global gastronomy.

Tharshan Selverajah: Winner of the Best Baguette in Paris Award

The Parisian baguette holds a cherished place in French cuisine, renowned for its golden-brown crust, crisp exterior—especially when fresh—and soft, airy interior. This iconic bread is a staple of Parisian life, often appearing on travellers' must-experience lists when visiting the city. More than just a culinary delight, the baguette embodies the essence of French culture and daily living. In November 2022, UN cultural body UNESCO awarded the baguette world heritage status.

In 2006, a 20-year-old Tharshan Selverajah fled Sri Lanka's civil war and sought refuge in France, a country and culture entirely unfamiliar to him. 17 years, later in 2023, he rose above 172 other shortlisted competitors to win the coveted Best Baguette in Paris award—an honour that not only crowned him the city's finest baguette maker but also one-year contract to supply baguettes to the Élysée Palace, the residence of the French President, not to mention the €4,000 that came with the award.

In May 2024, Paris honoured him by selecting Tharshan as a torchbearer for the 2024 Summer Olympics and he became the first person of Sri Lankan Tamil origin to receive the honour of being chosen as torchbearer for an Olympic event.

Feeing war-torn Sri Lanka, Tharshan found work in an Italian restaurant, where he often struck up conversations with the owner of a local bakery who came in for lunch. When the restaurant shut down, leaving Tharshan unemployed, the baker extended an invitation: why not try his hand at making bread instead? Intrigued by the offer, Tharshan joined the bakery, but the transition was anything but easy. He didn't speak French and had no experience in bread-making. Yet, despite the language barrier and his lack of formal training, he was determined—not just to become a skilled baker, but to make a name for himself and his craft. In 2016, after years of learning and refining his skills, he took a bold step and purchased the bakery, *Au Levain des Pyrénées*, from his boss and mentor. With ownership came an even bigger ambition: winning the prestigious Best Baguette in Paris competition.

Tharshan first entered the competition in 2018 and secured third place. Though impressive, it wasn't enough for him. He spent the next several years perfecting his technique, patiently waiting for the right moment to try again.

In 2023, he returned to the competition with renewed confidence. Out of 1,305 participating bakeries, his baguette was crowned the best in Paris. News of his victory spread before he and his team had even processed what had happened. The next morning, when he arrived at his bakery in the 20th arrondissement, a line of eager customers stretched down the block. By noon, they had completely sold out of traditional baguettes.

Since his win, Tharshan has expanded his business, opened a second bakery and built a brand around his bread. He attributes his success to one key ingredient: happiness. "When you bake with happiness," he says, "the bread turns out to be a winner."

Tanesh Thanaratnam: *Coupe de France du Burger* Regional Winner

The Coupe de France du Burger is an annual culinary competition in France that celebrates the creativity and expertise of burger chefs from across the country. Organized by Socopa, a prominent meat brand, the event brings together talented professionals who compete regionally before advancing to the national finals. The competition not only highlights innovative burger creations but also sets culinary trends within the French food scene.

In 2025, Tanesh Thanaratnam, a Tamil chef born in Paris to parents who fled Sri Lanka's civil war, made a significant impact at the Coupe de France du Burger. Representing Île-de-France, he won the regional title with his innovative creation, "*Le Tissot de La Varenne*," a burger inspired by classic French cuisine. The burger featured a carrot cake-style bun, beef cheek simmered in its own juices, a creamy sauce, rustic Limousin meat, mature black cheddar, candied kumquat, and fried carrot tops, achieving a perfect balance between soft and crispy textures.

Tanesh's journey to the national finals was remarkable. Competing against four other contenders in the Paris regional finals during the 10th anniversary of the French Burger Cup, he secured his place among the top five in the national finals, ultimately being placed fifth.

Raised in a challenging part of Paris, Tanesh's path to culinary success was unconventional. Without formal culinary qualifications, he began his journey at the age of 24, learning on the job and working in 20 different restaurants over a decade.

His determination and passion for French cuisine propelled him to the position of head chef. Reflecting on his experience, Tanesh stated, "I work three times harder than the locals, and I'm delighted that the hard work has paid off." Tanesh Thanaratnam's ascent in the French culinary scene underscores the profound impact of dedication. His achievements demonstrate that perseverance can lead to extraordinary accomplishments.

Tharsiny 'Thas' Thanendran: Finalist *Den Store Bagedyst*

Den Store Bagedyst, the Danish adaptation of the British television show *The Great British Bake Off*, has been captivating audiences since its debut in 2012. In this competition, amateur bakers undertake a series of challenges designed to impress a panel of judges with their baking prowess. Each week, one contestant is eliminated, culminating in a final where the top baker is crowned champion.

In 2023, Tharsiny "Thas" Thanendran, a 27-year-old Tamil baker and mechanical engineer from Copenhagen, showcased her exceptional baking skills by reaching the final of *Den Store Bagedyst*. Although she did not clinch the title, Thas became a favourite among both judges and viewers, earning two Master Baker aprons during the competition.

Balancing her professional and personal life, Thas attributes her success to her adeptness at organizing and prioritizing tasks. These skills have been invaluable, not only in managing large-scale projects at her workplace but also in executing time-sensitive recipes during the baking challenges.

Born in Denmark to Tamil parents who fled Sri Lanka's civil war, Thas holds her cultural roots in high regard. She acknowledges that her upbringing has significantly shaped her identity and achievements. In 2015, Thas moved to Copenhagen to pursue her studies in mechanical engineering and has since advanced to the role of Global Project Manager at Novo Nordisk.

Tharsiny "Thas" Thanendran's remarkable achievements as mechanical engineer and celebrated baker serve as an inspiration to the pursuit of one's passions while engaged in a rewarding professional career.

SPORTING HEROES

In the Zone: Sporting Standouts

From the margins of displacement to the heart of national pride, a new generation of Tamil sportsmen is making its mark in countries where their parents once sought sanctuary from the violence of the Sri Lankan state. Born to families shaped by trauma and resilience, these athletes are not only excelling in their chosen sports but are also redefining what it means to belong. Their presence on national teams and elite platforms signals more than just individual achievement—it is a quiet yet powerful testament to uprootal, adaptation, and the ability to thrive. Whether on the football pitch, cricket field, or athletics track, these young Tamils are carving out space in arenas once seen as unreachable, carrying with them the hopes of a community that has long been overlooked.

Rigivan Ganeshamoorthy: Strength in Stillness

In 2024, Rigivan Ganeshamoorthy, an Italian Tamil, made a stunning international debut at the Summer Paralympics, clinching the gold medal in the F52 discus throw with a new Paralympic world record of 27.06 metres. His performance was nothing short of extraordinary. He first shattered the existing world record with a second-round throw of 25.48 metres, then broke his own mark minutes later with a 25.80-metre throw. But it was his later attempt—an astonishing 27.06 metres—that sealed his victory, marking his third consecutive world record in a single event and securing Italy's gold.

A year earlier, in 2023, Rigivan had already established himself as a national force, winning the Italian Paralympic titles in the shot put F55 and the discus throw F54–F55. He also claimed the national title in javelin, underlining his versatility and dominance in field events.

Born in Rome to Tamil parents who had fled Sri Lanka's civil conflict, Rigivan was diagnosed with Guillain-Barré syndrome at the age of 18—a neurological disorder causing muscle weakness and sensory changes. His condition worsened in 2019 after a fall, leading to extended hospitalization at Santa Lucia Hospital in Rome. It was during this time that he explored adaptive sports, initially trying wheelchair basketball and fencing. He found wheelchair basketball to be too physically demanding. Eventually, he discovered field events—a space where his strength, focus, and discipline could truly shine.

Beyond his athletic prowess, Rigivan endeared himself to the public with his humility and wit. In a post-competition interview that went viral, he charmed viewers with his candid remarks and dedication of his victory to his mother, his hometown of Rome, and its coastal district. In every way, he has become more than a champion; he is a symbol of quiet resilience and pride for both Italy and the global Tamil diaspora.

Amuruthaa 'Amu' Surenkumar: Batting for the Future

In March 2024, British Tamil teenager Amuruthaa Surenkumar made history as the first professional Tamil cricketer to represent the English national team making her debut in an under-19 match against Sri Lanka. Amu, as she is affectionately known, hails from Bournemouth, the largest town in Dorset.

From a young age, Amu's skill with both the bat and ball were closely noted. Her prodigious cricketing talent was first spotted by North London CC, which she first joined as a 7-year-old. In 2021, aged just 14-years-old, she becomes the youngest player to be selected for an academy squad in a regional women's cricket competition involving eight teams from all over England. After a string of impressive performances for the Sunrisers academy, she won a professional contract with the team last year. She made an impact straight away, claiming two wickets in two balls on her debut, and powering her team to victory against in July 2023.

Amu's talents were recognised early in her career by Martin Issitt, a prominent figure in English cricket administration known for his dedication to youth and women's cricket. Reflecting on her early promise, Issitt remarked in 2021, "Her natural abilities and dedication to developing her cricket amazed us all from the first time we saw her."[96]

Cricket runs deep in Amu's family. Her father, S Surenkumar, a passionate cricketer himself, played for his alma mater, St John's College in Jaffna, while her mother, Logini, is also a former player. Amu has championed gender equality in sport, declaring in 2021, "I want to push gender equality in cricket, for example more media coverage of women's cricket and getting more girls and women to pick up a bat and ball and play the game."[97]

With her remarkable rise and strong sense of purpose, Amurutha Surenkumar stands as an inspiration to young cricketers everywhere.

---

[96]https://www.hamhigh.co.uk/sport/21333742.north-london-teenager-sets-sights-professional-cricket/
[97]https://www.hamhigh.co.uk/sport/21333742.north-london-teenager-sets-sights-professional-cricket/

Kenirujan 'Kenu' Suthakaran – The Tamil Tiger of the Cage

On 30 August 2024, Kenirujan Suthakaran claimed the Bantamweight title at FightStar Championship (FSC), one of the UK's leading Mixed Martial Arts (MMA) promotions, by knocking out Abdul Basith in the second round. He went on to successfully defend his title on 21 February 2025, defeating Adam Raja by unanimous decision. These victories marked Kenu as a rising force in British MMA.

Born and raised in South East London, Kenu is deeply rooted in his Tamil identity. He references it often—on social media, in interviews, and inside the cage—using hashtags like #Tamil and #TamilTiger, and proudly dedicating his wins to his heritage. His nickname, 'Tamil Tiger,' was given to him by his university coach, James Dixon—a label Kenu has embraced as a symbol of strength and resilience.[98]

Family plays a central role in his life and career. He often speaks of the support he receives from his parents and siblings, and of his mother's traditional Tamil meals that fuel his training. By sharing elements of Tamil culture with his audience—from cuisine to values—Kenu not only celebrates where he comes from but reclaims space for his identity in a sport not always known for such visibility.

Kenu's journey into the world of combat sports was driven by a mix of early passion, relentless personal discipline, and a strong sense of cultural identity. He began training in karate as a child, quickly progressing to full-contact competition. At just 14, he clinched a title at the International World Karate Association World Championships in the United States—a formative moment that deepened his commitment to martial arts and set the stage for a lifelong pursuit of excellence.

Until March 2024, Kenu balanced this passion with a career as a manufacturing engineer. Today, however, his focus lies firmly in the world he helped build: he is a gym owner, coach, and content creator.

Outside the cage, Kenu has made a name for himself as a Mixed Martial Arts coach and analyst

---

[98] *Day Of a Fighter in Training Camp Kenu Suthakaran*, https://www.youtube.com/watch?v=UkAbtgn_ohE&t=1s

Vimal Yoganathan: Footballer, Trailblazer

On 17 September 2024, *The Guardian* hailed 18-year-old Vimal Yoganathan as a trailblazer, poised to inspire a new generation of South Asian footballers. His debut for Manchester United in the Carabao Cup was not just a personal milestone but a moment of profound significance for the Tamil community in the UK—one largely absent from the world of football. "It would be a big moment for the community if I played," Vimal reflected, "and obviously it would raise a lot more awareness and gain a lot more attention." Yet, he remained grounded, choosing to let his performance speak louder than words. "I'm not putting all of that pressure on the Tamil community—I want to focus on football." Candid about the underrepresentation of Tamils in the sport, he recalled, "I don't think I met a single Tamil footballer growing up—not in Sunday league and definitely not in academy football." With quiet determination, Vimal is breaking barriers, both on and off the pitch.

Standing at 6ft 3in (191cm), Vimal Yoganathan is striking—not just for his height, which is uncommon among South Asians—but for the quiet determination that has defined his journey. The son of Sri Lankan Tamil parents, Vimal was raised in the small village of Trelawnyd in North Wales, far removed from the glare of professional football. His talent emerged early; by the age of six, he had already caught the attention of Liverpool scouts. Within a year, he joined the club's shadow squad, and at eight, he officially entered Liverpool's academy—laying the foundation for a promising career. He later moved to Barnsley, where he played for the Under-16s and went on to play a key role in the club's Under-18 division title win in 2023.

On 8 August 2023, Vimal made his professional debut for Barnsley in an English Football League (EFL) Cup match against Tranmere Rovers, coming on as a 65th-minute substitute. That moment marked more than just a personal milestone—it was historic. With that appearance, Vimal became the first player of Tamil heritage to feature in a professional senior game in English football.

Proud of his roots and deeply grateful to his parents, Vimal credits their support as vital to his success. They drove him to training sessions and matches across the country, nurturing his dream even when the odds seemed steep.

Challenging the stereotype that British Asian families value academics over athletics, he told the BBC, "Being a footballer wasn't only my dream—it was also theirs."⁹⁹ His rise shines a light on a wider issue: the underrepresentation of South Asians in British football. In 2023, only 22 professional players of South Asian heritage aged 17 or over played across England's top four leagues—roughly 1% of the 5,000 professional footballers in the country.

---

⁹⁹ *England's First Tamil footballer aims for the top*, https://www.bbc.com/news/articles/c4gm91v838jo

A Story of a Returnee[100]

Mainthan returned to his hometown bearing memories from the day he left. His home, Kankesanthurai, now lay in shambles—reduced to a small section of a sprawling military base in the North.

It wasn't just his town. Virtually every Tamil who returned to resettle found their villages and towns completely transformed. Public buildings, private homes, fences, streets, wells, and waterways ravaged, destroyed, or left in ruins by military action. Moreover, these settlements redesigned by the military to serve its ongoing occupation. The streets, fences, and buildings that had evolved organically demolished to make way for extensive military complexes, the unique character of small towns and villages erased beyond recognition.

This is exactly what had happened to Mainthan's hometown.

It was a common experience for all returnees. Some found only a pile of rocks where their house once stood; others discovered their former homes had been transformed into military commanders' residences—or reduced to mounds of stones from dismantled sentry posts. The walls that once enclosed their properties were gone, roads replaced by playing fields or training camps. A well that once provided life-giving water might have vanished or been replaced by something unrecognizable. Entire temples had disappeared—sometimes replaced by Buddha statues. In some cases, the only thing a returnee possessed was a key to a home that no longer existed.

Many villages had been merged with neighbouring settlements, their boundaries redrawn and absorbed into vast military zones. Nameboards that once displayed village names now pointed to military bases. Towns, hamlets, and streets bore military designations, while remaining fences were marked with GPS coordinates.

Driven by nostalgia, Veenai Mainthan had returned home—only to be confronted with a place unrecognizably transformed.

Kankesanthurai was no ordinary town—it held deep political and economic significance for Eelam Tamils, along with ideological and spiritual importance. Situated on the Bay of Bengal, alongside Mylitty and Parithithurai, these port towns once supplied over 45 percent of the

---

[100] From the foreword by Nilanathan to the second edition of the *Veenai Mainthani's Tholanthupona Vasanthangal* (Lost Springs) translated by the author.

island's fish production, both before and during the war.

Recalling his hometown's past glories and the renowned figures it produced, Mainthan was overcome with grief—this was neither the town nor the people he had once known.

Like many uprooted individuals of the first generation, he remained caught between two worlds—nostalgia for his homeland and the realities of life in his adopted country. That same longing had once fuelled wartime fundraising, and continues to shape contemporary Tamil politics.

Many like Veenai Mainthan—the first generation of the uprooted—live amphibious lives, suspended between two realities. They return to their childhood villages hoping to spend their final days there, yet most are elderly and dependent on healthcare unavailable in Sri Lanka. Nor can they bring themselves to leave their grandchildren behind, making a permanent return impossible.

Still, they return each winter, like migratory birds, to relive old memories.

About the Author

Ana Pararajasingham is an independent researcher and writer with a longstanding interest in justice, displacement, and identity—issues that have shaped both his personal journey and professional work.

In 2005, he edited *Sri Lanka: Ground Realities*. From 2007 to 2009, he served as Director of Programmes at the Centre for Just Peace and Democracy (CJPD), a Switzerland-based action-research centre. During his tenure, he authored *Sri Lanka's Endangered Peace Process and the Way Forward* (2007) and edited *Sri Lanka: 60 Years of "Independence" and Beyond* (2009).

In 2019, he published *Sri Lanka: A Victor's Peace*, a collection of essays originally featured in international journals and newspapers during the decade following the end of Sri Lanka's civil war.

Between 1990 and 2006, he was an Office Bearer with the Australasian Federation of Tamil Associations (AFTA), serving first as Secretary and later as Chairman.

He lives in Sydney, Australia.

www.ingramcontent.com/pod-product-compliance
Lightning Source LLC
Chambersburg PA
CBHW071956290426
44109CB00018B/2043